RIGHT TO EDUCATION

RIGHT TO EDUCATION
Retrospect and Prospects

Edited by
Noushad Husain

SHIPRA

Rs. 1250

ISBN: 978-81-7541-627-7

First Published in India in 2014

Right to Education: Retrospect and Prospects

Published by:

SHIPRA PUBLICATIONS
LG 18-19, Pankaj Central Market,
I.P. Ext., Patparganj, Delhi 110092, India
Ph.: 011- 2223 5152, 2223 6152
Email: info@shiprapublication.com
www.shiprapublication.com

Acknowledgements

First of all I thank a lot of my indebtedness to **"God for His Mercy"** because without the mercy of God the present book could not be completed. He gave me direction, knowledge, support and patience to edit this book.

I thank all the scholars for their valuable contribution to this timely volume. I would also like to show my gratitude toward all those authors and publishers whose works have been consulted, quoted and abstracted to make the book up-to-date and useful.

With great pleasure, I express my grateful thanks to my beloved father Mr. Zakir Huswain, mother, Mrs. Aishya Begum, wife Razda Khan, son Arsh Husain, Mr. Aleem Khan, Mrs. Naseem Khan, Brother Shahab Husain and other family members for their encouragement and support.

In the end, I am grateful to Mr. D. Kumar, Shipra Publications for publishing this book within the shortest time with accuracy and style.

Lastly, I offer this book to teachers, students, teacher educators, parents, civil society organizations, NGOs, Panchayati Raj Institutions, Local Government bodies, who want to realize the expectations of the RTE Act and fulfilling the dream of providing free and compulsory quality education to all children.

Dr. Noushad Husain

Contents

Introduction

The role of education in facilitating social and economic progress is well recognized. It opens up opportunities leading to both individual and group entitlements. Education, in its broadest sense of development of youth, is the most crucial input for empowering people with skills and knowledge and giving them access to productive employment in future. Improvements in education are not only expected to enhance efficiency but also augment the overall quality of life.

Education is both a human right in itself and a means for realizing and promoting other human rights. Education can be defined in a broad sense to imply "the entire process of social life by means of which individuals and social groups learn to develop consciously within, and for the benefit of, the national and international communities, and the whole of their personal capacities, attitudes, aptitudes and knowledge".

The great English poet William Wordsworth has rightly said, "Child is the father of man". This is perhaps because the child has all the potential to develop into a full man. That is why the most valuable belief is the belief in children who overtake the next generation from the present one. The children have the Right to Education because it is education that sharpens their innate abilities and converts them into responsible citizens. It is therefore, necessary that the parents and the society should protect the child with utmost care. A very conducive environment free from hunger, disease and oppression needs to be ensured for children in which they can have the full opportunity to grow in full bloom. The recently enacted Right to Education (RTE) Act, 2009 in India is an important step and defining event in that direction.

After a persistent struggle and prolonged wait, the Right to Education Act is finally implemented from the 1st April 2010. The Central Government has published a "Model Rules" for its effective implementation in all the states. However, while the Model Rules provide a framework; the actual regulations for the implementation are not as yet final.

The Right to Education, characterized as a Fundamental Right, can be considered an 'upstream' right in the sense that it determines whether other rights can actually be exercised. None of civil, political, economic and social rights can be exercised by individuals unless they receive a certain minimum education, without which their access to such rights remains illusory and theoretical. Therefore, among economic and social rights, the Right to Education holds a central place. No one will deny that education is not the basis for development nor will anyone deny that education which implied receptiveness and access to others is the best instrument to combat all forms of discrimination, particularly as against the women, minorities, children and others. Education has much to contribute to both in developing the human's personality and national development. It provides valuable developmental opportunities to children. Yet millions of children remain deprived of educational opportunities. Although children's Right to Education is internationally recognized, it is not completely fulfilled in many parts of the world. Out of school children represent a broken promise affecting the fortunes of the children, their education system, their health and that of their families and the overall development of the potential of the countries where they live. Without an elaborate and properly structured system of education, children are less likely to be healthy, strong or safe to fully participate in the activities of their communities or raise healthy children themselves one day. Without giving children their Right to Education, countries are less likely to achieve other optimum development goals.

The right to education has a solid basis in the international law on human rights. A general right to education was directly formulated for the first time in the Universal Declaration of Human Rights (UDHR) in Article 26. Later, the right to education was rearticulated at the universal level in Article 13 of the International Covenant on Economic, Social and Cultural Rights (ICESCR) and Article 28 of the Convention on the Rights of the Child (CRC), which both guarantee the right of everyone to compulsory and free primary education.

In India, gender, regional, social, economic and other disparities hamper children's progress towards the attainment of a quality education. Many of the children who do not have access to school and those who are excluded, marginalized or otherwise vulnerable such as children from poor and rural areas, girls and children with disabilities face particular challenges in gaining access to quality education and performing well to complete the Primary and Elementary Education. India is a party to UN Declaration on the Rights of Child, 1959 as well as to the Convention of the Rights of Child, 1989. Accordingly it adopted achild friendly policy and made Elementary Education a Fundamental Right in its Constitution through Eighty Sixth Amendment in 2002. Even then the UNICEF Report of 2005, on the state of the world's children under the title, 'Childhood under Threat', speaks about India that millions of Indian children are deprived of their rights to survival, health, nutrition, education and safe drinking water. The landmark passing of the

Right of Children to Free and Compulsory Education Act (RTE), 2009 marks a historic moment for the children of India. The RTE Act imposes an obligation on all the states of Indian federation to ensure the Right to Education to all its children by implementing the Act's provisions.

The passing of the Right of Children to Free and Compulsory Education (RTE) Act 2009 marks a historic moment for the children of India. The Fundamental Right to Education, as incorporated in our Constitution under Article 21A, became operative from April 1, 2010. This demonstrates national commitment to the education of children and to the future of India. The Act is a building block to ensure that every child has his orher right to get a quality elementary education honored.

The RTE Act provides a solid platform to reach the unreached with specific provisions for disadvantaged groups, such as child laborers, migrant children, children with special needs, or those who have a "disadvantage owing to social, cultural, economic, geographical, linguistic, gender or such other factors."

The RTE Act is a historic piece of legislation because it gives a legal right to free education to children between the ages of six and fourteen and makes the government responsible for providing it. The Supreme Court has upheld the reservation of 25 per cent of seats in private unaided schools under the Rights to Education Act. But the fact is that over 80 percent of children in rural India study in government schools. Therefore, while the spirit behind the reservation of seats is laudable, the priority and focus of India's education systems should be on what needs to be done to improve the quality of education in government schools, where most of the children are enrolled. While most children have reasonable access to a school building, the RTE Act has rightly focus on availability of basic infrastructure, such as qualified teachers, classrooms, playgrounds, toilets and safe drinking water in these schools.

Educationists, thinkers, experts and critics from all over are divided in their response to the Act and the model rules. The reactions generated primarily go in two separate directions. One group believes that this Act is leading towards imminent centralization whereby the privatization of education will get further intensified. As a result of which, those under resourced and under privileged sections of society for whom the Act was more relevant and imperative, will end up getting carried further away from the folds of education.

The second group, on the other hand acknowledging the fact that the Act is not without its share of flaws and omissions, believes, that for the moment, we need to focus on the positive aspects of the Act and generate awareness and discussions around these provisions in order to make effective use of them. This group feels that we have to work intensively with the positive facets of the Act and gradually try to change the existent flaws into make them more favourable in the days to come.

While debates, discussions, deliberations and contestations will continue, yet, most will agree that in post independent India, this Act has brought in a new chapter in the sphere of education. No Act for public welfare however, can be effectively implemented merely through the provisions of legislation. Acceptance of a legal framework and ensuring appropriate usage of its legal provisions requires a massive amount of public awareness. What is required is a synergized coordination among all those who are a part of and/or are associated with the vast government education system of our country.

As a consequence of the implementation of this Act, a paradigm shift in the education system is imminent in the days to come. It is essential for the society to understand the nature and the direction of this shift. Parents, Teachers, Civil Society Organizations, NGOs, Panchayati Raj Institutions, Local Government Bodies etc. all need to understand their duties, roles and responsibilities as envisaged in the Act. In addition, they also need to keep a keen eye to watch for the effective implementation of the Act in society. In realizing the expectations of the Act and fulfilling the dream of providing quality education to all children, the teacher has a very critical role to play.

The present book is edited in order to generate large scale awareness on the Right to Education Act, leading to rise of opinions, discussions, debates and the formulation of a constructive discourse on the same. The book presents field stories of actual implementation of the Act, the experiences and difficulties faced. Standing at this threshold of such a massive change in the education system, if this book is able to answer some questions that arise in the minds of our readers and enables them to determine their roles in this context, only then, we shall consider our small attempt as successful.

The book consists of 22 chapters related to different themes of right to education. An outstanding feature of this book is that it has been written in an easily understanding and simple language.

The first chapter "*Human Rights and the Implementation of Right to Education Act in Indian Context: Challenges and Remedies*" by Dr. Noushad Husain discusses in detail about right to education. The author first of all gives a historical outline about the right to education then he explains the global strategies and political commitment to the realization of right to education. The author explains the concept of RTE Act, 2009, its strengths and weaknesses. The paper is an attempt to explore key lacunae in the context of the RTE Act and suggests improvements to address them. The author discusses the supporting mechanisms, administrative imperatives and implementation challenges that need to be addressed if such policy improvements are to yield results on the ground.

The chapter "*Right to Education: Some Historical Landmarks*" by Dr. Noushad Husain describes the various human rights based approaches that may contribute to the realization of the right to education. The author presents a wonderful historical picture about the historical development of the right to education.

The Right to Education legislation has a long and chequered history, having been subjected to numerous rounds of heated debate and philosophical and semantic alterations. The next chapter entitled "*Right to Education: The Indian Constitutional Perspective*" by Dr. Noushad Husain discusses in detail about the historical decisions of Indian constitution related to right to education. The article gives a timeline of the RTE Act in India.

The chapter "*Right to Education: A Conceptual Framework*" by Noushad Husain presents the historical evolution of the concept of right to education in India. The author presents constitutional provisions related to education. He further listed out some important Articles related to education, minorities, equality, Gender and Vulnerable Groups and religion.

At present, we are facing many problems related to the implementation of RTE Act in India. Though the Right to Education Act is a great start, government officials are now beginning to understand the challenges they face in implementing it. The chapter "*Right to Education Act: A Stepping Stone towards Visionary Developed India*" by Wadudul Haque Siddique discusses some serious lacunas of RTE Act and gives suggestions for Improving the Loopholes of RTE Act.

Primary education is the most important constituent of the whole process of education policy. It helps to produce a literate and numerate population that can deal with problems at home and at work and to serve as a foundation upon which further education is built. RTE act helps us to realize quality elementary education to every citizen in the country and helps to achieve revolutionary changes in the right direction. The chapter "*Towards a Progressive Nation: The Role of RTE Act*" by Jeena K.G. Describes that how RTE Act helps to achieve quality elementary education to all.

In order to meet the challenges and surmount the hurdles that stand in the way of implementing Right to Education Act, it is needful to concentrate all efforts with full dedication and commitment. Efforts should be focused on qualitative improvement of the whole programme. The chapter "*RTE Implementation: Some Problems and Concerns*" by Charu Saini describes that for education to be a meaningful right, it must be available, accessible, acceptable, and adaptable.

The chapter "*Right to Education Act 2009: Critical Gaps and Challenges in Its Implementation*" by Vanita Chopra, Aarti Bhatnagar and Sonal Chabra discusses that if want to make RTE ACT a true reality then, it would be necessary to overhaul the entire education system. The authors of the chapter suggest some important factors for qualitative improvement with respect to RTE Act 2009.

Present system of Education fails to provide Education based on Equality and social justice, this inequality leads to increase in class distinction and widens the gap between classes and masses which increase the danger of national fragmentation. The another chapter "*Right to Education and the Common School System*" by Akthar Parveen provides an insight into the concept of Common School System and Right to Education.

Under the clause12 (1) (c) of RTE Act, 2009 mandates for private schools to admit a quarter of their class strength from weaker section and disadvantaged groups of society. The Act under reference directs all schools, including the ones run as private ventures, to reserve 25 per cent of the available seats for students from socially and economically backward families. That means, quarter of students in classes are to be from the marginalized section of society. The another interesting chapter entitled "*Facets of RTE in Teachers' Perception and Its Impact on Self Concept of Students Enrolled in Unaided Schools under RTE Act*" by Talmeez Fatma Naqvi is a challenging attempt to analyze the effects of the teachers' perception on self-concept of the children from socially and economically backward families admitted in the private schools under RTE, Act.

The successful implementation of the RTE Act, 2009 depends on the well qualified and well informed teachers. Their will power and ability to perform will decide the future of this Act. The responsibility of making them able and competent mainly lies on the shoulders of the teacher education institutions of our country. The chapter "*Responsibilities of Teacher Education Institutions for Preparing Effective Teachers for Implementing the Right to Education (RTE) Act*" by Sajid Jamal highlights and discusses the responsibilities of the teacher education institutions to make RTE a successful human right act.

The next chapter "*Perception of Teachers: An Important Factor in Determining the Success of RTE*" by Manju Negi, Sonal Chabra and Ravneet Gaur is an empirical study, which was conducted on a sample of 100 elementary teachers selected from 10 privately managed schools of Delhi. This study describes the perception of elementary teachers regarding the right to education act very comprehensively. As we know very well that for the success of RTE Act, teachers play an imperative role. So, the results of this study are very useful and it will provide some important factors to plan the future strategies regarding RTE Act in India.

It is an undeniable fact that India is a multi-cultural society marked by numerous regional and local variants. Here the hierarchies based on caste, economic status and gender are prominent features which deeply influence children's access to education. The chapter "*Right to Education and SC & STs: Surveying the Landscape from Below*" by Talmeez Fatma Naqvi highlights and discusses the actual position of the children belonging to backward class.

According to the author, the backward section of our society i.e. SC and ST is in the hand of upper class hostile teachers and alien curriculum and poor fellow do not understand and take as a right. It is the ground reality that our government only gave the right to be literate to the poor section of the society not the right to education.

Shabana Ashraf based on her analysis on a selected sample of elementary teachers, explains the need to equipped the elementary teachers to understand the need of growing demand of quality education, they should be able to act as a facilitator of knowledge to their learners, they must be act as mediating agents through when curriculum is transacted and knowledge is co-constructed along with learners, they should connect knowledge to outside the boundaries of classroom and enrich the curriculum with familiar or local experiences by making it less textbook cantered through her empirical study entitled "*A Study of Awareness of Elementary Teachers towards RTE Act*".

The chapter entitled "*Making the Right to Education Meaningful: The 4As Framework*" by Dr. Noushad Husain clarifies the 4As framework for right to education. After discussing the core elements of right to education, the author clarifies the concepts of rights and obligations. The author explains deeply that to check the fulfilment of right to education, the 4As framework can be used satisfactory. The chapter is sum up to analyze the RTE Act, 2009 in the light of the 4As framework.

Prof. D. Venkateshwarlu through his chapter "*Inclusion of Diverse Learners: Issues and Challenges*" explains that to make inclusion possible, the present education system, educational structure and educational practices need to be more flexible, more inclusive and more collaborative.

The chapter "*Right to Education and Children with Disabled (CWD): From Social Exclusion to Social Inclusion through Inclusive Education*" by Indrajeet Dutta discusses the issue of inclusive education regarding to disabled children. The author first provides a brief history of inclusive education then he list out the different rights of disabled persons provided by international conventions. After that he presents the current status of education of disabled children. At the last, he point out the significant barriers and challenges in the implementation of inclusive education for disabled children and to remove these challenges and barriers he discusses some important strategies.

The chapter entitled "*Attitude of Society towards HIV/AIDS Impacting Child Education*" by G.K. Tripathi seeks to underline the way the perception of HIV/AIDS afflicted people contravenes human rights and children's right to be educated along with making suggestions to overcoming the dreaded entity through education.

The RTE Act was come into effect from 1st April 2010. Three years are almost passed we have achieved a lot in these three years but still lot needs to be done. Another chapter "*Right to Education: Some Critical Issues*" by Neeti

Dutta highlights some of the major issues related to RTE act which is needs to be addressed immediately for effective implementation.

There are a number of barriers to achieving the MDGs target of all children receiving primary school education. One of the most pervasive is a shortage of facilities and teachers, often due to financial constraints. ICTs can help overcome these shortages in an efficient and economical way for countries facing budgetary limitations. The chapter "*The Role of ICTs in Achieving the Universal Primary Education* by Dr. Noushad Husain discusses in detail about how the countries especially developing countries like India can use the ICTs to achieve the goal 2 of the MDGs i.e. to achieve universal primary education.

The chapter "*A Rights Based Approach to Education*" by Dr. Noushad Husain and Afaque Nadeem Khan presents a conceptual framework for promoting the right to education.

The chapter "*The Right to Education: Financial Implications*" by Shobhit Wadhwa and Sucheta Arora Wadhwa highlights and discusses the financial issues regarding the implementation of RTE. Because, RTE is a milestone for the achievement of long awaited Universalisation of education, it is quite clear that there are many obstacles in the path of success. The funding of any project is the lifeblood of the project and in that sense RTE is suffering from acute anaemia. The authors of this chapter, at the last concluded that there is immediate requirement of resolving the differences among the various authorities of education and coordination between finance ministry and HRD ministry should be established to overcome the financial challenges in the path of RTE.

1

Human Rights and the Implementation of Right to Education Act in Indian Context

Challenges and Remedies

Noushad Husain

The first word revealed in the Quran was "**Iqra**" READ! Seek knowledge! Educate yourselves! Be educated. When the Quran began to be revealed, the first word of its first verse was 'Iqra' that is, read. Allaah says, (that means): "Read! In the Name of your Lord Who has created (all that exists). He has created man from a clot (a piece of thick coagulated blood). Read! And your Lord is the Most Generous. Who has taught (the writing) by the pen. He has taught man that, which he knew not." [*Quran*, 96: 1-5]

The importance of education is a non-disputable matter. Education is the knowledge of putting one's potentials to maximum use. One can safely say that a human being is not a human being in the proper sense till he/she is educated. This importance of education is basically for two reasons. The first is that the training of a human mind is not complete without education. Education makes man a right thinker. It tells man how to think and how to make decision. The second reason for the importance of education is that only through the attainment of education, man is enabled to receive information from the external world; to acquaint himself with past history and receive all necessary information regarding the present. Without education, man is as though living in a closed room; and with education, he finds himself in a room with all its windows open towards the outside world.

Education is the vehicle by which a child grows to be an independent adult. It is also the means by which cultural values are transmitted and the child is bound to his or her family, community and society. The right to education has a special value as it enables children to increase their chances of having their other rights fulfilled. According to Katarina Tomaševski, the former UN Special Rapporteur on the Right to Education, "the Right to

Education functions as a multiplier, enhancing all rights and freedoms when it is guaranteed while jeopardizing them all when it is violated."

The realization of the Right to Education assumes double importance for minority and indigenous children. First, because these children are often socially excluded and discriminated against, the 'multiplying' effect of the right to education is of particular relevance to break or perpetuate the cycle of exclusion and marginalization. Second, by enabling the transmission of values and culture, the right to education has a key function in the preservation of minorities' and indigenous peoples' cultures, hence, their existence as distinct groups.

The main objective behind writing this chapter is to make the readers understand the concept of RTE Act, 2009, its strengths and weaknesses. This chapter will attempt to explore key lacunae in the context of the RTE Act and suggest improvements to address them. I will also discuss the supporting mechanisms, administrative imperatives and implementation challenges that need to be addressed if such policy improvements are to yield results on the ground.

Policies on Education: EFA and MDGs

The Education for All (EFA) initiative and the Millennium Development Goals (MDGs) are the two most important global policies on education. They have great influence on how countries design and implement their education programmes to deliver this basic service (McMillan, 2011).

In 1990, the Jomtien World Conference on Education for All (EFA) set the goal of universal primary education for year 2000. This commitment was reaffirmed for 2015 at the World Education Forum 2000 in Dakar. Six new targets were set to meet by this date; the goals 1, 2, 5 and 6 being the most relevant to this chapter.

Aware of the importance of education, UNESCO launched in 1990 the Education for All (EFA) initiative. Its six goals aim to provide quality basic education to all children, youth and adults (UNESCO, 2011). In 2000, the United Nations Millennium Declaration set eight Millennium Development Goals (MDGs) to eradicate poverty. The MDG 2 on achieving universal primary education and MDG 3 on eliminating gender inequality in primary and secondary schools are particularly relevant to education as a human right. Hence, EFA and MDGs are the two most important global policies on education, which give governments an incentive to fulfil their duties of providing universal compulsory free education to all children.

Education as a Human Right

Education has been formally recognized as a human right since the adoption

Table 1.1: Education for All (EFA) Goals

EFA Six Goals
Goal 1 "Expanding and improving comprehensive early childhood care and education, especially for the most vulnerable and disadvantaged children."
Goal 2 "Ensuring that by 2015 all children, particularly girls, children in difficult circumstances and those belonging to ethnic minorities, have access to, and complete, free and compulsory primary education of good quality."
Goal 3 "Ensuring that the learning needs of all young people and adults are met through equitable access to appropriate learning and life-skills programmes."
Goal 4 "Achieving a 50 per cent improvement in levels of adult literacy by 2015, especially for women, and equitable access to basic and continuing education for all adults."
Goal 5 "Eliminating gender disparities in primary and secondary education by 2005, and achieving gender equality in education by 2015, with a focus on ensuring girls' full and equal access to and achievement in basic education of good quality."
Goal 6 "Improving all aspects of the quality of education and ensuring excellence of all so that recognized and measurable learning outcomes are achieved by all, especially in literacy, numeracy and essential life skills."

of the Universal Declaration of Human Rights in 1948. This has since been affirmed in numerous global human rights treaties, including the United Nations Educational, Scientific and Cultural Organization (UNESCO) Convention against Discrimination in Education (1960), the International Covenant on Economic, Social and Cultural Rights (1966) and the Convention on the Elimination of All Forms of Discrimination against Women (1981). These treaties establish an entitlement to free, compulsory primary education for all children; an obligation to develop secondary education, supported by measures to render it accessible to all children, as well as equitable access to higher education and a responsibility to provide basic education for individuals, who have not completed primary education. Furthermore, they affirm that the aim of education is to promote personal development, strengthen respect for human rights and freedoms, enable individuals to participate effectively in a free society and promote understanding, friendship and tolerance. The right to education has long been recognized as encompassing not only access to educational provision, but also the obligation to eliminate discrimination at all levels of the educational system, to set minimum standards and to improve quality. In addition, education is necessary for the fulfilment of any other civil, political, economic or social right.

The United Nations Convention on the Rights of the Child (1989) further strengthens and broadens the concept of the right to education, in particular through the obligation to consider in its implementation the Convention's four core principles: non-discrimination; the best interests of the child; the right to life, survival and development of the child to the maximum extent possible; and the right of children to express their views in all matters affecting them and for their views to be given due weight in accordance with their age and maturity *(Marta, 1997).*

The Right to Education: A Human Need, a Human Right

Like all other human rights, the right to education "[c]and have a bearing on both relations between the individual and the state and between individuals themselves." (Sepulveda *et al.*, 2004). Hence, it is important to establish that the right to education shares characteristics with other human rights. It is:

- Inherent and Inalienable: as established by the UDHR and other texts, everyone is entitled to the right to education by virtue of being human, irrespective of their race, ethnicity, sex/gender, age, nationality, socio-economic condition, health status, etc.
- The right to education is inter-connected to all other human rights and is, therefore, indivisible from them.
- The right to education is equally applicable to all. In this regard, although there may be some limitations provided by law, in principle, the right to education is a universal entitlement.

Human Right Based Approach (HRBA) to Education

UNICEF developed a rights-based conceptual framework applied to education. According to this framework, the right to education has three main interdependent dimensions: the right of access to education, the right to quality education, and the right to respect in the learning environment. Ensuring universal access to school is not enough, because it does not guarantee that children acquire the skills and knowledge they need to lead lives they consider valuable. Thus, quality education requires school processes and curriculum to be relevant and address the needs of children. A human-right based education should also recognize and respect children's rights at school. This, in turn, is likely to positively impact retention rates and empower children (UNICEF, 2007). Each of these three sections has central criteria that must be met. Table 1.2 summarizes these elements.

Right to Education Bill (RTE)

India's biggest legislative accomplishment in education is the 2009 Right of

Table 1.2: HRBA to Education

Rights-based conceptual framework for education	
1. The right of access to education	• Education throughout all stages of childhood and beyond • Availability and accessibility of education • Equality of opportunity
2. The right to quality education	• A broad, relevant and inclusive curriculum • Rights-based learning and assessment • Child-friendly, safe and healthy environments
3. The right to respect in the learning environment	• Respect for identity • Respect for participation rights • Respect for integrity

Source: UNICEF 2007, p. 28.

Children to Free and Compulsory Education Act. This Act is also known as the Right to Education Bill, and came into force on April 1, 2010 (DSS, 2010).

The Right to Education Bill (RTE) constitutes an unprecedented law because it gives the right to education the same legal status as the right to life (ICBSE 2010). It clearly states that no child should be denied admission to school due to lack of birth certificates and other documents. It also states that children need to be enrolled in classes according to their age and knowledge level. Furthermore, students are entitled to receive special training in order to be at par with their classmates. Children admitted in a school have the right to free education until they complete standard VIII, even after they turn 14 years old (RTE, 2009).

RTE also prohibits admission exams, and private schools must reserve 25 per cent of their enrolment for children from poor families. No seat in this quota must be left vacant. The state will subsidize private schools at the average per learner cost in the public schools (Govinda, 2011). Thus, at least on paper, RTE eliminates many of the obstacles preventing underprivileged children from accessing formal education.

Under RTE, the government carries out community surveys and tries to get help from NGOs for compiling a list of all out-of-school children. The government gives the final list to the principals of local schools, so that they can ensure that the children in their respective areas get enrolled. Given that RTE firmly states that every child between 6 and 14 years old (without exception) should be enrolled in a formal school, the government stopped funding organizations providing NFE.

The number of out-of-school children has decreased by an impressive amount, from 29 million in 2002-2003 to nine million in 2006 (Govinda, 2008). In fact, the EFA Global Monitoring Report of 2008 considers India as one of the 28 developing countries that have the highest chances of achieving universal enrolment by 2015 (Ward 2011, p. 544). Despite the tremendous display of efforts, India still faces major challenges in universal education, primarily due to poverty and discriminatory practices. Scheduled Castes, Scheduled Tribes and other minorities, such as Muslims and women, are generally disadvantaged in most states (Govinda, 2008). In order to successfully address these challenges, "Routine input-oriented strategies must give way to new imaginative initiatives that reach out to under-served areas and marginalized populations" (Govinda, 2008).

The AEPs selected for this research focus on disadvantaged groups that the government is unable to reach: pavement children, slum children and migrant children of construction workers. As a member of the international community, India is responsive to the Education for All initiative and the MDGs, which press for equal access to quality education. Thus, it is in the government's interest to make sure that the Sarva Shiksha Abhiyan programme and the Right to Education Bill are successfully implemented. The AEPs selected and their strategies to reach highly deprived children are, thus, greatly shaped by these two national policies.

The Right of Children to Free and Compulsory Education Act, 2009

In August 2009, the Parliament passed the historic Right of Children to Free and Compulsory Education (RTE) Act, 2009. The new law must be seen from the perspective of children. It provides a justiciable legal framework that entitles all children between the ages of 6-14 years to an education of reasonable quality, based on principles of equity and non-discrimination. It provides for children's right to free and compulsory admission, attendance and completion of elementary education. More importantly, it provides for the child's right to education that is free from fear, stress and anxiety. There are several provisions in the Act, including for example, provisions prohibiting corporal punishment, detention and expulsion which need to be fore-fronted to ensure that we move towards a system that, as the National Policy on Education states, provides "*a warm, welcoming and encouraging approach for children to learn*" (NPE, 1986/92). The most important aspect, however, is to ensure that the teaching-learning process is free from stress and anxiety (Sec. 29), with obvious implications for curricular reform. Testing and school grading systems need to be reviewed to motivate children to deepen and widen their learning. The RTE Act also lays down the responsibilities of the teachers. The teacher accountability systems would need to ensure that children are learning and that their right to learning in an environment that is free from stress and anxiety is not violated. We can understand the Right to Education Act easily with the help of Figure 1.1 given below:

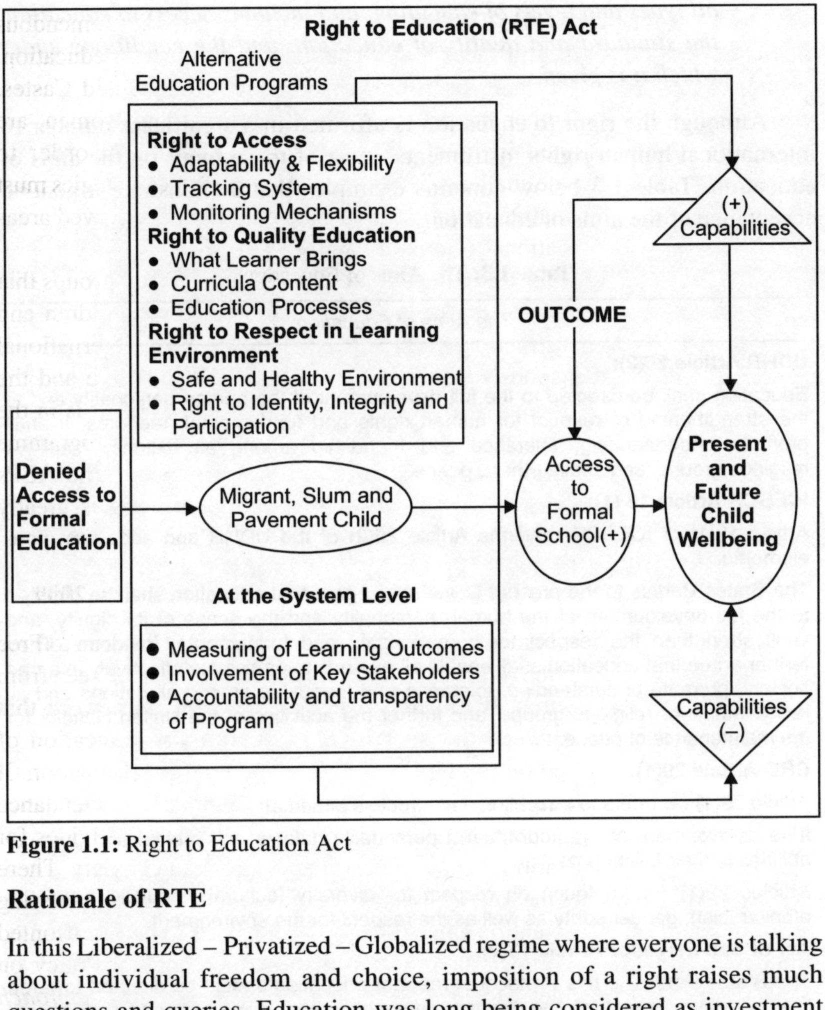

Figure 1.1: Right to Education Act

Rationale of RTE

In this Liberalized – Privatized – Globalized regime where everyone is talking about individual freedom and choice, imposition of a right raises much questions and queries. Education was long being considered as investment good, which raises stock of human capital (Becker, 1962 & Schultz, 1962). Therefore, the return to education should play the key role in attracting the choice of the individual as he himself would be the beneficiary of that good.

The Aims of the Right to Education

The only definition of "education" included in an international convention is set forth in the Convention against Discrimination in Education:

For the purposes of this Convention, the term 'education' refers to all types and levels of education, and includes access to education, the standard and quality of education, and the conditions under which it is given.

Although the right to education is affirmed in a significant number of international human rights instruments, most of these focus on the aims of education. Table 1.3 below contains examples that demonstrate a general acceptance of the aims of education.

Table 1.3: The Aims of Education

The Aims of Education
UDHR Article 26(2):
Education shall be directed to the full development of the human personality and to the strengthening of respect for human rights and fundamental freedoms. It shall promote understanding, tolerance and friendship among all nations, racial or religious groups, and shall further...peace.
ICESCR Article 13 (1):
Article 13(1) of ICESCR reaffirms Article 26(2) of the UDHR and adds two more elements:
The States Parties to the present Covenant...agree that education shall be directed to the full development of the human personality and the sense of its dignity, and shall strengthen the respect for human rights and fundamental freedoms. They further agree that education shall enable all persons to participate effectively in a free society, promote understanding, tolerance and friendship among all nations and all racial, ethnic or religious groups, and further the activities of the United Nations for the maintenance of peace.
CRC Article 29(1):
Article 29(1) (a) refers to education as a process aimed at:
[t]he development of the [individual's] personality, talents and mental and physical abilities to their fullest potential.
Articles 29(1) (c)–(e) touch on respect for diversity (cultural, linguistic, religious, ethnic/racial), gender parity as well as the respect for the environment.
Act of San Salvador Article 13(2):
The States Parties to this Protocol agree that education should be directed towards the full development of the human personality and human dignity and should strengthen respect for human rights, ideological pluralism, fundamental freedoms, justice and peace. They further agree that education ought to enable everyone to participate effectively in a democratic and pluralistic society and achieve a decent existence and should foster understanding, tolerance and friendship among all nations and all racial, ethnic or religious groups and promote activities for the maintenance of peace.

As already indicated, most human rights instruments state that education "shall be directed to the full development of the human personality." Thus, the implication is that the right to education is a precondition of human development. Also, in its General Comment, CESCR noted that the right to education is a means through which "marginalized adults and children can lift themselves out of poverty and obtain the means to participate fully in their communities." Nevertheless, as already articulated by the UNSRE, even when considering the important link between education and poverty reduction, a rights based approach ('RBA') to education requires education to be considered "[a]s an end in itself rather than a means for achieving other ends." From the outset, a RBA to realize education implies a commitment to counter social exclusion and discrimination as defined in various international human rights treaties and the Convention against Discrimination in Education.

The aims of education have been further re-affirmed by government and civil society at the international and regional level. In April 2000, the World Education Forum adopted the *Dakar Framework for Action*. Article 7 of the *Framework* states.

We hereby collectively commit ourselves to the attainment of the following goals:

- expanding and improving comprehensive early childhood care and education, especially for the most vulnerable and disadvantaged children;
- ensuring that by 2015 all children, particularly girls, children in difficult circumstances and those belonging to ethnic minorities, have access to and complete free and compulsory primary education of good quality;
- ensuring that the learning needs of all young people and adults are met through equitable access to appropriate learning and life skills programmes;
- achieving a 50 per cent improvement in levels of adult literacy by 2015, especially for women, and equitable access to basic and continuing education for all adults;
- eliminating gender disparities in primary and secondary education by 2005, and achieving gender equality in education by 2015, with a focus on ensuring girls' full and equal access to and achievement in basic education of good quality; and
- improving all aspects of the quality of education and ensuring excellence of all so that recognized and measurable learning outcomes are achieved by all, especially in literacy, numeracy and essential life skills.

Governing Principles of RTE

Keeping in view the mandate of the RTE Act, particularly the need to provide to all children of the country education of equitable quality, in the preparation of this report, the committee has been guided by the following principles:

(1) ***Holistic View of Education:*** As interpreted in National Curriculum Framework 2005, with implications for a systemic revamp of the entire content and process of education with significant implications for curriculum, teacher education, educational planning and management.

(2) ***Equity:*** To mean not only equal opportunity, but also creation of conditions in which the disadvantaged sections of the society – children of SC, ST, Muslim minority, landless agricultural workers and children with special needs, etc. – can avail of the opportunity.

(3) ***Access:*** Not to be confined to ensuring that a school becomes accessible to all children within specified distance, but implies an understanding of the educational needs and predicament of the traditionally excluded categories—the SC, ST and others sections of the most disadvantaged groups, the Muslim minority, girls in general, and children with special needs. This interpretation of access has been viewed by the Committee as an indispensable stipulation of the Act.

(4) ***Gender Concern:*** Implying not only an effort to enable girls to keep pace with boys, but to view education in the perspective spelt out in the National Policy on Education 1986/92; i.e., a decisive intervention to bring about a basic change in the status of women.

(5) ***Centrality of Teacher:*** To motivate them to innovate and create a culture in the classroom, and beyond the classroom, that might produce an inclusive environment for children, specially for girls from oppressed and marginalized backgrounds.

(6) ***Moral Compulsion:*** It is imposed through the RTE Act on parents, teachers, educational administrators and other stakeholders. Rather than shifting emphasis on punitive processes, the Committee has abided by this general tenor of the Act.

(7) ***Convergent and Integrated System of Educational Management:*** It is the prerequisite for implementation of the RTE law. All states must move in that direction as speedily as feasible.

(8) ***Adherence to RTE Stipulations*****:** Even where it seemed difficult to adhere to the timeframe laid down in the RTE Law, the Committee worked to find practical solutions for adherence to the Act's stipulations.

The RTE Act, 2009 Provides for

- The right of children to free and compulsory education till completion of elementary education in a neighbourhood school.
- It clarifies that 'compulsory education' means obligation of the appropriate government to provide free elementary education and ensure compulsory admission, attendance and completion of elementary education to every child in the six to fourteen age group. 'Free' means that no child shall be liable to pay any kind of fee or

charges or expenses, which may prevent him or her from pursuing and completing elementary education.

- It makes provisions for a non-admitted child to be admitted to an age appropriate class.
- It specifies the duties and responsibilities of appropriate Governments, local authority and parents in providing free and compulsory education, and sharing of financial and other responsibilities between the Central and State Governments.
- It lays down the norms and standards relating to, *inter alia,* Pupil Teacher Ratios (PTRs), buildings and infrastructure, school working days, teacher working hours.
- It provides for rational deployment of teachers by ensuring that the specified pupil teacher ratio is maintained for each school, rather than just as an average for the State or District or Block, thus ensuring that there is practically no urban-rural imbalance in teacher postings. It also prohibits deployment of teachers for non-educational work, other than decennial census, elections to local authority, state legislatures and parliament, and disaster relief.
- It provides for appointment of appropriately trained teachers, i.e., teachers with the requisite training and academic qualifications.
- For children in 6-14 age group, it prohibits (i) physical punishment and mental harassment, (ii) screening procedures for admission, (iii) capitation fees, (iv) private tuition by teachers, (v) running of schools without recognition,
- It provides for the following penalties:
  - ➢ For charging capitation fee: fine up to 10 times the capitation fee charged;
  - ➢ For resorting to screening during admission: ₹ 25,000 for first contravention; ₹ 50,000 for each subsequent contravention; and
  - ➢ For running a school without recognition: fine up to ₹ one lakh, and in case of continuing contravention ₹ 10,000 for each day during which the contravention continues.
- It provides for development of curriculum in consonance with the values enshrined in the Constitution, and which would ensure the all-round development of the child, building on the child's knowledge, potentiality and talent and making the child free of fear, trauma and anxiety through a system of child friendly and child centred learning.
- It provides for protection and monitoring of the child's right to free and compulsory education and redressal of grievances by the National and State Commissions for Protection of Child Rights, which shall have the powers of a civil court.

Rules for Implementation of the RTE Act

The model rules for implementation of the Act, as approved by the HRD Ministry and circulated to all states, highlight the responsibilities of State Governments, local authorities, school management, parents and teachers. These are:

1. That State Governments or local authorities will determine neighbourhood schools by undertaking household surveys and school mappings. Such agencies shall ensure that no child is subjected to caste, class, religious or gender abuse at school.

2. Local authorities will conduct household surveys and maintain a record of all children in their jurisdiction. The record will contain detailed information on children and their parents, and will specify whether they belong to weaker sections or disadvantaged group, or have a disability.

3. The State Government or local authority will identify children with disabilities and children from disadvantaged groups every year. Unaided and private schools shall ensure that children from weaker sections and disadvantaged groups shall not be segregated from other children in the classroom, nor shall their classes be held in places and timings different from classes held for other children.

4. Such children shall not be treated differently from the rest of the children in any manner pertaining to entitlements and facilities like textbooks, uniforms, library, ICT facilities, extra-curricular activities and sports, the rules say.

5. The school management committee or local authority will identify drop-outs or out-of-school children above six years of age and admit them in classes appropriate to their age after special training. The duration of the training shall be for three months and can be extended to two years. After admission, these children will continue to receive special attention by teachers for successful integration into the class "academically and emotionally", the rules say.

6. The State Government and local authorities will establish primary schools within a walking distance of one km from the neighbourhood. In case of Class VI to VIII children, the school should be within a walking distance of three km from the neighbourhood.

7. Private schools will reserve 25 per cent of their seats for poor children, and provide free education to them. The Government will reimburse the cost according to the per-child expenditure fixed by it.

8. The rules prescribe a formula to calculate per-child expenditure. The annual recurring expenditure incurred by the State Government on elementary education in respect of all schools established, owned or controlled by it or by the local authority, divided by the total number of children enrolled in all such schools, shall be the per-child expenditure.

9. In the absence of schools in small hamlets, the State Government shall

make adequate arrangements like free transportation and residential facilities. For physically challenged children, the State Government will make arrangement for their smooth transport and schooling.

10. Every child between the ages of 6 to 14 years irrespective of gender and social category has the right to free and compulsory education. The education given to this age group would be the ground work for their future and would act as a stepping stone towards the visionary developed India.

11. Any cost that prevents a child from accessing school will be borne by the State, which shall have the responsibility of enrolling the child as well as ensuring attendance and completion of eight years of schooling.

12. No child shall be denied admission for want of documents; no child shall be turned away if the admission cycle in the school is over and no child shall be asked to take an admission test. Children with disabilities will also be educated in the mainstream schools.

13. Further, all private schools shall be required to enrol children from weaker sections and disadvantaged communities in the incoming class to the extent of 25 per cent of their enrolment, by simple random selection. No seats in this quota can be left vacant.

14. These children will be treated on par with all the other children in the school and subsidized by the State at the rate of average per learner costs in the government schools. All schools will have to prescribe to norms and standards laid out in the Act and no school that does not fulfil these standards within three years will be allowed to function.

15. All private schools will have to apply for recognition, failing which they will be penalized to the tune of ₹ one lakh and if they still continue to function will be liable to pay ₹ 10,000 per day as fine.

16. The National Commission for Protection of Child Rights (NCPCR) has been mandated to monitor the implementation of this historic Right.

Challenges in the Implementation of RTE Act, 2009

The main challenges in the implementation of RTE Act, 2009 are as follows:

- Some State governments have said that they do not have the funds to implement the Act. The governments have also observed that they do not have adequate control over private schools to compel them to reserve quota of seats as laid down.
- Many unaided private schools have petitioned the Supreme Court, challenging the 25 per cent reservation of seats as "unconstitutional" and "violating fundamental rights of unaided private educational institutions."
- Shortfall of trained teachers will be a big challenge. The average students-to-teacher ratio in a classroom at present stands at 50:1.

The Act spells out that this ratio should be 30:1, which means that at least twelve lakh trained teachers will be required within six months of notification of the Act.

Key Issues to Monitor and Analyze in Assessing Support for Education

More emphasis should be given to the three aspects of education:

Right to Education

- The right to education shall be ratified through legally binding documents, through the Constitution or legally binding Act. The Act should have a particular focus on discrimination and guarantee that primary education is free of charge;
- Secondary education should be made generally available and accessible to all; higher education should be made equally accessible to all on the basis of capacity.
- Assess indirect costs and to what extent they hinder all children to participate in education
- Educational systems should be inclusive of girls and boys alike, irrespective of ethnicity, disability and location of residence. Educational strategies shall be based on solid analyses of the out-of-school population and strategies on how to include them.
- Disaggregated data shall be used as evidence to guide educational policies, plans, budgets and to an equitable resource distribution between different forms of education, out of school population and districts.

Rights in Education

- The learner shall have the right to receive quality education in order to read, write, numeracy and basic life skills.
- The learner should learn to respect human rights, fundamental freedoms, own culture and language, respect for natural resources, tolerance, equity of sexes, and living in peace.
- Education shall be in line with the dignity of human rights. Punishments, unfair treatment and discrimination due to gender, disability, HIV, pregnancy, etc. should be made illegal.
- Learning environment shall be safe and healthy.
- Teacher's training shall incorporate knowledge of human rights, participatory methods, child friendly pedagogies, including knowledge on how to meet the needs of learners with various limitations (in the classroom and/or with support from specialized services).
- Enable participation of learners and students to influence the quality and organization of education.

Rights through Education

- Education should promote values of peace, tolerance, equality of sexes, and friendship among all people, ethnic, national and religious groups and persons of indigenous origin and respect for the natural environment
- Learners should be equipped with relevant skills and self-confidence to be able to participate meaningfully in democratic processes, exercise their political and civic rights, keep healthy and earn a living.

Norms and Standards as per the RTE Act

The RTE Act clearly lays down norms and standards for the physical infrastructure and human resource required to implement the Act.

Table 1.4: Norms and Standards as per the RTE Act

	1. Number of Teachers	
	Admitted Children	*Numbers of Teachers*
A. I to V Class	0-60	2
	61-90	3
	91-120	4
	121-200	5
	>150	5 plus one head teacher
	>200	PTR (excluding head teacher) not to exceed 40
B. VI –VII class	• At least one teacher per class so that there is at least one teacher each for science and mathematics, social studies and languages. • At least one teacher for every 35 children. • Where admission of children is above 100, a full-time head teacher and part time instructors for art education, health and physical education, and work education.	
	2. Building	
All-weather buildings consisting of at least one classroom for every teacher and an office-cum-store-cum head teacher's room, barrier-free access, separate toilets for boys and girls, safe and adequate drinking water for all children, a kitchen where the mid-day meal is cooked in school, a playground and arrangements for securing the school building by a boundary wall or fencing.		
	3. Minimum of Working Days/Instructional Hours in an Academic Year	
A. Working Days	I–V class VI–VIII class	220 Working Days
B. Instructional Hours	I–V class VI–VIII class	1000 Instructional Hours
4. Minimum number of working hours per week for teacher – 45 teaching hours (Including Preparation Hours).		
5. Teaching and learning equipments to be provided to each class as required.		
6. Library providing newspapers, magazines and books on all subjects available.		
7. Play materials, games and sports equipments to be provided for each class as required.		

RTE Roadmap

The RTE provides a legally enforceable rights framework with certain unambiguous time targets that Governments must adhere to. For example, the Act mandates that every child in the six to fourteen age group shall have a right to free and compulsory education in a neighbourhood school. The Act also provides that if a school does not exist in an area or limit prescribed as the neighbourhood, the appropriate Government and the local authority shall establish a school in this area within a period of three years. Therefore, all children-girls and boys-children from disadvantaged groups and economically weaker sections, children with special needs, children involved in child labour and so on, must be in a school within three years time starting from 1 April 2010. This provision in the RTE Act is applicable to the SSA goals on access and universalization of elementary education. The following timeframes, mandated by the RTE Act, become immediately applicable to SSA:

Table 1.5: Time Frames of RTE Act

Activity	*Time Frame*
Establishment of neighbourhood schools	3 years (by 31 March 2013)
• Provision of school infrastructure All weather school buildings • One-classroom-one-teacher • Office cum-store-cum-Head teacher room • Toilets and drinking water facilities • Barrier free access • Library • Playground • Fencing/boundary walls	3 years (by 31 March 2013)
Provision of teachers as per prescribed PTR	3 years (by 31 March 2013)
Training of untrained teachers	5 years (by 31 March 2015)
All quality interventions and other provisions	With immediate effect

Right to Education: Future Course of Action

The Right of Children to Free and Compulsory Education Act (2009) has come into force since April 2010 and the RTE Act provides the legislative framework for "Universalization of Elementary Education (UEE)". MHRD had set up a committee to prepare model rules under the RTE Act. The model rules were shared with the States in the meeting of State Education Secretaries. The central rules titled "The Right of Children to Free and Compulsory Education Rules 2010" were notified in the Official Gazette on 9 April 2010.

As a follow-up of RTE Act, the Central government has issued notifications authorizing the National Council for Teacher Education to lay down the minimum qualifications for a person to be eligible for appointment as a teacher. Since then, the NCTE has notified teachers' qualifications under the RTE Act. The Central government also authorized the National Council of Educational Research and Training to develop a framework of national curriculum for elementary education. With the recommendation of the committee for implementation of RTE and resultant revamp of SSA, the SSA's framework of implementation has been revised and its norms have been modified to align them with the requirement of RTE Act, 2009. The financial outlays for implementing the combined RTESSA programme are as given in Table 1.6. The fund sharing pattern between the Centre and the State has been revised with a new funding pattern of 65:35, (90:10 for North-eastern states) applicable for a period of five years with effect from 2010-11.

Normative Standards on the Right to Education

Here, we outline the components of the right to education that can be drawn from international as well as regional human rights instruments. In this regard, a combination of all the normative standards on the right to education contained in international human rights law point to a clearly defined set of elements and components (Fig. 1.2).

Table 1.6: Total Requirement Approved under RTE

Year	*Total*	*Recurring*	*Non-Recurring*	*% Recurring*	*% Non-Recurring*
2010-11	40503	29247	11256	72%	28%
2011-12	43904	33303	10601	76%	24%
2012-13	48151	37948	10203	79%	21%
2013-14	487443	40798	7945	84%	16%
2014-15	49931	42345	7586	85%	15%
Total	2,31,233	1,83,641	47,592	79%	21%

Source: MHRD Annual Report, 2010-11.

In the same way, the language around the aims of education is consistent in most international human rights instruments, it is also clear that there is a minimum level of education that should be compulsory, free and available to all. In this regard, it is possible to assert that this is one of the core elements of the right to education. Thus, a more detailed analysis of each component is provided below.

Loopholes in the Right to Education (RTE) Bill

The 2009 Right to Education (RTE) Bill is a very important law for all children to exercise their right to go to school. It addresses some of the most pressing obstacles preventing disadvantaged children from getting admission in schools, such as showing an identity document or birth certificates. Despite its important contribution, the RTE has loopholes that negatively affect the most underprivileged children.

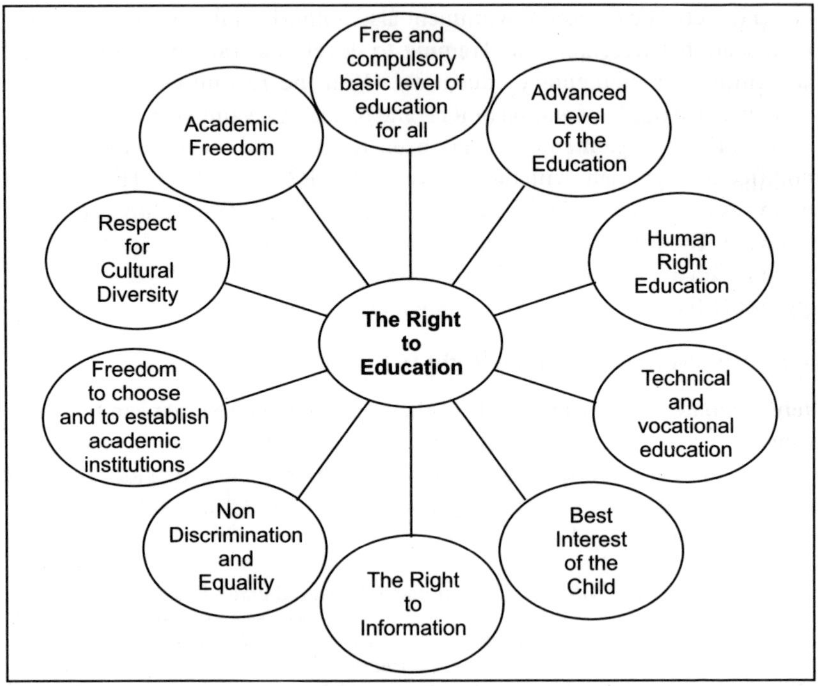

Figure 1.2: A basic level of education should be compulsory and free for all

The law says that no child from age six to fourteen years should be denied access to formal education, and focuses on getting as many children as possible enrolled into formal schools, i.e. the quantitative outcome. However, it does not pay attention to the process required to achieve the outcome, which is a vital component of the Human Rights-Based Approach. The RTE seems to disregard the fact that formal schooling is not a suitable solution for all children. This law does not take into account the factors affecting disadvantaged children and their capability to access education. Since the RTE recognizes formal education as the only legitimate one, the government stopped funding NGOs (like DSS) that were operating successful non-formal education programmes.

The RTE pushes for formal education, but it does not provide mechanisms that genuinely address the needs of the most disadvantaged children. Under the RTE there is no policy about procedures and strategies to sustainably retain in school those children enrolled under this law. Furthermore, it does not provide special curricula that help former out-of-school children to successfully cope with the formal system. Finally, there is no budget allocation to sustain a monitoring mechanism to evaluate the progress of these children after entering the formal system.

Furthermore, a major loophole is that at the time of admission, the RTE prioritizes the age of children over their knowledge level. This means that the government wants children to be enrolled in the standard that is appropriate to their age despite having a much lower knowledge level than that of their peers. For instance, an illiterate 10-year old child should be admitted to Class I for the first year if one looks at knowledge level, but the year after he or she should be enrolled in the standard corresponding to their age (i.e. Class VI). Teachers should provide extra support before or after class in order to help the child catch up with their peers. However, this is an unrealistic goal because the child lacks the capacity to absorb so many concepts in one year, and he or she is not used to studying so many hours a day. Public school teachers are unable to pay personal attention to children having trouble learning because they are in charge of a much larger number of students, and in practice, they do not provide the extra assistance that the law requires.

In a nut shell, the serious lacunae and contradictions in the RTE Act are as follows:

This Act:

- ***allows*** the authorities to dilute the meaning of Free Education in an ad-hoc manner;
- ***distorts*** the concept of Neighbourhood School recommended by the Kothari Commission (1966) and resolved by the Parliament in the National Policy on Education-1986 (as modified in 1992), thereby authorizing the government to compel the poor children to study in inferior quality schools;
- ***maintains*** Sarva Shiksha Abhiyan's discriminatory multi-layered school system;
- ***permits*** the government to build schools of entirely unacceptable, ambiguous and sub-standard norms and standards;
- ***continues*** with inferior quality education for almost three-fourths of the children, particularly girls and disadvantaged;
- ***undermines*** the universally accepted pedagogic role of mother tongue in acquiring knowledge and learning languages other than one's mother tongue, including English;
- ***discriminates*** between the children studying in government schools and the private unaided schools in various ways. This is bound to lead to further deterioration of the quality of education in the government schools, making private schools, both aided and un-aided, even more expensive and inaccessible to a wide section of the society. The worst sufferers of such discrimination will be the girls, thereby leading to increased gender disparity;

- ***aims*** at demolishing the government school system under the pretext of providing free education to the weaker sections on 25 per cent of the seats in private schools. On several grounds, it is clear that this misconceived provision would not give any benefit whatsoever to the deprived children even in the short term;
- ***legitimizes***, through the above-named provision of 25 per cent reservation in private schools, the 'free market' policy of school vouchers and Public Private Partnership;
- ***refuses***, by not including the financial estimates for implementation of the Bill in the Financial Memorandum, to explicitly accept the full obligations of the Bill; and
- ***promotes*** unregulated privatization and commercialization of school education.

In conclusion, the RTE is mainly concerned with quantitative results that show that India is close to achieving universal education for all children. However, the law has significant loopholes that make it seem as though this initiative lacks a sincere commitment to prevent dropouts. The efforts of the Indian government to facilitate access to formal schools do not have a large impact if they cannot ensure that children stay in school and complete compulsory education, which grants them the necessary skills and capabilities to lead valuable lives.

Suggestions for Implementation of the RTE Act

To take the advantages of RTE Act, the successful implementation of RTE Act is necessary and for the successful integration of RTE Act, the suggestions can be categorized under four broad areas:

Awareness

Awareness among communities about the Act is one of the key aspects for its successful implementation. At present, awareness among people about the Act is low. Unless people understand its contours, there will be limited initiative and ownership on their part. Civil society can play a much larger role in creating this awareness.

Capacity Development

Capacity development is required at various levels to operationalize the Act. At the community level, SMCs and *Panchayat Raj* Institutions (PRIs) need to be trained about their roles and responsibilities; strengthening of systems and human resource development is also needed to make efficient use of available resources, and most importantly, teachers should be trained to impart child-centred education.

Management

Management functions should be reviewed and bottlenecks in implementation of the Act identified. Planning and monitoring of programmes is as important as improving the quality of education imparted. Both require different set of skills.

Four tiers in the management structure need to be strengthened and empowered to make implementation of the Act more effective.

- The Centre should also address state-specific concerns and provide support, if required. If some states are dragging their feet in implementing the Act, the Centre can demand its implementation by linking it with the SSA and other development grants.
- The State Commission for Protection of Child Rights (SCPCR), which is the monitoring agency for implementation of the Act in different states, has not been effective in many of them. It is therefore important to ensure that an effective SCPCR is in place.
- Local authorities need to play a crucial role. Effective implementation of the Act will depend on how effective *Gram Panchayats* (GPs) and *Nagar Palikas* are. They need to be given sufficient resources to implement the Act.
- There should be a bottom-up approach and more autonomy given to schools. These should then be monitored through independent mechanisms.

Innovations

There have been many innovations in the area of classroom transactions and distribution of entitlements from which one can learn. Today, technology can be put to good use to collect information and make planning more need-based. For example, the Delhi Government has initiated online attendance of teachers. The register closes at a specified time and teachers, who do not mark their presence up to that time, are marked absent. Similarly, teachers desirous of seeking transfers can make online requisitions and even give their preference for the schools to which they wish to be transferred. This helps to streamline the process of attendance and transfers.

Conclusion

To quote Justice P.N. Bhagwati, Former Chief Justice of India:

> *"The child is a soul with a being, a nature and capacities of its own, who must be helped to find them, to grow into their maturity, into a fullness of physical and vital energy and the utmost breadth, depth*

and height of its emotional, intellectual and spiritual being; otherwise there cannot be a healthy growth of the nation."

It is an established fact that basic education improves the level of human well-being, especially with regard to life expectancy, infant mortality and nutritional status of children. Social justice and equity are by themselves strong arguments for providing basic education for all. Education is an effective instrument not only for the development of one's personality, but also for the sustained growth of the nation. Elementary education in India, therefore, is the foundation for the development of every citizen and the nation as a whole. Making quality elementary education available to all has been one of the important concerns of the government.

The right to education is both a human right in itself and an indispensable means of realizing other human rights. Consequently, it must be placed among the priorities of all governments. Once more, it is for citizens and social movements to remind their governments of their responsibilities and to demand that the right to quality education becomes a reality.

Ensuring the right to education in India requires decisive progress towards universal access to free quality education, with continuity throughout the primary and secondary levels. This implies transforming schools into a space for the full development of students as rights-holders. In order to achieve this, political commitment and increased investment are required from all stakeholders (state, private sector, donors), as well as more efficient institutional management, an improved curricula and a rights-based understanding of school governance. In addition, it is critical to improve the efficiency of available resources, particularly by reducing repetition and dropout rates.

It is also crucial to ensure a more equitable distribution of educational opportunities at all levels of the school system so as to avoid discrimination based on social class, gender, capacities, ethnicity or area of residence. Access to quality preschool education must be ensured for children between the ages of three and six. In addition to playing a key role in children's development, pre-school education also prepares students and improves results at the primary level. Of equal importance is the need to carry out an in-depth review of the critical factors that limit the quality of education. The aim should be to design strategies—with the participation of teachers and communities—that can improve curricular relevance and ensure that students are equipped with the skills required in a world of intense social and cultural transformations. It is fundamental to promote an ethical commitment to justice and equality of opportunities among students, developing attitude of solidarity, respect and responsibility towards others.

References

1. Chauhan, C.P.S. (2009). Education for All in India: A Second Look, *International Journal of Lifelong Education,* vol. 28, no. 2, pp. 227-240.
2. Door Step School (DSS) (2010). *Annual Report 2010-2011*. Mumbai and Pune.
3. Govinda, R. *Implementing Right to Education Act in India: Major issues and challenges.* http://www.create-rpc.org/pdf_documents/RGovindaBangladeshconference2011.pdf
4. Govinda, R. (2008). Education for All in India: Assessing Progress towards Dakar Goals, *Prospects: quarterly review of comparative* education, vol. 38, no. 3, pp. 431-444.
5. McMillan, L.K. (2011). What is Right? Two Variations for Interpreting the Right to Education', *International Review Education*, vol. 1, no. 56, pp. 531-545.
6. Marta, S.P. (1997). The Convention on the Rights of the Child, in Office of the High Commissioner for Human Rights, United Nations Institute for Training and Research, and United Nations Staff College Project, *Manual on Human Rights Reporting under Six Major International Human Rights Instruments*, United Nations, Geneva. p. 427.
7. Parth, J.S. (2009). The Right of Children to Free and Compulsory Education Bill, 2008, Suggestions from the Centre for Civil Society. http://www.ccsindia.org/.
8. Planning Meeting: Research on Child Labour in South Asia, Jaipur, June 18, 2000 CUTS-CITEE, Jaipur, http://www.cuts-international.org/linkages-Meeting-18.htm.
9. Sadgopal, A (2008). Education Bill: dismantling rights. *The Financial Express*, 9 November, 2008.
10. The Right of Children to Free and Compulsory Education Act (RTE) 2009 (the whole of India, except the State Jammu and Kashmir). http://education.nic.in/elementary/free%20and%20compulsory.pdf.
11. UNESCO (2005). Education for All Global Monitoring Report 2005 - The Quality Imperative. Paris, EFA Global Monitoring Report Team. http://portal.unesco.org/education/en/.
12. UNESCO (2011). *Education for All (EFA).* http://www.unesco.org/new/en/education/themes/leading-the-international-agenda/education-for-all/.
13. UNICEF (2007). *A Human Rights-Based Approach to Education for All,* UNICEF, New York. http://unesdoc.unesco.org/images/0015/001548/154861e.pdf.
14. Ward, M. (2011). Aid to Education: The Case of Sarva Shiksha Abhiyan in India and the Role of Development Partners, *Journal of Education Policy*, vol. 26, no. 4, pp. 543-556.

2

The Right to Education
Some Historical Landmarks

Noushad Husain

Education is globally recognized as a fundamental human right and people with access to education can develop the skills, capacity and confidence to secure other rights. The right to education thus acts as an enabling right that functions as the voice through which rights can be claimed and protected. It is therefore an important stepping stone to improve the social situation of the people. The right to education is recognized, promoted and protected at all levels from national, regional to international. Education is the primary vehicle by which economically and socially marginalized adults and children can lift themselves out of poverty and obtain the means to participate fully in their communities. Education has a vital role in empowering women, safeguarding children from exploitative and hazardous labour and sexual exploitation, promoting human rights and democracy, protecting the environment, and controlling population growth *(Sinha, 2008)*.

The right to education has a solid basis in the international law on human rights. It has been laid down in several universal and regional human rights documents. Examples are the Universal Declaration on Human Rights (Article 26), the European Convention on Human Rights and Fundamental Freedoms (Article 2 of the First Protocol), the UNESCO Convention against Discrimination in Education and the International Covenant on Economic, Social and Cultural Rights (Articles 13 and 14).

The right to education can be characterized as an 'empowerment' right. Such a right provides "the individual with control over the course of his or her life, and in particular, control over (.) the state." In other words, exercising an empowerment right enables a person to experience the benefit of other rights. It is an empowerment right, because of its links with other rights: "The key to social action in defence of rights, (.) is an educated citizenry, able to spread its ideas and to organize in defence of its rights." Civil and political rights such as freedom of expression, freedom of association or the right to political participation, only obtain substance and meaning when a person is educated.

In short, the right to education contributes in an important way to the essence of promoting human rights, *i.e.,* living in dignity. Through its links with other rights, the right to education accentuates the unity and interdependence of all human rights. In 1948, the Universal Declaration of Human Rights ('UDHR') set the basis for the body of international human rights law that states that *"everyone has a right to education"*. During the last decade, the progressive development of a framework for the realization of the right to education has advanced.

This background chapter aims to assess various human rights based approaches that may contribute to the realization of the right to education.

Historical Development of the Right to Education

The literature indicates that the term 'education' has long been with humankind (Volio, 1979: 19), but the notion that education is a fundamental human right is a relatively new concept (Huberman, 1979: 57). Societies have been educating their learners for ages, for different aims. Learners might be educated to fulfil different roles in the home and in society. This, therefore, means that societies continually ask themselves different questions about what kind of education is necessary for the child (Mialaret, 1979: 48) and how relevant that particular kind of education would be for the child. Education became a matter of public concern and state responsibility only with the emergence of the secular state. A letter written by Thomas Jefferson to George Wythe in Paris in 1786, as quoted by Volio (1979: 22) and Starkey (1991: 42) reads as follows:

> *"I think by far the most important bill in our whole code is that for the diffusion of knowledge among people. No other sure foundation can be devised for the preservation of freedom and happiness... Preach! My dear sir, a crusade against ignorance; establish and improve the law for educating the common people."*

There can be no doubt that Jefferson placed a high value on education, as it is through education that people can be freed from ignorance. Laws had to be passed to enforce such ideals and to ensure that people receive education.

In the sixteen and seventeenth century, philosophers such as John Locke and Jean-Jacques Rousseau adumbrated in their writings the modern concept of the individual's right to education. They advocated a parental obligation to educate children, until they become of age and are able to make full and proper use of their freedom and faculties. Education was perceived and conceived as pre-existing or as a natural right, which is superior to the positive law. This means that the right to education is a human right that man has by virtue of his or her being human and parents have the obligation to nurture, protect and to provide children with basic education in order to prepare them for life (Hodgson, 1998: 7; Wringe, 1981: 140). This idea is evidenced by the following quotation:

> "...*Giving children an education suitable to their station in life: a duty pointed out by reason, and of far the greatest importance of any. For it is not easy to imagine or allow, that a parent has conferred any considerable benefit upon his child, by bringing him into the world, if he afterwards entirely neglects his culture and education and...leads a life useless to others and shameful to himself* (Hodgson, 1998: 8)."

The right to education emerged rather belatedly in the history of civil liberties, despite its importance (Volio, 1979: 19). Civil liberty instruments, such as the English Bill of Rights of 1689, the Virginia Declaration of Rights of 1776, the American declaration of Independence of 1776 and the French Declaration of the Rights of Man of 1789 focused on the rights to life, freedom, equality, private property, freedom of expression and religious beliefs. These instruments did not contain any specific mention of the human right to education (Volio, 1979:19; Hodgson, 1998:9).

During the course of the nineteenth century the development of liberalism and socialism placed education in the catalogue of human rights. The liberalist concept of human rights focused on the duty of parents to provide education, their freedom to choose the education of their children within the limits established by law and the duty of the state to guarantee that every child receives education by means of compulsory school attendance and legal regulation of school curricula (Nowak, 1995: 192).

At the international level, the right to education has been recognized by a number of universal and regional instruments, adopted particularly after World War II. To mark the importance of education, different countries recognized the right to education and included it in their Constitutions.

The human right to education was not fully proclaimed at the international level until after the World War II. At that time the human right to education was recognized in international and regional instruments and in customary law and appeared most prominently in the hierarchy of human rights (Hodgson, 1998: 39). The progress made in the recognition of the right to education has resulted in the fact that it is now recognized and reaffirmed in some detail by major international human rights instruments (UDHR, CDE, CRC and ICSECR) (Daudet and Singh, 2001: 13). International states have agreed, by ratifying several declarations, conventions and covenants, that they will uphold human rights and protect the rights of their citizens, including the rights of learners to education. Once human rights instruments are ratified, they become legally binding on the state that ratified them (Balton, 1992: 211; Dorr, 1994: 10). Some of these human rights instruments are explained below:

Chronology of Development of the Right to Education

In a nutshell, the chronology of the development of the Right to Education is as follows:

Table 2.1: Tracing the Development of the Right to Education Act Internationally

Year	*Event*
1924	The Declaration of Geneva
1948	In the Universal Declaration of Human Rights education is declared a basic right of every human being.
1958	Convention Concerning Discrimination in Respect of Employment and Occupation
1959	The Declaration of the Rights of the Child is adopted by the UN General Assembly. Education is declared as the right of every child.
1960–1966	UNESCO's World Regional Conferences on Education.
1969	The International Convention on the Elimination of All Forms of Racial Discrimination enters into force, proclaiming the right of all to education, regardless of race or ethnicity.
1976	The International Covenant on Economic, Social and Cultural Rights enters into force, guaranteeing the right to education for all.
1981	The Convention on the Elimination of All Forms of Discrimination against Women enters into force, calling for equal rights in education.
1985	The Third World Conference on Women. Education is declared the basis for improving the status of women.
1990	The World Declaration on Education for All in Jomtien, Thailand. The conference, co sponsored by UNDP, UNESCO, UNICEF, the World Bank and later UNFPA, presented a global consensus on an expanded vision of basic education.
1993	The E-9 Education Summit in New Delhi, India. Representatives of the Governments of the nine most populous nations in the developing world (Bangladesh, Brazil, China, Egypt, India, Indonesia, Mexico, Nigeria and Pakistan) pledge to achieve the goal of universal primary education by the year 2000.
1994	The World Conference on Special Needs Education: Access and Equality in Salamanca. Participants declare that all countries should incorporate special needs education into their domestic education strategy.
1994	The International Conference on Population and Development. Participating states commit themselves to promote and attain universal and equitable access to quality education to help eradicate poverty, promote employment and foster social integration, with a particular emphasis on girls' education.
1996	The Amman Affirmation at the Mid-decade meeting of the International Consultative Forum on Education for All.
2000	The Dakar Framework for Action adopted at the World Education Forum in Senegal.

International Human Rights Instruments on the Right to Education

There are many international instruments and tools that can be used to canvass various dimensions of the right to education. This paper lists the main instruments, interpretative tools and documents that set the basis of the right to education in its present-day form. The following international instruments protect and promote the right to education:

The Declaration of Geneva (1924)

Although the Declaration of Geneva of 1924 does not specifically make reference to the right of learners to education, it does lay some foundations for such a right. Principle V states that a child must be brought up in the consciousness that its talent must be devoted to the service of its fellow men (Arajarvi, 1992: 410; Detrick, 1999: 427; Hodgson, 1998: 11; Van Bueren, 1995: 7 and Van Bueren, 1998: 3).

The Universal Declaration of Human Rights (UDHR) (1948)

According to the first sentence of Article 26 of the UDHR (1948) "*Everyone has the right to education*". This article refers to both adults and learners and to education in the broad sense (Arajarvi, 1992: 406). Article 26 of the Universal Declaration of Human Rights is given below:

1. *Everyone has the right to education. Education shall be free, at least in the elementary and fundamental stages. Elementary education shall be compulsory. Technical and professional education shall be made generally available and higher education shall be equally accessible to all on the basis of merit.*
2. *Education shall be directed to the full development of the human personality and to the strengthening of respect for human rights and fundamental freedoms. It shall promote understanding, tolerance and friendship among all nations, racial or religious groups, and shall further the activities of the United Nations for the maintenance of peace.*
3. *Parents have a prior right to choose the kind of education that shall be given to their children.*

It includes all activities by which human beings transmit to their descendants a body of knowledge and skills and a moral code, however elementary, which will enable that group to subsist in the particular conditions of its characteristic environment and ethics (M'Bow, 1979: 7; Detrick, 1999: 475). This declaration provides the foundation for both moral and legal principles in education. Although it was not recognized as being legally binding, it covers the political and moral scope of human rights resolutions by which member states to the declaration must abide. In order to make it binding, it was necessary that its major principles should also be taken up in an instrument such as a covenant. The importance of the UNESCO conventions, declarations and programmes adopted on the right to education, lies in the fact that firstly they reaffirm certain principles enshrined in the basic text of the conventions and then these are given concrete substance; otherwise, they would remain 'mere principles' whose application would not be clear. Secondly, they ensure that member states commit to the right to education by updating the principles for reaffirming that right (Daudet and Singh, 2001: 14).

Convention (No. 111) Concerning Discrimination in Respect of Employment and Occupation (1958)

The International Labour Organization (ILO)'s Convention Concerning Discrimination in Respect of Employment and Occupation declares as its aim the promotion of "*equality of opportunity and treatment in respect of employment and occupation, with a view to eliminating any discrimination in respect thereof,*" and calls upon education to assist in securing this. States are required to "*enact such legislation and to promote such educational programmes as may be calculated to secure the acceptance and observance of this policy*" (Article 3).

The UN Declaration on the Rights of the Child (UNDRC) (1959)

In its preamble, the UNDRC reaffirms the proclamation made in the UDHR of 1948 that everyone is entitled to the rights enshrined in the declaration without distinction of any kind. The first direct reference in an international human rights instrument to the child's right to education is in Principle 7 of the UNDRC. This principle proclaims that "*the child is entitled to receive education, which shall be free and compulsory at least in the elementary stage.*" (Arajarvi, 1992: 411; Detrick, 1999: 472 and Van Bueren, 1998: 5), but it does not include provisions with regard to the quality of education. The Articles 28 and 29 of UNDRC are as follows:

Article 28

1. *States Parties recognize the right of the child to education, and with a view to achieving this right progressively and on the basis of equal opportunity, they shall, in particular:*
   (a) *Make primary education compulsory and available free to all;*
   (b) *Encourage the development of different forms of secondary education, including general and vocational education, make them available and accessible to every child, and take appropriate measures, such as the introduction of free education and offering financial assistance in case of need;*

(c) *Make higher education accessible to all on the basis of capacity by every appropriate means;*

(d) *Make educational and vocational information and guidance available and accessible to all children;*

(e) *Take measures to encourage regular attendance at schools and the reduction of drop-out rates.*

2. *States Parties shall take all appropriate measures to ensure that school discipline is administered in a manner consistent with the child's human dignity and in conformity with the present Convention.*
3. *States Parties shall promote and encourage international cooperation in matters relating to education, in particular with a view to contributing to the elimination of ignorance and illiteracy throughout the world and facilitating access to scientific and technical knowledge and modern teaching methods. In this regard, particular account shall be taken of the needs of developing countries.*

Article 29

1. *States Parties agree that the education of the child shall be directed to:*

(a) *The development of the child's personality, talents and mental and physical abilities to their fullest potential;*

(b) *The development of respect for human rights and fundamental freedoms, and for the principles enshrined in the Charter of the United Nations;*

(c) *The development of respect for the child's parents, his or her own cultural identity, language and values, for the national values of the country in which the child is living, the country from which he or she may originate, and for civilizations different from his or her own;*

(d) *The preparation of the child for responsible life in a free society, in the spirit of understanding, peace, tolerance, equality of sexes, and friendship among all people, ethnic, national and religious groups and persons of indigenous origin;*

(e) *The development of respect for the natural environment.*

2. *No part of the present Article or Article 28 shall be construed so as to interfere with the liberty of individuals and bodies to establish and direct educational institutions, subject always to the observance of the principle set forth in paragraph 1 of the present Article and to the requirements that the education given in such institutions shall conform to such minimum standards as may be laid down by the State.*

The Convention against Discrimination in Education (CDE) 1960

A further international recognition of the right to education came with the adoption of the CDE in Paris by the UN General Conference of UNESCO in 1960, which came into force in 1962. The convention reaffirms Article 7 of the UDHR, which asserts the general principle of non-discrimination and proclaims in Article 26 that every person has the right to education. The convention also reaffirms the UNESCO Constitution that advocates the ideals of equality of educational opportunity without regard to race, sex or any other discrimination in education, but it also promotes equality of opportunity and equal treatment for all. It allows the establishment and maintenance of private educational institutions based on language, religion and cultural beliefs, as long as their purpose is not to discriminate or exclude other groups of persons and provide that they offer a quality and level of education equal to those provided by public authorities Article 2 (c) of the CDE of 1960.

Article 3 and Article 4 of the Convention against Discrimination in Education (1960) is:

- *In order to eliminate and prevent discrimination within the meaning of this Convention, the States Parties thereto undertake:*
  (a) *To abrogate any statutory provisions and any administrative instructions and to discontinue any administrative practices, which involve discrimination in education;*
  (b) *To ensure, by legislation where necessary, that there is no discrimination in the admission of pupils to educational institutions;*
  (c) *Not to allow any differences of treatment by the public authorities between nationals, except on the basis of merit or need, in the matter of school fees and the grant of scholarships or other forms of assistance to pupils and necessary permits and facilities for the pursuit of studies in foreign countries;*
  (d) *Not to allow, in any form of assistance granted by the public authorities to educational institutions, any restrictions or preference based solely on the ground that pupils belong to a particular group;*
  (e) *To give foreign nationals resident within their territory the same access to education as that given to their own nationals.*

Article 4 of the Convention against Discrimination in Education (1960) related to Equality of opportunity in education is given below:

- *The States Parties to this Convention undertake furthermore to formulate, develop and apply a national policy, which, by methods appropriate to the circumstances and to national usage, will tend to promote equality of opportunity and of treatment in the matter of education and in particular:*

(a) *To make primary education free and compulsory; make secondary education in its different forms generally available and accessible to all; make higher education equally accessible to all on the basis of individual capacity; assure compliance by all with the obligation to attend school prescribed by law;*

(b) *To ensure that the standards of education are equivalent in all public educational institutions of the same level, and that the conditions relating to the quality of the education provided are also equivalent;*

(c) *To encourage and intensify by appropriate methods the education of persons, who have not received any primary education or who have not completed the entire primary education course and the continuation of their education on the basis of individual capacity;*

(d) *To provide training for the teaching profession without discrimination.*

Article 5 of the Convention against Discrimination in Education (1960) related to the choice of education is as follows:

1. *The States Parties to this Convention agree that:*

(a) *Education shall be directed to the full development of the human personality and to the strengthening of respect for human rights and fundamental freedoms; it shall promote understanding, tolerance and friendship among all nations, racial or religious groups, and shall further the activities of the United Nations for the maintenance of peace;*

(b) *It is essential to respect the liberty of parents and, where applicable, of legal guardians, firstly to choose for their children institutions other than those maintained by the public authorities, but conforming to such minimum educational standards as may be laid down or approved by the competent authorities and, secondly, to ensure in a manner consistent with the procedures followed in the State for the application of its legislation, the religious and moral education of the children in conformity with their own convictions; and no person or group of persons should be compelled to receive religious instruction inconsistent with his or their convictions;*

(c) *It is essential to recognize the right of members of national minorities to carry on their own educational activities, including the maintenance of schools and, depending on the educational policy of each State, the use or the teaching of their own language, provided however:*

(i) *That this right is not exercised in a manner, which prevents the members of these minorities from understanding the culture and language of the community as a whole and from participating in its activities, or which prejudices national sovereignty;*

(ii) *That the standard of education is not lower than the general standard laid down or approved by the competent authorities; and*

(iii) *That attendance at such schools is optional.*

2. *The States Parties to this Convention undertake to take all necessary measures to ensure the application of the principles enunciated in paragraph 1 of this Article.*

The International Covenant on Economic, Social and Cultural Rights (ICESCR) (1966)

The ICESCR of 1966 covers the right to education comprehensively, especially Articles 13 and 14, as they set out the aims of education systems and the content of education. Article 14 deals more specifically with the provision of free primary education, Article 13 (2) corresponds with Article 26 (1) of the UDHR (1948) and points out that "*primary education shall be compulsory and available to all.*" (Daudet & Singh, 2001: 7; Detrick, 1999: 474; Singh, 2003: 16 and Van Bueren, 1998: 72).

Articles 13 and 14 of the International Covenant on Economic, Social and Cultural Rights (1966) related to the right to education are given below:

Article 13

1. *The States Parties to the present Covenant recognize the right of everyone to education. They agree that education shall be directed to the full development of the human personality and the sense of its dignity, and shall strengthen the respect for human rights and fundamental freedoms. They further agree that education shall enable all persons to participate effectively in a free society, promote understanding, tolerance and friendship among all nations and all racial, ethnic or religious groups, and further the activities of the United Nations for the maintenance of peace.*
2. *The States Parties to the present Covenant recognize that, with a view to achieving the full realization of this right:*

(a) *Primary education shall be compulsory and available free to all;*

(b) *Secondary education in its different forms, including technical and vocational secondary education, shall be made generally available and accessible to all by every appropriate means, and in particular by the progressive introduction of free education;*
(c) *Higher education shall be made equally accessible to all, on the basis of capacity, by every appropriate means, and in particular by the progressive introduction of free education;*
(d) *Fundamental education shall be encouraged or intensified as far as possible for those persons, who have not received or completed the whole period of their primary education;*
(e) *The development of a system of schools at all levels shall be actively pursued, an adequate fellowship system shall be established, and the material conditions of teaching staff shall be continuously improved.*

3. The States Parties to the present Covenant undertake to have respect for the liberty of parents and, when applicable, legal guardians to choose for their children schools, other than those established by the public authorities, which conform to such minimum educational standards as may be laid down or approved by the State and to ensure the religious and moral education of their children in conformity with their own convictions.
4. No part of this Article shall be construed so as to interfere with the liberty of individuals and bodies to establish and direct educational institutions, subject always to the observance of the principles set forth in paragraph 1 of this Article and to the requirement that the education given in such institutions shall conform to such minimum standards as may be laid down by the State.

Article 14

Each State Party to the present Covenant, which, at the time of becoming a Party, has not been able to secure in its metropolitan territory or other territories under its jurisdiction compulsory primary education, free of charge, undertakes, within two years, to work out and adopt a detailed plan of action for the progressive implementation, within a reasonable number of years, to be fixed in the plan, of the principle of compulsory education, free of charge, for all.

Convention on the Elimination of all forms of Discrimination against Women (1979)

The women's rights convention from 1979, known as the Convention on the Elimination of all forms of Discrimination against Women, and often abbreviated as CEDAW, obliges state parties to:

> "*...take all appropriate measures to eliminate discrimination against*

women in order to ensure to them equal rights with men in the field of education and in particular to ensure, on the basis of equality of men and women:. The elimination of any stereotyped concept of the roles of men and women at all levels and in all forms of education by encouraging co-education and other types of education which will help to achieve this aim and, in particular, by the revision of textbooks and school programs and the adaptation of teaching methods..." (Article 10)

The Convention on the Rights of the Child (CRC) (1989)

The international convention concerning the child's right to education is the CRC adopted by the United Nations General Assembly in 1989. This convention contains numerous provisions with regard to education. Whereas Article 13 (3) obliges the state parties to ensure that disabled learners have access to education and training, Article 29 (1) (a) provides for the aims and purposes of education and states that education shall be directed to the development of the child's personality, talents and physical and mental ability. Article 30 guarantees the monitoring of education and states that learners must not be denied the right to use their language, observe their culture and profess their religious beliefs (Arajarvi, 1992: 417; Detrick, 1999: 471-472; Hodgson, 1998: 44; Tomasevski, 2003: 54 and Van Bueren, 1998: 16).

Article 28 of the Convention on the Rights of the Child (1989) is as follows:

1. *States Parties recognize the right of the child to education, and with a view to achieving this right progressively and on the basis of equal opportunity, they shall, in particular:*
   (a) *Make primary education compulsory and available free to all;*
   (b) *Encourage the development of different forms of secondary education, including general and vocational education, make them available and accessible to every child, and take appropriate measures, such as the introduction of free education and offering financial assistance in case of need;*
   (c) *Make higher education accessible to all on the basis of capacity by every appropriate means;*
   (d) *Make educational and vocational information and guidance available and accessible to all children;*
   (e) *Take measures to encourage regular attendance at schools and the reduction of drop-out rates.*
2. *States Parties shall take all appropriate measures to ensure that school discipline is administered in a manner consistent with the child's human dignity and in conformity with the present Convention.*

3. *States Parties shall promote and encourage international co-operation in matters relating to education, in particular with a view to contributing to the elimination of ignorance and illiteracy throughout the world and facilitating access to scientific and technical knowledge and modern teaching methods. In this regard, particular account shall be taken of the needs of developing countries.*

World Declaration on Education for All: The Jomtien Conference (1990)

In 1990, delegates from 155 countries agreed at the World Conference on Education for All, in Jomtien, Thailand to universalise primary education and massively reduce illiteracy before the end of the decade. The Jomtien Conference (1990) was a reply to diminishing coverage of primary education in the 1980s. The 1980s can be seen as a lost decade due to debt and structural adjustments that had brought earlier progress in education to a halt. The Jomtien Conference helped move education back to the centre of the international development agenda. Progress towards Education for All (EFA) has, however, been much slower than those, who attended the Jomtien Conference had hoped, and moving closer to the new century, it became clear that the aims set in Jomtien would fail. In 2000, 104 million school-aged children were still not in school. The majority of them were girls and 94 per cent were living in developing countries – mostly in South Asia and Sub-Saharan Africa.

The 1990 World Conference on Education for All held in Thailand declared that the effective provision of basic education for all depends on political commitment and political will backed by appropriate and supportive fiscal, economic, trade, labour, employment and health policies. The main points of this conference related to basic learning needs are given below:

1. *Every person—child, youth and adult—shall be able to benefit from educational opportunities designed to meet their basic learning needs. These needs comprise both essential learning tools (such as literacy, oral expression, numeracy, and problem- solving) and the basic learning content (such as knowledge, skills, values and attitudes) required by human beings to be able to survive, to develop their full capacities, to live and work in dignity, to participate fully in development, to improve the quality of their lives, to make informed decisions, and to continue learning. The scope of basic learning needs and how they should be met varies with individual countries and cultures, and inevitably, changes with the passage of time.*
2. *The satisfaction of these needs empowers individuals in any society and confers upon them a responsibility to respect and build upon their collective cultural, linguistic and spiritual heritage, to promote*

the education of others, to further the cause of social justice, to achieve environmental protection, to be tolerant towards social, political and religious systems which differ from their own, ensuring that commonly accepted humanistic values and human rights are upheld, and to work for international peace and solidarity in an interdependent world.

3. *Another and no less fundamental aim of educational development is the transmission and enrichment of common cultural and moral values. It is in these values that the individual and society find their identity and worth.*
4. *Basic education is more than an end in itself. It is the foundation for lifelong learning and human development on which countries may build, systematically, further levels and types of education and training.*

International Commission on Education for the 21st Century—Learning: The Treasure Within (1996)

The opinion of the international commission on Education for the twenty-first century was as follows:

> "*Education is coming to occupy an ever larger place in people's lives as its role among the forces at work in modern society's increases. There are several reasons for this. The traditional division of life into separate periods—childhood and youth devoted to schooling, adulthood and working life, and retirement—no longer corresponds to things as they are today and corresponds still less to the demands of the future. Today, no one can hope to amass during his or her youth an initial fund of knowledge which will serve for a lifetime. The swift changes taking place in the world call for knowledge to be continuously updated, and at the same time, the initial education of young people is tending to become more protracted. A shorter working life, shorter working hours and a longer expectancy of life after retirement are also increasing the time available for other activities.*"

The commission further said:

> "*Education, too, is changing fast. More and more opportunities for learning out of school are occurring in all fields, while skills, in the traditional sense of the term, are giving way in many modern sectors of activity to the ideas of developing competence and adaptability. The traditional distinction between initial education and continuing education therefore needs to be reconsidered. Continuing education*

that is really in harmony with the needs of modern societies can no longer be defined in relation to a particular time of life (adult education as opposed to the education of the young, for instance) or to too specific a purpose (vocational as opposed to general). The time to learn is now the whole lifetime, and each field of knowledge spreads into and enriches the others. As the twenty-first century approaches, education is so varied in its tasks and forms that it covers all the activities that enable people, from childhood to old age, to acquire a living knowledge of the world, of other people and themselves. [.] It is this educational continuum, coextensive with life and widened to take in the whole of society that the Commission has chosen to refer to in this report as 'learning throughout life'. A key to the twenty-first century, learning throughout life will be essential for adapting to the evolving requirements of the labour market and for better mastery of the changing timeframes and rhythms of individual existence."

Millennium Development Goals (MDGs) (2000)

Access to education is also affirmed in the Millennium Development Goals (MDGs), agreed in 2000 following the Millennium Summit and intended to be achieved by 2015. MDG2 is to "Achieve universal primary education" and MDG3 is to "Promote gender equality and empower women".

Millennium Development Goals

- **Goal 2:** Achieve universal primary education
- **Target 2A:** Ensure that all boys and girls complete a full course of primary schooling

Indicators

2.1 Net enrolment ratio in primary education
2.2 Proportion of pupils starting grade 1, who reach last grade of primary
2.3 Literacy rate of 15-24 year-olds, women and men

- **Goal 3:** Promote gender equality and empower women
- **Target 3A:** Eliminate gender disparity in primary and secondary education preferably by 2005, and at all levels by 2015.

Indicators

3.1 Ratios of girls to boys in primary, secondary and tertiary education
3.2 Share of women in wage employment in the non-agricultural sector
3.3 Proportion of seats held by women in national parliament

The Dakar Framework for Action (2000)

The World Education Forum, held in Dakar from 26 to 28 April 2000, was the largest evaluation ever undertaken in the field of education. Altogether, 164 countries were represented, besides 150 civil society groups, including NGOs. The preparations for the forum had been particularly thorough. A considerable mass of information had been collected emphasizing a highly contrasted situation from one country to another, with some countries having made remarkable progress, while others were experiencing growing difficulties in various areas of education. The breakthrough outcome of the forum had been the adoption of the Dakar Framework for Action.

Education for All adopted at the World Education Forum, (Dakar, Senegal, 26 to 28 April 2000) expresses the commitment of the entire international community to the full realization of the right to education. The Dakar Framework for Action sets out six goals for achieving basic education for all by 2015:

> **Goal-I:** *Expanding and improving comprehensive early childhood care and education, especially, for the most vulnerable and disadvantaged children.*

All young children must be nurtured in safe and caring environments that allow them to become healthy, alert and secure and be able to learn. The past decade has provided more evidence that good quality early childhood care and education, both in families and in more structured programmes, have a positive impact on the survival, growth, development and learning potential of children. Such programmes should be comprehensive, focusing on all of the child's needs and encompassing health, nutrition and hygiene as well as cognitive and psycho-social development. They should be provided in the child's mother tongue and help to identify and enrich the care and education of children with special needs. Partnerships between governments, NGOs, communities and families can help ensure the provision of good care and education for children, especially for those most disadvantaged, through activities centred on the child, focused on the family, based within the community and supported by national, multi-sectoral policies and adequate resources.

Governments, through relevant ministries, have the primary responsibility of formulating early childhood care and education policies within the context of national EFA plans, mobilizing political and popular support, and promoting flexible, adaptable programmes for young children that are appropriate to their age and not mere downward extensions of formal school systems. The education of parents and other caregivers in better child care, building on traditional practices, and the systematic use of early childhood indicators, are important elements in achieving this goal.

Goal-II: *Ensuring that by 2015 all children, particularly girls, children in difficult circumstances and those belonging to ethnic minorities, have access to and complete free and compulsory primary education of good quality.*

All children must have the opportunity to fulfil their right to quality education in schools or alternative programmes at whatever level of education is considered 'basic'. All states must fulfil their obligation to offer free and compulsory primary education in accordance with the United Nations Convention on the Rights of the Child and other international commitments. The international agreement on the 2015 target date for achieving Universal Primary Education (UPE) in all countries will require commitment and political will from all levels of government. For the millions of children living in poverty, who suffer multiple disadvantages, there must be an unequivocal commitment that education be free of tuition and other fees, and that everything possible be done to reduce or eliminate costs such as those for learning materials, uniforms, school meals and transport. Wider social policies, interventions and incentives should be used to mitigate indirect opportunity costs of attending school. No one should be denied the opportunity to complete a good quality primary education because it is unaffordable. Child labour must not stand in the way of education. The inclusion of children with special needs, from disadvantaged ethnic minorities and migrant populations, from remote and isolated communities and from urban slums, and others excluded from education, must be an integral part of strategies to achieve UPE by 2015.

While commitment to attaining universal enrolment is essential, improving and sustaining the quality of basic education is equally important in ensuring effective learning outcomes. In order to attract and retain children from marginalized and excluded groups, education systems should respond flexibly, providing relevant content in an accessible and appealing format. Education systems must be inclusive, actively seeking out children who are not enrolled, and responding flexibly to the circumstances and needs of all learners. The EFA 2000 Assessment suggests a wide range of ways in which schools can respond to the needs of their pupils, including affirmative action programmes for girls that seek to remove the obstacles to their enrolment, bilingual education for the children of ethnic minorities, and a range of imaginative and diverse approaches to address and actively engage children, who are not enrolled in school.

Goal-III: *Ensuring that the learning needs of all young people and adults are met through equitable access to appropriate learning and life skills programmes.*

All young people and adults must be given the opportunity to gain the knowledge and develop the values, attitudes and skills that will enable them to develop their capacities to work, to participate fully in their society, to take control of their own lives and to continue learning. No country can be expected to develop into a modern and open economy without a certain proportion of its work force having completed secondary education. In most countries this requires an expansion of the secondary system.

Young people, especially adolescent girls, face risks and threats that limit learning opportunities and challenge education systems. These include exploitative labour, the lack of employment, conflict and violence, drug abuse, school-age pregnancy and HIV/AIDS. Youth-friendly programmes must be made available to provide the information, skills, counselling and services needed to protect them from these risks.

All young people should be given the opportunity for ongoing education. For those who drop out of school or complete school without acquiring the literacy, numeracy and life skills they need, there must be a range of options for continuing their learning. Such opportunities should be both meaningful and relevant to their environment and needs, help them become active agents in shaping their future and develop useful work-related skills.

Goal-IV: *Achieving a 50 per cent improvement in levels of adult literacy by 2015, especially for women, and equitable access to basic and continuing education for all adults.*

All adults have a right to basic education, beginning with literacy, which allows them to engage actively in, and to transform the world in which they live. There are still some 880 million people, who cannot read or write in the world; two-thirds are women. The fragile levels of literacy acquired by many new literates compound the problem. Yet the education of adults remains isolated, often at the periphery of national education systems and budgets.

Adult and continuing education must be greatly expanded and diversified, and integrated into the mainstream national education and poverty reduction strategies. The vital role that literacy plays in lifelong learning, sustainable livelihoods, good health, active citizenship and in improving the quality of life for individuals, communities and societies must be more widely recognized. Literacy and continuing education are essential for women's empowerment and gender equality. Closer linkages among formal, non-formal and informal approaches to learning must be fostered to respond to diverse needs and circumstances of adults.

Sufficient resources, well-targeted literacy programmes, better trained teachers and the innovative use of technologies are essential in promoting these activities. The scaling up of practical, participatory learning methodologies developed by non-government organizations, which link literacy with empowerment and local development, is especially important. The success of adult education efforts in the next decade will be essentially demonstrated by substantial reduction in disparities between male/female and urban/rural literacy rates.

> **Goal-V:** *Eliminating gender disparities in primary and secondary education by 2005, and achieving gender equality in education by 2015, with focus on ensuring girls' full and equal access to and achievement in basic education of good quality.*

Gender-based discrimination remains one of the most intractable constraints in realizing the right to education. Without overcoming this obstacle, Education for All cannot be achieved. Girls are a majority among out-of-school children and youth, although in an increasing number of countries, boys are at a disadvantage. Even though the education of girls and women has a powerful trans-generational effect and is a key determinant of social development and women's empowerment, limited progress has been made in increasing girls' participation in basic education.

International agreement has already been reached to eliminate gender disparities in primary and secondary education by 2005. This requires that gender issues be mainstreamed throughout the education system, supported by adequate resources and strong political commitment. Merely ensuring access to education for girls is not enough; unsafe school environments and biases in teacher's behaviour and training, teaching and learning processes, and curricula and textbooks often lead to lower completion and achievement rates for girls. By creating safe and gender-sensitive learning environments, it should be possible to remove a major hurdle to girls' participation in education. Increasing levels of women's literacy is another crucial factor in promoting girls' education. Comprehensive efforts, therefore, need to be made at all levels and in all areas to eliminate gender discrimination and to promote mutual respect between girls and boys, women and men. To make this possible, changes in attitudes, values and behaviour are required.

> **Goal-VI:** *Improving every aspect of the quality of education, and ensuring their excellence so that recognized and measurable learning outcomes are achieved by all, especially in literacy, numeracy and essential life skills.*

Quality is at the heart of education, and what takes place in classrooms and other learning environments is fundamentally important to the future well-being of children, young people and adults. A quality education is one that satisfies basic learning needs, and enriches the lives of learners and their overall experience of living.

Evidence over the past decade has shown that efforts to expand enrolment must be accompanied by attempts to enhance educational quality if children are to be attracted to school, stay there and achieve meaningful learning outcomes. Scarce resources have frequently been used for expanding systems with insufficient attention to quality improvement in areas, such as teacher's training and materials development. Recent assessments of learning achievement in some countries have shown that a sizeable percentage of children are acquiring only a fraction of the knowledge and skills they are expected to master. What students are meant to learn has often not been clearly defined, well-taught or accurately assessed.

Governments and all other EFA partners must work together to ensure basic education of quality for all, regardless of gender, wealth, location, language or ethnic origin. Successful education programmes require: (1) healthy, well-nourished and motivated students; (2) well-trained teachers and active learning techniques; (3) adequate facilities and learning materials; (4) a relevant curriculum that can be taught and learned in a local language and builds upon the knowledge and experience of the teachers and learners; (5) an environment that not only encourages learning, but is welcoming, gender-sensitive, healthy and safe; (6) a clear definition and accurate assessment of learning outcomes, including knowledge, skills, attitudes and values; (7) participatory governance and management; and (8) respect for and engagement with local communities and cultures.

Conclusion

In this chapter, I have sought to clarify various human rights instruments that contribute and make education a right at global and state levels. This chapter is an attempt to equip the readers with an overview of the historical and recent events related to the development of right to education. It also acquaints them with some of the issues surrounding the right to education to make education a fundamental right of each child. To sum up, there is an utmost need for realizing that provision for universal access to quality school education is the groundwork of development and a fundamental condition in the process of creating India as a knowledge society.

References

1. Arajarvi, P. (1992). Article 26. In Eide, A., Alfredson, G., Melander, G., Rehof, L. and Rosas, A. (Eds.). *The Universal Declaration of Human Rights: A Commentary*. London: Scandinavian University Press: 405-428.
2. Balton, D.A. (1992). Human Rights in Classroom. Teaching the Convention on the Right of the Child. *Social Education*, 56 (4), 210-212.

3. Convention against Discrimination in Education, Adopted by the General Conference at its eleventh session, 14 December 1960, Paris, UNESCO, 1960.
4. Daudet, Y. and Singh, K. (2001). *The Right to Education: Analysis of UNESCO.* Standard Setting Instruments. Paris: UNESCO.
5. Delors *et al., Learning: The Treasure Within, Report to UNESCO of the International Commission on Education for the Twenty-first Century,* pp. 99-100, Paris, UNESCO Publishing, 1996.
6. Detrick, S. (1999). *Commentary on the United Nations Convention on the Rights of the Child.* The Hague: Matinus Nijhoff Publishers.
7. Dorr, N. (1994). An Introduction to Human Rights Development since 1945. In Hefferman, L., Kingston, J. & Robinson, M. (Eds.). *Human Rights. A European Perspective.* Ireland Black Rock: The Round Hall Press: 1-20.
8. Hodgson, D. (1998). *The Human Right to Education.* Ashgate: Dartmouth Publishers.
9. Huberman, A.M. (1979). The Present Situation and Future Prospects. In Mialaret, G. (Ed.). *The Child's Right to Education.* Paris: UNESCO: 57-76.
10. International Covenant on Economic, Social and Cultural Rights, OHCHR website, http://www2.ohchr.org/english/law/cescr.html
11. M'Bow, A.M. (1979). Introduction. In Mialaret, G. (Ed.). The Child's Right to Education. Paris: UNESCO: 9-19.
12. Mialaret, G. (1979). What Kind of Education? In Mialaret, G. (Ed.). *The Child's Right to Education.* Paris: UNESCO: 47-53.
13. Nowak, M. (1995). The Right to Education. In Eide, A. & Krause, K. (Eds.). *Economic, Social and Cultural Rights.* Boston. Kluwer Academic Publishers: 189-211.
14. Singh, K. (2003). The Right to Education: Foundation for Education for All (EFA). *Idea Newsletter,* April-September: 16-17.
15. Starkey, H. (1991). *The Challenge of Human Right education.* Great Britain: Cassell Education Ltd.
16. The International Covenants on Human Rights and Optional Protocol, pp. 8-9, New York, United Nations Office of Public Information, 1976.
17. The Universal Declaration of Human Right, UN website, *http://www.un.org/en/documents/udhr/index.html*
18. Tomasevski, K. (2003). Education Denied: Costs and Remedies. London: Zed Books.
19. UNESCO (1990). *World Declaration on Education for All and Framework for Action to Meet Basic Learning Needs.* Paris: UNESCO.
20. UNESCO (2000). *Dakar Framework for Action. Education for All: Meeting our Collective Commitments.* Text adopted by the World Education Forum Dakar, Senegal, 26-28 April, 2000. http://www.unesco.org/education/efa/ed_for_all/dakfram_eng.shtml
21. United Nations Committee on Economic, Social and Cultural Rights (1999). *General Comment on the Implementation of Article 13, CESR.* E/C.12/1999/10. http://www.cesr.org/ESCR/gencomment13.htm
22. United Nations Committee on Economic, Social and Cultural Rights (2002, March). *The Constitutional Provisions on the Right to Education and Modernizing/developing*

National Legislation in Keeping with the State Obligation/government Responsibility under the Dakar Framework for Action: E/C.12/2002/SA/2. http://www.unhchr.ch/tbs/doc.nsf/0/b64ee7a93883d174c1256bb9004168e6?Opendocument

23. United Nations Committee on Economic, Social and Cultural Rights (2003). *General Comment No. 5, Persons with disabilities, (Eleventh session, 1994), U.N. Doc E/1995/22 at 19 (1995), reprinted in Compilation of General Comments and General Recommendations Adopted by Human Rights Treaty Bodies, U.N. Doc. HRI/GEN/1/Rev.6 at 24 (2003). http://www1.umn.edu/humanrts/gencomm/epcomm5e.htm*
24. Universal Declaration of Human Rights Adopted and Proclaimed by the General Assembly of the United Nations on the Tenth Day of December 1948, Final Authorized Text. New York, United Nations, 1950.
25. Van Bueren G. (1995). International Law on the Right of the Child. Boston: Matinuss Nijhoff Publishers.
26. Van Bueren G. (1998). *International Document on Children's Right* Thousand Okas: Matinuss Nijhoff Publishers.
27. Volio, F. (1979). The Child's Right to Education: A Survey. In Mialaret, G. (Ed.). *The Child's Right to Education*. Paris: UNESCO: 19-33.
28. World Bank (2003). Education for All: Including Children with Disabilities.
29. World Bank (2006). World Development Report 2006, "Equity and Development".
30. World Conference on Education for All, Meeting Basic Learning Needs, Jomtien, Thailand, 1990, *World Declaration on Education for All,* Article 1, New York, Inter-Agency Commission (UNDP, UNESCO, UNICEF, World Bank) for the World Conference on Education for All, 1990.
31. Wringe, C.A. (1981). *Children's Rights: A Philosophical Study*. London: Routledge/Kegan Paul.

3

The Right to Education

The Indian Constitutional Perspective

Noushad Husain

The Indian Constitution is known to be a document committed to social justice. As per expert opinion, literacy forms the cornerstone for making the provision of equality of opportunity a reality. The Indian Constitution has therefore recognized education as the essence of social transformation, as is evident from its education specific Articles.

The Right to Education legislation has a long and chequered history, having been subjected to numerous rounds of heated debate and philosophical and semantic alterations. It was tailored into existence in the period following the passage of the 86th Constitutional Amendment in 2002, which declared Education a fundamental right of all children in the age-group of 6-14. A participatory process of inviting comments from members of the public yielded several different drafts of the bill in the subsequent years until finally, in 2008, the Union Cabinet stamped its seal of approval on it and it was placed before the *Rajya Sabha*, which passed it in July 2009. The bill then proceeded to the *Lok Sabha*, where it was passed in August 2009.

The Right of Children to Free and Compulsory Education Act, 2009 (RTE Act) has a long and chequered history. The right to education was discussed extensively during the drafting of the Constitution. The Constituent Sub-Committee on Fundamental Rights included the right to primary education as a fundamental right. However the Advisory Committee of the Constituent Assembly rejected this proposal and placed it in the category of non-justifiable fundamental rights (later known as Directive Principles of State Policy). The first official recommendation for the inclusion of a fundamental right to education was made in 1990 by the Acharya Ramamurti Committee. Thereafter, several political as well as policy level changes influenced the course of free and compulsory education. The country witnessed an increased international focus on its initiatives regarding free and compulsory education after its participation in the World Conference on Education for All in 1990. India also ratified the United Nations Convention on the Rights of the Child in 1992.

Historical Decisions of Indian Constitution Related to Right to Education

Right to Education has been recognized as a human right to be protected and preserved. Its importance has also been recognized by the framers of the Constitution under Article 44 of the Constitution. So as to convert a Right to Education into a fundamental right to education, the Courts in India played a vital role.

Case-I: Mohini Jain vs. Union of India, (1992) 3 SCC 666

The Supreme Court first recognized the right to education as a fundamental right in *Mohini Jain vs. Union of India* (1992) 3 SCC 666. In this case, the Supreme Court through a division bench comprising of justices Kuldip Singh and R.M. Sahai, deciding on the constitutionality of the practice of charging capitation fee. It was observed in this judgment that:

> *'Right to life' is the compendious expression for all those rights which the courts must enforce because they are basic to the dignified enjoyment of life. It extends to the full range of conduct which the individual is free to pursue. The right to education flows directly from right to life. The right to life under Article 21 and the dignity of an individual cannot be assured unless it is accompanied by the right to education. The State Government is under an obligation to make an endeavour to provide educational facility at all levels to its citizens.* (Para 12)

In this case, the observation of the court was:

> *The directive principles which are fundamental in the governance of the country cannot be isolated from the fundamental rights guaranteed under Part III. These principles have to be read into the fundamental rights. Both are supplementary to each other. The State is under a constitutional mandate to create conditions in which the fundamental rights guaranteed to the individuals under Part III could be enjoyed by all. Without making "right to education" under Article 41 of the Constitution a reality, the fundamental rights under Chapter III shall remain beyond the reach of large majority, which is illiterate.*

"Right to life" is the compendious expression for all those rights which the Courts must enforce because they are basic to the dignified enjoyment of life. It extends to the full range of conduct, which the individual is free to pursue. The right to education flows directly from right to life. The right to life under Article 21and the dignity of an individual cannot be assured unless it is accompanied by the right to education. The State Government is under an obligation to make an endeavour to provide educational facilities at all levels to its citizens.

The fundamental rights guaranteed under Part III of the Constitution of India including the right to freedom of speech and expression and other rights under Article 19 cannot be appreciated and fully enjoyed unless a citizen is educated and is conscious of his individualistic dignity.

The "right to education", therefore, is concomitant to the fundamental rights enshrined under Part III of the Constitution. The State is under a constitutional-mandate to provide educational institutions at all levels for the benefit of the citizens. The educational institutions must function to the best advantage of the citizens. Opportunity to acquire education cannot be confined to the richer section of the society.

Case-II: J.P. Unnikrishnan vs. State of Andhra Pradesh, 1993 SCC (1) 645

This rationality of case-I judgement was further examined by a five judge bench where the enforceability and the extent of the right to education was clarified. In 1993, the Supreme Court narrowed the ambit of the fundamental right to education as propounded in the Mohini Jain case in the case of *J.P. Unnikrishnan vs. State of Andhra Pradesh*, 1993 SCC (1) 645. The Court observed that:

> *"It would not be correct to contend that Mohini Jain was wrong in-so far as it declared that 'the right to education flows directly from right to life'. But the question is what is the content of this right? How much and what level of education is necessary to make the life meaningful? Does it mean that every citizen of this country can call upon the State to provide him education of his choice? In other words, whether the citizens of this country can demand that the State provide adequate number of medical colleges, engineering college and other educational institutions to satisfy all their educational needs? Mohini Jain seems to say, yes. With respect, we cannot agree with such a broad proposition. The right to education which is implicit in the right to life and personal liberty guaranteed by Articles 21 must be construed in the light of the directive principles in Part IV of the constitution. So far as the right to education is concerned, there are several articles in Part IV which expressly speak of it. Article 41 says that the 'State shall, within the limits of its economic capacity and development, make effective provisions for securing the right to*

> *work, to education and to public assistance in case of unemployment, old age sickness and disablement, and in other cases of undeserved want'. Article 45 says that 'the State shall endeavour to provide, within a period of ten years from the commencement of this Constitution, for free and compulsory education for all children until they complete the age of fourteen years'. Article 46 commands that 'the State shall promote with special care the educational and economic interest of the weaker section of the people, and, in particular, of the Schedule Castes and the Scheduled Tribes and shall protect them from social injustice and all forms of exploitation......'. The three Articles 45, 46 and 41 are designed to achieve the said goal among others. It is in the light of these Articles that the content and parameters of the right to education have to be determined. Right to education, understood in the context of Articles 45 and 41, means: (a) every child/citizen of this country has as right to free education until he completes the age of fourteen years and (b) after a child/citizen completes 14 years, his right to education is circumscribed by the limits of the economic capacity of the State and its development. We may deal with both these limbs separately* (Para 171)."

In order to treat a right as a fundamental right, it is not necessary that it should be expressly stated as one in Part III of the Constitution. The provisions of Part III and IV are supplementary and complementary to each other. Fundamental rights are but a means to achieve the goal indicated in Part IV and must be constructed in the light of the directive principles.

Though right to education is not stated expressly as a fundamental right, it is implicit in and flows from the right to life guaranteed under Article 21 having regard to the broad and expansive interpretation given by the Court. The right to education has been treated as one of transcendental importance. It has fundamental significance to the life of an individual and the nation. Without education being provided to the citizens of this country, the objectives set forth in the Preamble to the Constitution cannot be achieved. The Constitution would fail.

The fact that the Right to Education occurs in as many as three Articles in Part IV *viz.,* Articles 41, 45 and 46 shows the importance attached to it by the founding fathers. Even some of the Articles in Part III *viz.,* Articles 29 and 30 speak of education.

That right to education is implicit in the right to life is that the State cannot deprive the citizen of his right to education except in accordance with the procedure prescribed by law. The right to education, which is implicit in the right to life and personal liberty guaranteed by Article 21, must be constructed in the light of the Directive Principles in Part IV of the Constitution.

Right to Education, understood in the context of Articles 45 and 41, means: (a) every child/citizen of this country has a right to free education until he completes the age of fourteen years and (b) after a child/citizen completes 14 years, his right to education is circumscribed by the limits of the economic capacity of the State and its development.

The right to education, which flows from Article 21, is not an absolute right. It must be constructed in the light of directive principles. A true democracy is one where education is universal, where people understand what is good for them and the nation and know how to govern them. Articles 45, 46 and 41 are designed to achieve the said goal among others. It is in the light of these articles that the content and parameters of the right to education have to be determined. Right to education, understood in the context of Articles 45 and 41, means that every child/citizen of this country has a right to free education until he completes the age of fourteen years and (b) after a child/citizen completes 14 years, his right to education is circumscribed by the limits of the economic capacity of the State and its development. It is significant that among the several Articles in Part IV, only Article 45 speaks of a time-limit; no other article does. It is not a mere pious wish and the State cannot flout the said direction even after 44 years on the ground that the article merely calls upon it to "Endeavour to provide" the same and on the further ground that the said Article is not enforceable by virtue of the declaration in Article 37. The passage of 44 years—more than four times the period stipulated in Article 45—has converted the obligation created by the Article into an enforceable right. At least now, the State should honour the command of Article 45. It must be made a reality.

This does not, however, mean that this obligation can be performed only through the State schools. It can be also be done by permitting, recognizing and aiding voluntary non-governmental organizations, who are prepared to impart free education to children. This does not also mean that unaided private schools cannot continue. They can. Indeed, they too have a role to play. They meet the demand of that segment of population, who may not wish to have their children educated in State-run schools. They have necessarily to charge fees from the students.

While allocating the available resources, due regard should be had to the wise words of the Founding Fathers in Articles 45 and 46. Though the importance and significance of higher education cannot be denied, but there should be a proper balancing of various sectors of education.

The right to free education is available only to children until they complete the age of 14 years. Thereafter, the obligation of the State to provide education is subject to the limits of its economic capacity and development of the State. A citizen has a right to call upon the State to provide educational facilities to him within the limits of its economic capacity and development. The limits of economic capacity are ordinary speaking, matters within the subjective satisfaction of the State.

The obligations created by Articles 41, 45 and 46 of the Constitution can be discharged by the State either by establishing institutions of its own or by aiding, recognizing and/or granting affiliation to private educational institutions. Private educational institutions are a necessity in the present day context. It is not possible to do without them because the Governments are in no position to meet the demand—particularly in the sector of medical and technical education, which call for substantial outlays. While education is one of the most important functions of the Indian State, it has no monopoly therein. Private educational institutions—including minority educational institutions—too have a role to play.

Case-III: Bandhua Mukti Morcha, etc. vs. Union of India

The same has also been reiterated by the Hon'ble Supreme Court in *Bandhua Mukti Morcha, etc. vs. Union of India case where it* specifically referred to the earlier judgements made in this connection as under:

> *"In Maharashtra State Board of Secondary and Higher Education vs. K.S. Gandhi, right to education at the secondary stage was held to be a fundamental right. In J.P. Unnikrishnan vs. State of Andhra Pradesh, a constitution Bench had held education up to the age of 14 years to be a fundamental right.... It would be, therefore, incumbent upon the State to provide facilities and opportunity as enjoined under Article 39 (e) and (f) of the Constitution and to prevent exploitation of their childhood due to indigence and vagary."*

Case-IV: Anil Kumar Roy Sharma vs. State

In this case, the Court observed:

> *"The rights of a student below fourteen years to appear in class VIII board are a facet of right to education guaranteed under Article 21 of the Constitution."*

It is clear from the above remarkable judgements of the court that they have tried to make education a fundamental right.

Tracing the Development of the Right to Education Act in India

Ever since Independence, India has undertaken several initiatives to achieve universalization of elementary education, which has yielded mixed results. The Right to Education legislation in India has seen a chequered history in evolving from a directive principle to a fundamental right. In 1950, the

Constitution articulated its commitment to education through its Directive Principles of State Policy. The 86th Constitutional Amendment was followed by multiple rounds of discussions (tabling of Right to Free and Compulsory Education Bills by the NDA and UPA governments), which made education a fundamental right for children in the age group of 6-14 years. The Act was introduced in Rajya Sabha in December 2008. It was passed in the Lok Sabha on 4 August 2009 and the President gave his assent to it on 26 August 2009. The Act came into force on 1 April 2010 as a fundamental right in India. In short, the short history of RTE Act in India is given below:

Timeline of the RTE Act in India

- **1910:** Resolution moved by Gopal Krishna Gokhale in the Imperial Legislative Council seeking Free and Compulsory Primary Education.
- **1937:** Mahatma Gandhi makes a plea for universalization of education.
- **1944**: Sargent Plan to achieve universal elementary education by 1984.
- **1947:** Constituent assembly explores avenues to achieve universal elementary education
- **1950**: Directive Principles of State Policy (Article 45) directs state to endeavour to provide free and compulsory education to all children until fourteen years of age within a period of ten years Constitution of India introduced as Article 45, one of the Directive Principles of State Policy:
  - "The State shall endeavour to provide within a period of ten years from the commencement of this Constitution, for free and compulsory education for all children until they complete the age of fourteen years."
- **1968**: The first National Commission for education under Dr. Kothari submits its reports. Due to insignificant achievements, National Policy on Education urges serious efforts toward provision of free and compulsory education.
  - Introduced several far-reaching changes such as uniform curriculum for boys and girls.
  - Mathematics and Science as compulsory subjects.
  - It also proposed a Common School System [access to education should not be decided by wealth or class]
- **1976:** Constitution amendment making education a concurrent subject (responsibility of both State and Centre) was passed.
- **1986:** National Policy on Education resolves to provide all children free and compulsory education up to 14 years by 1995. National

policy on Education (NPE) endorsing Common School System (CSS) was formulated.

- Subsequent NPE's endorsed CSS, but it has never been implemented.
- Kothari Commission Report also called for a 20 year plan to implement CSS, starting with simultaneously improving quality of current schools while pushing the quality of ten per cent of schools to higher standards.

- **1992:** India becomes signatory to the UN Convention on Rights of the Child, which requires states to recognize the right of the child to education.
- **1993**: The Supreme Court in the case of *Unnikrishnan vs. State of Andhra Pradesh* ruled that the right to education is a fundamental right that flows from the Right to Life in Article 21 of the Constitution. The Supreme Court asked the state to honour the command of Article 45 of Constitution.
  - This judgement allowed that RTE comes out of Right to Life, and so included education as a right for children of ages 0 to 18.
- **1997:** Constitution Amendment making Education a fundamental right was introduced.
- **12 December 2002:** Public pressure generated after Unnikrishnan case spurs successive governments to make education a fundamental right. 86th Amendment 2002 makes elementary education a fundamental right. The Right to Education (RTE) Act is born. In 2002, the 86th Amendment to the Constitution introduced Article 21-A making the right to education a fundamental right. For the first time in independent India's history, a fundamental right had been added to the Constitution. Unlike other fundamental rights, the right to education required an enabling legislation to become effective. The RTE Act is this enabling legislation. The RTE Act came into force on 1 April 2010. The Constitution was amended (86th Amendment Act, 2002) to make free and compulsory education to all children in the 6-14 age group, as a Fundamental Right.
  - "The State shall provide free and compulsory education to all children of the age six to fourteen years in such as a way as the State may, by law, determine."
  - The 86th Amendment also modified Article 45, which reads as "The state shall endeavour to provide early childhood care and education for all children until they complete the age of six years."
  - This was deemed as diluting RTE since we went backwards from

0-18 to 6-14. Many proponents of the original right wanted the constitution to be amended again.

- **October 2003:** The Free and Compulsory Education for Children Bill, 2003 (NDA government). A first draft of the legislation envisaged in the above Article, viz., Free and Compulsory Education for Children Bill, 2003, was prepared and posted on http://education.nic.in in October, 2003, inviting comments and suggestions from the public at large.
- **2004:** The Free and Compulsory Education for Children Bill, 2004 (NDA government). Subsequently, taking into account the suggestions received on this draft, a revised draft of the Bill entitled Free and Compulsory Education Bill, 2004.
- **2005:** The Right to Education Bill, 2005 (June) (CABE Bill) (UPA I Government)
- **2005:** The Right to Education Bill, 2005 (August) (UPA I Government)
- **2005:** The Central Advisory Board of Education (CABE) committee report constituted to draft the Right to Education Bill submits its report.
- **June 2005:** The CABE committee drafted the 'Right to Education' Bill and submitted the same to the Ministry of HRD. MHRD sent it to the NAC where Mrs. Sonia Gandhi was the Chairperson. The NAC sent the Bill to PM for his observation.
- **July 2006:** Central legislation discarded. States advised to make their own Bills based on The Model Right to Education Bill, 2006 (UPA I government)
  - ➢ Formulates a Model Bill
  - ➢ Heavily diluted from the CABE committee Bill
  - ➢ Dropped all private school clauses
  - ➢ Dropped all neighbourhood school clauses
  - ➢ Dropped all financial obligations from the centre
  - ➢ Dropped any committee to oversee implementation
  - ➢ Suggests that individual states pass that as a legislation and implement

Why did the Government drop the bill?

- Main reason *given* was no money!
- Some instances of Central Government spending:
  - ➢ In the year 2004-05 an additional ₹ 5,010 crore was collected through the two per cent education cess for funding universal basic education, but only ₹ 2000 crore extra was spent for the purpose.

- ➢ The funds given in form of corporate subsidy (in terms of lost revenue generation) through the SEZ bill (which was passed in 2005) stands at ₹ 90,000 crore as per the Finance Ministry of India.
- ➢ Government has allocated ₹ 9,320 crore in 2005-06 for National highway Development Program (NHDP).
- ➢ Government has promised to spend an additional ₹ 20,000 crore (estimated) on increasing seats in higher education institutions over the next three years.

Forward to 2008, Just Prior to Elections

- The HRD Ministry's Working Group (WG) draft was sent to the concerned Ministries around February.
- Women and Child Welfare sent in its formal approval soon since the WG draft had made the National Commission for Child Rights (NCPCR) as the overseeing institution.
- The Finance Ministry approval followed by mid-March.
- The Law Ministry had many objections, including references to 'compulsion on the state' and the HRD Minister had to meet with the Law Minister and this ensured that the budget session of the Parliament deadline was missed.
- The Law Ministry finally sent in the formal draft on 8th July that retains:
    - ➢ the free and compulsory education objects,
    - ➢ the quality related chapter on content and process,
    - ➢ and a better mandatory schedule (some of the items that were to be 'prescribed' in the WG draft

  like playground, boundary wall etc. have also been made mandatory).
- But they continued to refuse to use the term 'equitable education', insisting that it is not justiciable.

Finally in August 2009: Nearly six years after the amendment, the Bill is cleared by the Cabinet. On 4 August 2009, the Right to Education Act is officially passed by the Parliament. Key provisions state that 25 per cent of admissions in all private schools will be provided free of cost to children from under-privileged areas. Then, Union Human Resources Development Minister Kapil Sibal says that the move is about the State's obligation to provide compulsory education. "This is a historic opportunity as there was never such a law in the last 62 years since Independence," he says.

- Rajya Sabha passes the bill and forwarded it to the Lok Sabha.
    - ➢ The passed bill from the Rajya Sabha was different from the one introduced.

- Lok Sabha passes the bill.
- Notified in the Gazette and Act in effect starting April 2010.
- **1 April 2010:** The Right of Children to Free and Compulsory Education Act as enacted by the Parliament comes into force. "We are committed to ensuring that all children, irrespective of gender and social category, have access to education. An education that enables them to acquire the skills, knowledge, values and attitudes necessary to become responsible and active citizens of India," says Prime Minister Manmohan Singh.
- **12 April 2012:** Supreme Court upholds the validity of the RTE Act and makes it clear that the Act would be implemented across the country. The court, however, exempted private unaided minority schools (such as schools run by religious institutions) from the Act stating that it would "infringe upon the fundamental freedom" of such schools.

Conclusion

It is identifiable that the Indian legislation is quite aligned to the international norms on the right to education and enshrinement of the right to education into national legislation rests clear. National norms also assure the education rights, which are available, accessible, acceptable and adaptable. But, having a legislation, which enshrines rights does not mean that the reality of those subjected to it will demonstrate the full realization of the right. The system presents pockets of success in the realization of education but "[these healthy segments of Indian education do not contradict the fact that the system as a whole is under severe strain, financially and institutionally, and needs to change and adjust, for more quality, efficiency and relevance" (Schwartzman 2004:27).

Legislation can be a tool for enhancing the realization of the right, but it does not ensure instant realization. In specific cases, the Indian judiciary played an important role in assuring the realization of the right to education, but to follow such a route does not ensure a sustainable educational system in which education is available, accessible, acceptable and adaptable. Each case is individual and the costs of using this method for accomplishing rights are high (Gupta, 2009).

References

Govt. of India (1992). National Policy on Education 1986 (with modifications undertaken in 1992) New Delhi: MHRD, Govt. of India.

Gupta, S. (2009). What are the different strategies and approaches to realize Right to Education (RTE) in India? Institute of Development Studies, University of Sussex.

J. Donnelly and R.E. Howard, 'Assessing national human rights performance: A theoretical framework', *Human Rights Quarterly*, Vol. 10, 1988, pp. 214-248, at p. 215.

M.C. Mehta vs. State of Tamil Nadu & Ors (1996). 6 SCC 756.

Ministry of Human Resources Development (2009). The Right of Children to Free and Compulsory Education Act 2009, New Delhi: MHRD.

Model Rules under the Right of children to free and compulsory Education Act (2009).http://mhrd.gov.in/sites/upload_files/mhrd/files/RTI_Model_Rules.pdf.

Mohini Jain vs. State of Karnataka 1992 AIR 1858.

P.A. Inamdar and Others vs. State of Maharashtra and Others (2005). (6) SCC 537.

Plan for Action for Human Rights Education. http://unesdoc.unesco.org/images/0014/001478/147853e.pdf.

Right of Children to Free and Compulsory Education Act (RTE), 2009 (35 of 2009). http://education.nic.in/.

Right to Education Act: Key Gaps in Policy and Implementation, Azim Premji Foundation (2011).

Sinha, M.K. (2008). Right to Education: Indian and International Practices. *Indian Journal of International Law*, pp. 188-207, 48:2.

T.M.A. Pai Foundation and others vs. State of Karnataka and others (2003). AIR (SC) 355.

The Constitution (Eighty-Sixth Amendment) Act (2002). http://indiacode.nic.in/coiweb/amend/amend86.htm.

The Constitution (Eighty-Sixth Amendment) Act (2002).http://indiacode.nic.in/coiweb/amend/amend86.htm.

The Right of children to free and compulsory Education Act, 2009 Clarification on Provisions. http://mhrd.gov.in/sites/upload_files/mhrd/files/RTE_Section_wise_rationale_rev_0.pdf.

UNESCO (1994). The Salamanca Statement and Framework for Action on Special Needs Education Paris: UNESCO.

Unni Krishnan, J.P. & Ors. vs. State of Andhra Pradesh & Ors 1993 AIR 217

Webliography

http://wdsbeta.worldbank.org
http://www.ibe.unesco.org
http://www.un.org/disabilities
http://www.education.nic.in/cd50years/g/W/16/0W160401.htm
http://www.education.nic.in/cd50years/y/3P/45/3P450301.htm
http://www.education.nic.in/cd50years/g/52/4U/524U0101.htm
http://www.education.nic.in/ssa/ssa_1.asp
http://www.indg.in/primary-education/policiesandschemes/the-national-policy-on-children
http://india.gov.in/spotlight/spotlight_archive.php?id=31
http://www.niua.org/Publications/newsletter/uf_english_apr-jun07.pdf

4

The Right to Education
A Conceptual Framework

Naushad Husain

The right to education is a universal entitlement to education, recognized by various Governments and NGO's as a human right that includes the right to free, compulsory primary education for all, an obligation to develop secondary education accessible to all, in particular by the progressive introduction of free secondary education, as well as an obligation to develop equitable access to higher education, ideally by the progressive introduction of free higher education. The right to education also includes a responsibility of Government to provide basic education for individuals, who have not completed primary education. In addition to these, access to educational provisions, the right to education encompasses the obligation to rule out discrimination at all levels of the educational system, to set minimum standards and to improve quality of education.

Meaning and Definition

Rights

Rights are legal, social, or ethical principles of freedom or entitlement; that is, rights are the fundamental normative rules about what is allowed of people or owed to people, according to some legal system, social convention, or ethical theory. Rights are of essential importance in such disciplines as law and ethics, especially theories of justice and deontology

Rights are often considered fundamental to civilization, being regarded as established pillars of society and culture and the history of social conflicts can be found in the history of each right and its development. According to the Stanford Encyclopaedia of Philosophy, "Rights structure the form of governments, the content of laws, and the shape of morality as it is currently perceived." The connection between rights and struggle cannot be overstated—

rights are not as much granted or endowed as they are fought for and claimed, and the essence of struggles past and ancient are encoded in the spirit of current concepts of rights and their modern formulations.

The specific enumeration of rights has differed greatly in different periods of history. In many cases, the system of rights promulgated by one group has come into sharp and bitter conflict with that of other groups. In the political sphere, a place in which rights have historically been an important issue, constitutional provisions of various states sometimes address the question of who has what legal rights. Modern conceptions of rights often emphasize liberty and equality as among the most important aspects of rights, though conceptions of liberty and equality frequently differ. In abstract sense, rights refer to justice, ethical correctness, or harmony with the RULES OF LAW or the principles of morals, whereas in concrete legal sense, it refers to a power, privilege, demand, or claim possessed by a particular person by virtue of law.

Education

Education narrowly refers to formal institutional instructions. Generally, international instruments use the term education in a narrow sense. The Article 1(2) of the UNESCO's *Convention against Discrimination in Education (1960)* has defined the term "education" to mean "all types and levels of [formal] education, [including] access to education, the standard and quality of education, and the conditions under which it is given."

In a wider sense, education may describe "all activities by which a human group transmits to its descendants a body of knowledge and skills and a moral code which enable the group to subsist." In this sense, education refers to the transmission to a subsequent generation of those skills needed to perform tasks of daily living, and further passing on the social, cultural, spiritual and philosophical values of the particular community. The wider meaning of education has been recognized in Article 1(a) of UNESCO's 1974 Recommendation concerning Education for International Understanding, Co-operation and Peace and Education relating to Human Rights and Fundamental Freedoms. The article states that education implies:

> "*the entire process of social life by means of which individuals and social groups learn to develop consciously within, and for the benefit of, the national and international communities, the whole of their personal capabilities, attitudes, aptitudes and knowledge.*"

The European Court of Human Rights has defined education in a narrow sense as "teaching or instructions. in particular to the transmission of knowledge and to intellectual development" and in a wider sense as "the whole process whereby, in any society, adults endeavour to transmit their beliefs, culture and other values to the young."

International Legal Basis of Right to Education

The rise of democratism, socialism, liberalism and secular states in the nineteenth century led to promote education as a matter of citizen's right and incorporate it in Constitutions and legislations of various countries. For example, the Constitution of the German Empire of 1849 had provisions relating to educational rights, and the 1870 Education Act of England and Wales established a system of public education in the country. The right to education is law in Article 26(1) of the Universal Declaration of Human Rights (UDHR, 1948) which states:

> "*Everyone has the right to education. Education shall be free, at least at the elementary and fundamental stages. Elementary education shall be compulsory. Technical and professional education shall be made generally available and higher education shall be equally accessible to all on the basis of merit, and technical and professional education shall be made generally available.*"

In Europe, Article 2 of the first Protocol of 20 March 1952 to the European Convention on Human Rights states that the right to education is recognized as a human right and is understood to establish an entitlement to education. Article 10 of the European Social Charter guarantees the right to vocational education.

Articles 13 and 14 of the International Covenant on Economic, Social and Cultural Rights (ICESCR) also set out detailed formulations of the right to education. Article 13 contains a general statement that everyone has the right to education and that edu-cation should contribute to the full development of the human personality. It also specifically stipulates that Primary education shall be compulsory and available free to all. According to the ICESCR, the right to education includes the right to free, compulsory primary education for all, an obligation to develop secondary education accessible to all in particular by the progressive introduction of free secondary education, as well as an obligation to develop equitable access to higher education in particular by the progressive introduction of free higher education. The right to education also includes a responsibility to provide basic education for individuals, who have not completed primary education. In addition to these accesses to educational provisions, the right to education encompasses also the obligation to eliminate discrimination at all levels of the educational system, to set minimum standards and to improve quality.

Articles 28 and 29 of the Convention on the Rights of the Child (CRC) deal with the right of the child to education. CRC is similar to the provisions contained in ICESCR. In addition, it states that school discipline should be administered in a manner consistent with a child's human dignity.

The right to education is inherent in UNESCO's constitutional mandate.

RTE has been reaffirmed in the 1960 UNESCO Convention against Discrimination in Education, which stipulates that states parties must undertake to formulate, develop and apply a national policy which will tend to promote equality of opportunity and treatment, and, in particular, to make primary education free and compulsory. In addition, it recognizes parents' right to freely choose their children's educational institutions and to ensure the re-ligious and moral education of their children in conformity with their own convictions.

Historical Evolution of the Concept of Right to Education in India

Pre-Independence

The right to education issue has been debated in India for more than a century. A substantial part of the memorandum presented by Mahatma Jotirao Phule to the Indian Education Commission (i.e. the Hunter Commission) in 1882, dwelt upon how the British Government's funding of education tended to benefit "Brahmins and the higher classes" while leaving "the masses wallowing in ignorance and poverty." Another attempt to get elementary education recognised as a right was made way back in 1909 when G.K. Gokhale introduced a Bill under the Indian Council Act of 1909, to make primary education compulsory, with State funding. However, the Bill was defeated by a large majority. While addressing the legislatures, Gokhale made the observation that the issue would keep coming up again and again until all children realised their right to free and compulsory education. In 1937, at the National Education Conference held at Wardha (Maharashtra), Mahatma Gandhi had to use all powers at his command to persuade the Ministers of Education of the newly elected Congress governments of seven provinces to give priority to basic education (under *Nai Talim)* of seven years and allocate adequate funds for this purpose. The Wardha Conference passed four resolutions among which the first one stated, "That free and compulsory education be provided for seven years on a nation-wide scale." This resolution on free and compulsory education was reiterated by the 51st annual session of Indian National Congress held at Haripura in February, 1938.

In this way, the concept of Right developed in India during the freedom movement with the demand for self governance and total independence from the colonial rule that culminated into Part III of the Indian Constitution on 'Fundamental Rights'.

Post-Independence

In 1950, the country adopted its own Constitution, which provided Fundamental Rights to equality, to freedom, against exploitation, to freedom of religion, to constitutional remedies and cultural and educational rights of the minorities. The right to free and compulsory education was retained in

Part IV of the Constitution that incorporates the Directive Principles of State Policy. Article 45 of Part IV of the Constitution declared: "The State shall endeavour to provide, within a period of ten years from the commencement of this Constitution, for free and compulsory education for all children until they complete the age of fourteen years." The 1980s and the 1990s saw a very liberal interpretation of Article 21 of the Indian Constitution by the Indian judiciary. The most relevant of them from education point of view was the Supreme Court's Unnikrishnan Judgement (1993). The Court ruled that Article 45 of the Directive Principles of State Policy must be read in harmonious conjunction with Article 21 since right to life and personal liberty loses its meaning if a child is deprived of elementary education (Unnikrishnan vs. State of Andhra Pradesh, 1993, Supreme Court of India 217). Thus, this judgement made right to free and compulsory education as good as a fundamental right. In other liberal interpretations of Article 21, the Court elevated to the status of fundamental rights, right to environment protection, to public health, to food and shelter and to rehabilitation in the case of bonded labourers. The Supreme Court also held that economic and financial constrains could be a ground for restricting the State from making provisions of post-basic and higher education, but *not* elementary education.

The Unnikrishnan Judgement activated several civil society groups to demand the incorporation of right to education as a Fundamental Right in Part III of the Constitution. The government finally agreed to bring a bill to amend the Constitution in order to elevate right to education to the status of a fundamental right. This became the new Article 21A of the Constitution in December 2002, which reads: "The State shall provide free and compulsory education to all children of the age 6 to 14 years in such manner as the State may, by *law*, determine. Notably, the Amendment was rightly introduced after Article 21, keeping in view the connection between this right and right to life. This was in the spirit of the interpretation of Article 21 by the Supreme Court of India. Many legal luminaries and educationists have emphasized the wide ramifications of the right to education, Justice (Retd.) J.S. Verma, the former Chief Justice of India and also the former Chairman of the National Human Rights Commission, observes that providing free elementary education is an 'essential sovereign function' of the welfare state. Justice (Retd.) V.R. Krishna Iyer (2005) has observed that education is a cardinal component of human dignity, and access to it is enshrined in the Indian Constitution.

The expert group set up by the Government of India after the Unnikrishnan Judgement, on the financial implications of RTE, with economist Tapas Majmudar as Chair person, chose the right-based approach to providing elementary education. The report said: "From being an incremental development goal in the process of Education for All, universalization of elementary education has in consequence of the Unnikrishnan Judgement, now become the legal right of every Indian child… entitlements sanctioned by the Constitution cannot be deferred by the State at its convenience. The State has to make the necessary reallocation of resources, by superseding other important claims, if necessary, in a manner that the justiciable entitlement can become a reality."

The Indian parliament on 4 August 2009 passed the Right of Children to Free and Compulsory Education Act or Right to Education Act (RTE). It describes the modalities of the provision of free and compulsory education for children between 6 and 14 in India under Article 21A of the Indian Constitution. India became one of 135 countries to make education a fundamental right of every child when the Act came into force on 1 April 2010. The law came into effect in the whole of India except the state of Jammu and Kashmir from 1 April 2010. According to this law, all children, irrespective of gender and social category, have access to education; an education that enables them to acquire the skills, knowledge, values and attitudes necessary to become responsible and active citizens of India." Thus, the 86th Constitutional Amendment Act 2002 made education a Fundamental Right for children in the age group of 6-14 years by providing that "the State shall provide free and compulsory education to all children of the age of six to fourteen years in such manner as the State may, by law, determine."

Education related Constitutional Provisions

Constitution is the fundamental law of the country, reflecting the underlying and unifying values of society. It spells out the basic rights of each person; it serves as a framework for all other laws and policies, and cannot be easily changed. However, it can be amended and updated through a democratic process, and it is important to keep it alive, by popularising and using it, and by campaigning for its reform or amendment, if necessary. The most relevant articles are given here, but we should encourage reading the Constitution in its totality.

The State is the main agency in any claim to the right to education: it is the prime duty-bearer and the prime implementer; it is the guarantor; and it is the state's signature in relation to the international norms and standards, which binds it to respect, protect and fulfil the right to education. The state must, therefore, be judged or challenged on its central text on the right to education, whether this is the Constitution, the laws or the policies.

Articles related to Education

Article 21A. *The State shall provide free and compulsory education to all children of the age of six to fourteen years in such manner as the State may, by law, determine.* (Eighty-Sixth Amendment Act, 2002)

Article 41. Right to work, to education and to public assistance in certain cases.

The State shall, within the limits of its economic capacity and development, make effective provision for securing the right to work, to education and to public assistance in cases of unemployment, old age, sickness and disablement, and in other cases of undeserved want.

Article 45. Provision for free and compulsory education for children.

(1) *The State shall endeavour to provide, within a period of ten years from the commencement of this Constitution, for free and compulsory education for all children until they complete the age of fourteen years.*

(2) *The State shall endeavour to provide early childhood care and education for all children until they complete the age of six years.* (Eighty-Sixth Amendment Act, 2002)

Article 46. Promotion of educational and economic interests of Scheduled Castes, Scheduled Tribes and other weaker sections.

The State shall promote with special care the educational and economic interests of the weaker sections of the people, and, in particular, of the Scheduled Castes and the Scheduled Tribes, and shall protect them from social injustice and all forms of exploitation.

Article 51 A. (k) *Who is a parent or guardian to provide opportunities for education to his child or, as the case may be, ward between the age of six and fourteen years.* (Eighty-Sixth Amendment Act, 2002)

Articles related to Minorities

Article 29. Protection of interests of minorities.

(1) *Any section of the citizens residing in the territory of India or any part thereof having a distinct language, script or culture of its own shall have the right to conserve the same.*

(2) *No citizen shall be denied admission into any educational institution maintained by the State or receiving aid out of State funds on grounds only of religion, race, caste, language or any of them.*

Article 30. Right of minorities to establish and administer educational institutions.

(1) *All minorities, whether based on religion or language, shall have the right to establish and administer educational institutions of their choice.*

(1A) *In making any law providing for the compulsory acquisition of any property of an educational institution established and administered by a minority, referred to in clause (1), the State shall ensure that the amount fixed by or determined under such law for the acquisition of such property is such as would not restrict or abrogate the right guaranteed under that clause.*

(2) *The State shall not, in granting aid to educational institutions, discriminate against any educational institution on the ground that it is under the management of a minority, whether based on religion or language.*

Article 350 A. Facilities for instruction in mother-tongue at primary stage.

It *shall be the endeavour of every State and of every local authority within the State to provide adequate facilities for instruction in the mother-tongue at the primary stage of education to children belonging to linguistic minority groups; and the President may issue such directions to any State as he considers necessary or proper for securing the provision of such facilities.*

Article 15 (5) *Nothing in this Article or in Sub-clause (g) of Clause (1) of Article 19 shall prevent the State from making any special provision, by law, for the advancement of any socially and educationally backward classes of citizens or for the Scheduled Castes or the Scheduled Tribes in so far as such special provisions relate to their admission to educational institutions including private educational institutions, whether aided or unaided by the State, other than the minority educational institutions referred to in Clause (1) of Article 30.* (Ninety-Third Amendment Act, 2005)

Articles related to Equality

Article 14. Equality before law.

The State shall not deny to any person equality/ before the law or the equal protection of the laws within the territory of India.

Article 15. Prohibition of discrimination on grounds of religion, race, caste, sex or place of birth.

(1) *The State shall not discriminate against any citizen on grounds only of religion, race, caste, sex, place of birth or any of them.*

(2) *No citizen shall, on grounds only of religion, race, caste, sex, place of birth or any of them, be subject to any disability, liability, restriction or condition with regard to—*

   (a) *access to shops, public restaurants, hotels and places of public entertainment; or*

   (b) *the use of wells, tanks, bathing ghats, roads and places of public resort maintained wholly or partly out of State funds or dedicated to the use of the general public.*

(3) *Nothing in this Article shall prevent the State from making any special provision for women and children.*

(4) *Nothing in this article or in Clause (2) of Article 29 shall prevent the State from making any special provision for the advancement of any socially and educationally backward classes of citizens or for the Scheduled Castes and the Scheduled Tribes.*

Article 24. Prohibition of employment of children in factories, etc.

No child below the age of fourteen years shall be employed to work in any factory or mine or engaged in any other hazardous employment.

Articles related to Gender and Vulnerable Groups

Article 39. Certain principles of policy to be followed by the State.

The State shall, in particular, direct its policy towards securing

(a) *that the citizens, men and women equally, have the right to an adequate means of livelihood;*

(e) *that the health and strength of workers, men and women, and the tender age of children are not abused and that citizens are not forced by economic necessity to enter vocations unsuited to their age or strength;*

(f) *that children are given opportunities and facilities to develop in a healthy manner and in conditions of freedom and dignity and that childhood and youth are protected against exploitation and against moral and material abandonment.*

Articles related to Religion

Article 25. Freedom of conscience and free profession, practice and propagation of religion.

(1) *Subject to public order, morality and health and to the other provisions of this Part, all persons are equally entitled to freedom of conscience and the right to freely profess, practise and propagate religion.*

(2) *Nothing in this Article shall affect the operation of any existing law or prevent the State from making any law*

    (a) *regulating or restricting any economic, financial, political or other secular activity which may be associated with religious practice;*

    (b) *providing for social welfare and reform or the throwing open of Hindu religious institutions of a public character to all classes and sections of Hindus.*

Explanation I.—The wearing and carrying of kirpans shall be deemed to be included in the profession of the Sikh religion.

Explanation II.—In Sub-clause (b) of Clause (2), the reference to Hindus shall be construed as including a reference to persons professing the Sikh, Jaina or Buddhist religion, and the reference to Hindu religious institutions shall be construed accordingly.

Article 26. Freedom to manage religious affairs.

Subject to public order, morality and health, every religious denomination or any section thereof shall have the right

(a) *to establish and maintain institutions for religious and charitable purposes;*

(b) *to manage its own affairs in matters of religion;*

Article 28. Freedom as to attendance at religious instruction or religious worship in certain educational institutions.

(1) *No religious instruction shall be provided in any educational institution wholly maintained out of State funds.*

(2) *Nothing in Clause (1) shall apply to an educational institution, which is administered by the State, but has been established under any endowment or trust, which requires that religious instruction shall be imparted in such institution.*

(3) *No person attending any educational institution recognised by the State or receiving aid out of State funds shall be required to take part in any religious instruction that may be imparted in such institution or to attend any religious worship that may be conducted in such institution or in any premises attached thereto unless such person or, if such person is a minor, his guardian has given his consent thereto.*

Constitutional, Legal and National Policies/Statements for Universalization of Elementary Education (UEE)

As the RTE is related to Elementary Education, therefore, Constitutional, Legal and National Policies/Statements specified for UEE are given here. These have time and again upheld the cause of Universal Elementary Education.

Constitutional mandate 1950—"The State shall endeavour to provide, within a period of ten years from the commencement of this Constitution, for free and compulsory education to all children until they complete the age of 14 years."

National Policy of Education 1986—"It shall be ensured that free and compulsory education of satisfactory quality is provided to all children up to 14 years of age before we enter the twenty first century."

Unnikrishnan Judgement, 1993—"Every child/citizen of this country has a right to free education until he completes the age of fourteen years."

Education Ministers Resolve, 1998—"Universal elementary education should be pursued in the mission mode. It emphasized the need to pursue a holistic and convergent approach towards UEE."

National Committee's Report on UEE in the Mission Mode: 1999— UEE should be pursued in a mission mode with a holistic and convergent approach with emphasis on preparation of District Elementary Education Plans for UEE. It supported the fundamental right to education and desired quick action towards operationalization of the mission mode towards UEE.

References

1. ASER (2013); Annual Status of Education Report (ASER), Pratham, ASER Centre, New Delhi.
2. GOI; Model Rules under the Right of children to free and compulsory Education Act (2009) http://mhrd.gov.in/sites/upload_files/mhrd/files/RTI_Model_Rules.pdf.
3. GOI; The Constitution (Eighty-Sixth Amendment) Act. (2002) http://indiacode.nic.in/coiweb/amend/amend86.htm.
4. MHRD (1993); Department of Education: Learning without Burden: report of the National Advisory Committee (New Delhi).
5. MHRD (2009); The Right of Children to Free and Compulsory Education Act 2009, Ministry of Human Resources Development (New Delhi).
6. NCERT (1966); Education and National development: Report of the Education Commission 1964-66 Ministry of Education (New Delhi).
7. NCERT (2000, 2005); National Curriculum Framework National Council for Educational Research and Training (New Delhi).
8. NCERT (2005); National Focus Group on Examination Reforms, National Council for Educational Research and Training, Position Paper (New Delhi).

Webliography

1. http://en.wikipedia.org/wiki/Right_to_education
2. http://mhrd.gov.in/rte
3. http://mhrd.gov.in/sites/upload_files/mhrd/files/RTE_Section_wise_rationale_rev_0.pdf
4. http://unesdoc.unesco.org/images/0015/001548/154861e.pdf
5. http://www.ohchr.org/EN/ProfessionalInterest/Pages/CESCR.aspx
6. http://www.un.org/en/documents/udhr/index.shtml
7. http://www.unicef.org/publications/index_42104.html

5

The Right to Education Act

A Stepping Stone towards Visionary Developed India

Wadudul Haque Siddique

Education has its functionalism in almost all sphere of life. Its signification can never be marginalized. An educated society prepares the present generation for a bright future and enables the individual to galvanize the capacity of collective. More than 2300 years back Chanakya had said, *"That mother and that father are enemies, who do not give education to their children."* In the recent past Nelson Mandela had proclaimed, *"Education is the most powerful weapon which you can use to change the world."* What happens when a country of the size of India has over three million children living on the streets? Or has over 150 million children working as bonded labourers? Or one out of every six girl child does not live to see her 15th birthday? What happens when despite having a national policy for compulsory primary education, only 50 per cent of children have access to education?

It is a popular saying that "Education is both the means as well as the end to a better life," means, because it empowers an individual to earn his/her livelihood and the end because it increases one's awareness on a range of issues. But, unfortunately, in today's modern day scenario the subject of Education is actually used by our political leaders and legislators as the "means" for achieving the "end" common to them all political power. After all, it makes an integral part of their Election manifesto.

The Right of Children to Free and Compulsory Education Act, 2009, popularly known as the Right to Education (RTE) Act is a remarkable step forward in the field of education in India. However, some of the provisions of the Act, although included with noble intentions, will have unintended consequences that might counter some of the advantages of the new system itself as well as have ill effects on the very subjects of the Act, the children, most of whom are even unaware of the polity behind the legislation ruling them.

Right to Education (RTE) ACT

The Constitution (Eighty-sixth Amendment Act, 2002) inserted Article 21-A in the Constitution of India to provide free and compulsory education of all children in the age group of six to fourteen years as a Fundamental Right in such a manner as the State may, by law, determine. The Right of Children to Free and Compulsory Education (RTE) Act, 2009, which represents the consequential legislation envisaged under Article 21-A, means that every child has a right to full time elementary education of satisfactory and equitable quality in a formal school, which satisfies certain essential norms and standards.

Article 21-A and the RTE Act came into effect on 1 April 2010. The title of the RTE Act incorporates the words 'free and compulsory'. 'Free education' means that no child, other than a child, who has been admitted by his or her parents to a school, which is not supported by the appropriate Government, shall be liable to pay any kind of fee or charges or expenses, which may prevent him or her from pursuing and completing elementary education. 'Compulsory education' casts an obligation on the appropriate Government and local authorities to provide and ensure admission, attendance and completion of elementary education by all children in the 6-14 age group. With this, India has moved forward to a rights based framework that casts a legal obligation on the Central and State Governments to implement this fundamental child right as enshrined in the Article 21A of the Constitution, in accordance.

Key Strengths of the RTE Act

The main strengths of the RTE Act are given below:

***Assignation of State Responsibility*:** The Act clearly makes the state responsible for ensuring that every child, in the age group of 6 to 14, receives schooling for eight years, instead of merely shifting the onus for this to the parents, a majority of who are illiterate and mired in poverty.

***Specific Duties*:** The Act reiterates the role of the state, along with private and aided schools, to satisfy certain basic norms in terms of infrastructure, learning facilities and the academic calendar. This is important since the quality of inputs has bearing on education outcomes.

***Pupil Teacher Ratio*:** The Act mandates a minimum Pupil-Teacher Ratio and explicitly requires the same to be maintained in each school, rather than as an average over a block or a district.

***Teacher Qualifications*:** The Act prescribes the minimum qualifications of teachers and their academic responsibilities, along with the minimum quality of the content and process. This can positively impact the actual quality of education provided within our schools.

Suggestions for Improving the Loopholes of RTE

The Act also has several shortcomings and there are some, who will say that it is wholly inadequate. Like many other Acts and laws, the intentions of the RTE Act are very noble, but the key issues are around critical gaps in policy as well as implementation and enforcement issues. Attention may be drawn to the following issues, which may result in the RTE Act not delivering the promise of quality education for all.

Quality of Teachers and Teacher Education

While the Act lays down minimum criteria for teacher qualifications, it may be hard to expect quality improvement unless the foundations/principles, content and methodologies of pre- and in-service training of teachers are re-looked at and changed. In addition to this, there needs to be a tight mechanism to prevent mushrooming of innumerable sub-standard private teacher training colleges and institutes in the country.

Institutional Structures for Academic Support

The Act draws no attention to the existing shortcomings of the institutional structures for teachers' training and innovation. There should be more clear and strict provisions for capacitating the educational support structures, like the SCERT and DIET. Formation of a separate cadre of these organizations would greatly contribute towards professionalizing teaching. However, the RTE hardly talks of interventions required for the academic support structures themselves.

Ensuring Learning Outcomes and Competencies

While ensuring that every child, who traverses through the elementary education system, acquires a certificate of completion, the Act fails to guarantee that a child has acquired competencies deriving from said education process —no standards are set for monitoring and measuring learning outcomes—a case of guaranteeing graduation, but not education. The Act should also define a framework to measure the quality of education imparted.

Recognition Process for State Schools

Unlike for private schools, the process of attaining recognition for state schools is not prescribed. The Act does not mention the course of action that the State schools will have to face, in case of failure to adhere to minimum norms for quality mentioned in the schedule. There does not seem to be any penalty on the government specified for failing to meet its obligations.

Teacher Shortages and Financing

The financing of the RTE Act could prove to be a major obstacle in its effective implementation. After protracted negotiations between the Centre and the

States, it was decided that the financial burden would be shared in a 65:35 ratio. However, even one year after the Act came into force, the government of UP (the most populous state) stated that it did not have funds to implement the Act. The budgetary allocation for Sarva Shiksha Abhiyan (the vehicle for the implementation of the RTE Act) in the budget for 2011-12 is ₹ 21,000 crore, a mere ₹ 2,000 crore increase from the previous financial year. At present, the shortage of teachers is one of the greatest obstacles facing the implementation of the RTE Act. According to the Ministry of HRD, in order to meet the requirements of the RTE Act, 5.08 lakh additional teachers are required to be recruited. Given that hiring of new teachers and construction of new schools is mandated under the Act, it is yet to be seen if these can be accomplished with the given budgetary allocations.

Inadequate Grievance Redressal Mechanism

In order to make the RTE Act effective, it is necessary to establish the modalities through which rights under the RTE Act are protected and violations of the Act are to be dealt with, i.e., a system of registering, investigating and responding within a well-appointed time frame. Today, more than a year after the RTE Act came into force; this does not exist in most states. There is no designated authority for grievance redressal at the habitation level. Only eleven states have set up State Commissions for the Protection of Child Rights and Right to Education Protection Authorities.

Exclusion of Early Childhood Education (ECE)

Several studies on early childhood have shown that three to six years is the age when children need to be exposed to literacy-rich environment to enhance their literacy growth and children, who experience schooling for the first time at the age of six years, are clearly at a disadvantage. In the face of such evidence, it is necessary that RTE is enhanced to include Pre-School Education and its convergence with mainstream education.

Conclusion

In conclusion, we can say that RTE is really a stepping stone in the history of elementary education in India. Its success depends on the central government, state governments, policy makers, teacher educators, teachers, parents, social workers and NGOs. At present, we are facing many problems related to the implementation of RTE Act in India. Though the Right to Education Act is a great start, government officials are now beginning to understand the challenges they face in implementing it. They are searching for resources and partnerships to support the goals of the Act. Teacher development and trainings are being investigated and pursued. The future is bright in India in many areas and education can certainly be one of them. Some important suggestions to achieve the goal of RTE are given below:

- Parents, Teachers, Professionals, Social workers and NGOs should assist the government and competent authorities for the successful implementation of this Act.
- Seminars and workshops should be organized to generate awareness among rural people about RTE Act, 2009.
- Appropriate facilities should be provided by the government and competent authorities to the rural people of India.

References

1. Annual Status of Education Report 2011.
2. Bhargava, P.M.; *RTE ACT: Some Rights and Wrongs*.
3. Gupta, S.; What are the different strategies and approaches to Realize (RTE) Right to Education in India.
4. http://images2.asercentre.org/aserreports/ASER_2011/education_report_card.pdf.
5. http://www.thehindu.com/opinion/lead/article533475.ece?homepage=true.
6. http://www.right-to-education.org/sites/r2e.gn.apc.org/files/Shantanu_Gupta_RTE%20in%20India.pdf.
7. http://indiabudget.nic.in/ub2012-13/eb/sbe58.pdf.
8. http://www.asercentre.org/ngo-education-india.php?p=Spotlight%3A+ASER+2011.

6

Towards a Progressive Nation

The Role of RTE Act

Jeena K.G.

> *"Education is the most powerful weapon, which you can use to change the world"*
> — Nelson Mandela

Education unfolds child's potential to the optimum level. It refines character, enhances personality development in an all-round manner and it has the power of creating enlightened citizens and through them a progressive nation. The great thinker, swami Vivekananda sermonized that education is a panacea for all social evils. We are trying hard to give quality education at all levels in order to achieve our dream—a developed India in near future.

India is privileged that it has the treasure of younger human resource in comparison to other countries. This young human resource is an opportunity and, at the same time, a challenge before us, as we have the obligation of giving quality education to all. It is our responsibility to provide them quality education in order to mould them in the right manner and use this human resource for the betterment of society and, at large, for the progress of the nation.

Importance of Elementary Education

It is crystal clear that the quality of nation depends on the quality of education. While coming to quality of education, elementary education has paramount importance, as it forms the base and stepping stone to individual development. This fact is strengthened by J.P. Naik, an eminent educationist's observation, "The progress of primary education is one important index of the general, social and economic development of the country as a whole." Being the foundation of educational structure, the elementary education lays strong foundation for the child's physical, intellectual, emotional and social development. It helps in the eradication of adult illiteracy and makes the most significant contribution to the efficient functioning of our country. Kothari commission (1964-66) highlighted the importance of elementary education in its report, as "We believe that the provision of free and universal education for every child is an educational objective of the highest priority, not only on grounds of social justice and democracy, but also for raising the competence of the average worker and for increasing national productivity."

It is rightly said that "the child of today is the citizen of tomorrow." He or she is the builder of the country. It is through a well planned and well-implemented educational system that the child could be equipped to realize his/her potential and contribute effectively in national reconstruction. Therefore, investment in elementary education is essential for facilitating the physical, intellectual and emotional development of the child.

Education by its very nature influences the social, cultural, economic and political parameters. Real effect of democracy will become a mirage as long as a large part of the population remains excluded from the political process. Common causes of exclusion are insecurity and wide spread adult illiteracy. In general, literacy and education are important tools of effective political participation. Adult illiteracy in this country is to be removed by proper planning of elementary education for all.

The value of education not only lies in the person, who acquires it, but also for the society. For instance, when a young person from a deprived community acquires good education, the community gets the advantage. Hence, wide spread elementary education helps to resolve social problems and maintain good social order.

Studies have obviously shown that countries, which have made adequate provision for elementary education, are far ahead of those with inadequate provision. When we analyze the enrolment of children globally, 91 per cent of children of primary school age were enrolled in schools in 2010 and only nine per cent of the targeted population is excluded from access to education. It is seen that at the global level, the adjusted net enrolment rate has increased by seven percentage points between 1999 and 2010 (Figure 6.1).

But in India, the situation is different. Universalization of elementary education is the constitutional commitment in India. Efforts have been made in the past to achieve the goal, but despite spectacular quantitative expansion of educational facilities, the goal is still a far distant dream. Article 45 envisaged the Universalizsation of Elementary Education for all the children up to the age of 14 years within a time frame of ten years since the commencement of the Constitution. Actually, the aim was supposed to be achieved in 1960; later, NPE was established in 1986/92 and still the aim was not achieved. In

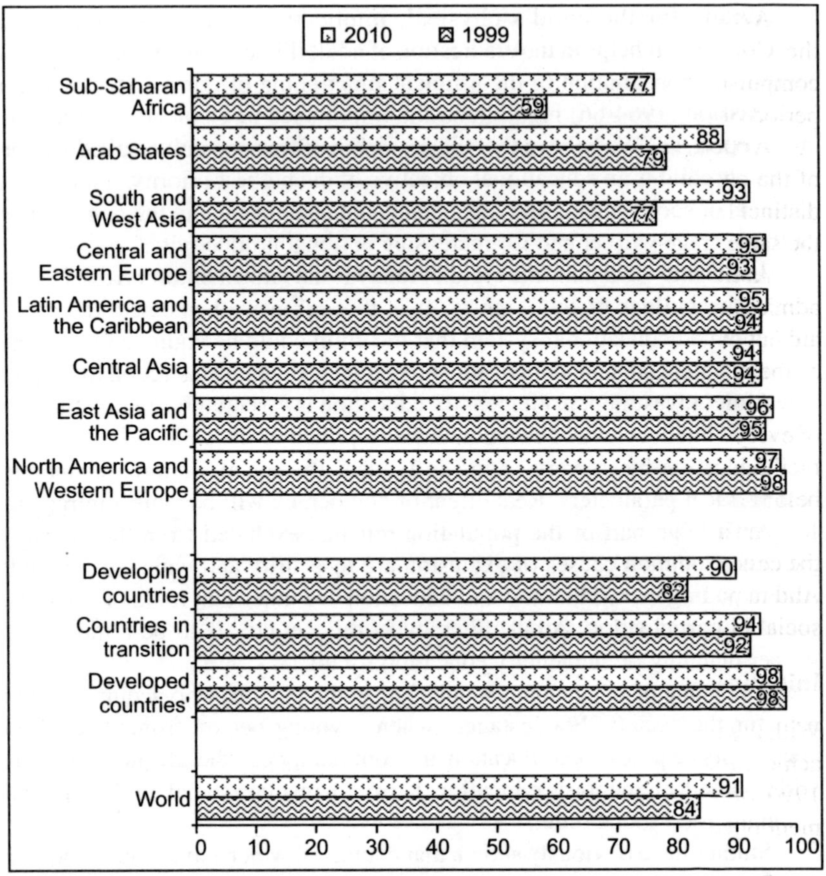

Source: UNESCO Institute for Statistics, May 2012.

Figure 6.1: Adjusted net enrolment rate in primary education, 1999 and 2010 (%)

this context, it's needless to mention that the achievement of this noble objective has been evading us for the past more than six decades.

Constitutional Provisions regarding Elementary Education

With a view to accelerating the pace of national development and promoting emotional integration, it is imperative to invest in education. The Constitution of India adumbrates that education is a tool for meeting the national challenges and it is geared towards the needs of democracy, socialism and secularism. Keeping this in mind, the Constitution made provisions for improving the present situation. Some of them are discussed below:

Article 45: The Article 45 in the Directive Principles of State Policy in the Constitution mandated the State to endeavour to provide free and compulsory education to all children up to the age of fourteen years in a period of ten years.

Article 29 (1): Article 29 (1) of the Constitution provides that any section of the citizens residing in the territory of India or any part thereof having a distinct language scripts or culture of its own shall have the right to conserve the same.

Article 29 (2): Article 29 (2) lays down that "no citizen shall be denied admission into any educational institution maintained by the state or receiving aid out of state funds on grounds only of religion, race, caste, language or any of them."

Article 350-A: Article 350-A lays down that "it shall be the endeavour of every State and of every local authority within the state to provide adequate facilities in the mother-tongue at the primary stage of education to children belonging to linguistic minority groups."

Article 46: As per the Article "state shall promote with special care for the educational and economic interests of the weaker sections of the people. And in particular, of the Scheduled Tribes (STs) and shall protect them from social injustice and all forms of exploitation."

Initiatives for Achieving UEE

With the formulation of NPE, India initiated a wide range of programmes for achieving the goal of UEE. These efforts were intensified in the 1980s and 1990s through several schematic and programme interventions, which are mentioned below:

- Minimum Levels of Learning (MLL),
- Operation Black Board (OBB),
- Shiksha Karmi Project (SKP),
- Andhra Pradesh Primary Education Project (APPEP)
- Bihar Education Project (BEP),
- U.P. Basic Education Project (UPBEP),
- National Programme of Nutritional Support to Primary Education (NP-NSPE) (Mid Day Meal scheme),
- Mahila Samakhya (MS),
- Lok Jumbish Project (LJP),
- Teacher Education through District Institutes of Education and Training,
- District Primary Education Programme (DPEP), and
- Sarva Shiksha Abhiyan (SSA).

Due to the continuous struggle in the past years for giving quality elementary education to all, made the situation much better. Now, there is a significant progress in access and enrolment of children in schools. The number of out-of-school children has reduced significantly. The gender gap in elementary education has narrowed and the percentage of children belonging to Scheduled Castes and Tribes enrolled is proportionate to their population. The Figure 6.2 shows increase in the enrolment of children in primary and upper primary schools.

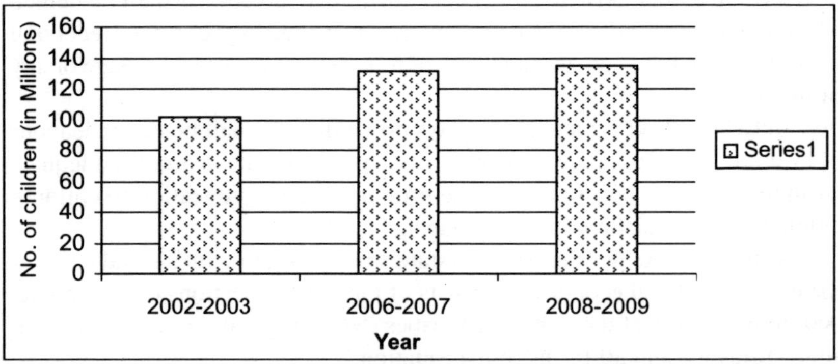

Figure 6.2: Enrolment of Children in Primary and Upper Primary Schools

Need of RTE Act

Elementary education has been the major concern of all nations, since it is the foundation of the entire structure of education and is directly related to the success of democracy. It is also considered as the foundation stone of human development and plays a significant role in democratic system. To promote social justice, equality, it will be necessary to provide equal opportunity for education to all not only in access, but also in the condition for success. The purpose is to remove prejudices and complexes transmitted through social environment and the accident of birth. RTE Act helps to achieve this important aim.

For providing quality elementary education to every citizen, the Constitution (Eighty-sixth Amendment Act, 2002) inserted Article 21-A in the Constitution of India to provide free and compulsory education of all children in the age group of six to fourteen years as a Fundamental Right in such a manner as the State may, by law, determine. The Right of Children to Free and Compulsory Education (RTE) Act, 2009, which represents the consequential legislation envisaged under Article 21-A, means that every child has a right to full time elementary education of satisfactory and equitable quality in a formal school, which satisfies certain essential norms and standards.

Education is both an indicator and an instrument of development, and its attainment is a major factor behind the accumulation of human capital. Education has long been identified as one of the most important determinants of economic growth. The economic returns from investment in education are typically high, both for individual and society due to increase in both cognitive and non cognitive skills.

Education is one of the most important life determining factors. It is both an end and means for socio economic development. It helps in the formation of social capital of high quality including human resource development. Education opens production possibilities and galvanizes a stagnating economy to reach the highest pinnacle of economic prosperity. So, education today is viewed as a holistic approach for economic transition and transformation. In this context, the RTE Act helps to achieve quality elementary education to every citizen. The need to address inadequacies in retention, residual access, particularly of un-reached children, and the questions of quality are the most compelling reasons for the insertion of Article 21-A in the Constitution of India and the passage of the RTE Act, 2009 in the Parliament. Article 21-A and the RTE Act came into effect on 1 April 2013. The title of the RTE Act incorporates the words 'free and compulsory'. 'Free education' means that no child, other than a child, who has been admitted by his or her parents to a school, which is not supported by the appropriate Government, shall be liable to pay any kind of fee or charges or expenses, which may prevent him or her from pursuing and completing elementary education. 'Compulsory education' casts an obligation on the appropriate Government and local authorities to provide and ensure admission, attendance and completion of elementary education by all children in the 6-14 age groups. With this, India has moved forward to a rights based framework that casts a legal obligation on the Central and State Governments to implement this fundamental child right as enshrined in Article 21A of the Constitution, in accordance with the provisions of the RTE Act.

How RTE Act Helps to Achieve Quality Elementary Education to All

The RTE Act helps to achieve quality elementary education to every citizen. For this, it gives a number of provisions. These are mentioned below:

Neighbourhood School

Universal access to elementary education requires schooling facilities within reasonable reach of all children. If schools are not located in or near the habitations where children reside, children are unlikely to complete schooling, even if they are formally enrolled in schools. The RTE Act provides children's access to elementary schools within the defined area or limits of neighbourhood. The RTE act mentions about neighbourhood school in its report, "The appropriate governments and local authorities shall establish, within the area or limits of a neighbourhood, a school, where it is not already established, within a period of three years from the commencement of the Act." Further, the Act places a compulsion on the State to ensure that no child from the weaker sections or disadvantaged groups is discriminated against in any manner or prevented from pursuing and completing elementary education.

Special Training for Out-of-School Children

The RTE Act makes specific provision for Special Training for age-appropriate admission of out-of-school children. A majority of out-of school children belong to disadvantaged communities: Scheduled Castes, Scheduled Tribes, Muslims, migrants, children with special needs, urban deprived children, working children, children in other difficult circumstances, for example, those living in difficult terrain, children from displaced families, and areas affected by civil strife, etc. need Special Training. Special Training for never enrolled children or those, who dropped out before completing elementary education would require an identification of children, who must be enrolled. For this, the State Government, Local Authority and School Management Committee will need to undertake a community level school mapping exercise. The neighbourhood and school mapping exercise will be followed by: (i) immediate enrolment in school; (ii) organisation of Special Training of flexible duration to enable the child to be at par with other children; (iii) actual admission of the child in the age-appropriate class on completion of Special Training, and his/her participation in all class activities; (iv) continued support to the child, once admitted to the regular school, so that the child can integrate with the class socially, emotionally and academically. The RTE Act also provides that such children shall continue to be provided free and compulsory elementary education even after they cross 14 years of age.

Learning in Age Appropriate Classes

The RTE Act (Section 4) stipulates age appropriate admission for out-of-school children, or those, who may have dropped out, so that older children do not lose self esteem by being made to sit in a designated class of younger children. It is in this context that the RTE Act provides for Special Training for out-of-school children, before being accommodated in an age-appropriate class.

RTE Emphasizes Constructivist Approach

The theory of constructivism is based on the idea that children learn better by actively constructing knowledge and by reconciling new information with previous knowledge. The constructivist perspective supports that learners learn through interaction with others. Learners work together as peers, applying their combined knowledge to the solution of the problem.

According to constructivist perspective, learning is determined by the complex interplay among learners' existing knowledge, the social context, and the problem to be solved. Instruction then refers to providing learners with collaborative situation in which they have both the means and the opportunity to construct 'new and situation-specific understanding.

Learning is not a passive receptive process but is, instead, an active meaning making process required to solve meaningful problems. Constructivist approach helps the learners make sense of the world around them. This is to be done through 'critical pedagogy', which foregrounds questions of inequality and justice and enables learners to undertake transformative action.

Pre-School Training

By realizing the importance of pre-school learning and early childhood care and its role in improving participation of children in schools, Section 11 of the RTE Act, 2009 makes provision for being engaged with pre-school education. It states: "With a view to prepare children above the age of three years for elementary education and to provide early childhood care and education for all children until they complete the age of six years, the appropriate Government may make necessary arrangement for providing free pre-school education to such children."

It may be concluded that education is an effective instrument not only for the development of one's personality, but also for the sustained growth of the nation. Therefore, elementary education in India is the foundation for the development of every citizen and the nation as a whole. By making quality elementary education available to every citizen of the country, it will help to boost up the progress of Nation. The importance of RTE Act can be understood with the help of Figure 6.3.

Conclusion

Education is considered to be the single most important factor in achieving rapid economic development and technological progress and in creating a social order founded on the values of freedom, social justice and equal opportunity. All the commissions and committees approved the significant role of education, especially primary education for bringing prosperity in the country. Primary education is the most important constituent of the whole process of education policy. It helps to produce a literate and numerate population that can deal with problems at home and at work and to serve as a foundation upon which further education is built. Higher education and training need to rest on a solid base, build by quality elementary education. The RTE Act helps us to realize quality elementary education to every citizen in the country and helps to achieve revolutionary changes in the right direction.

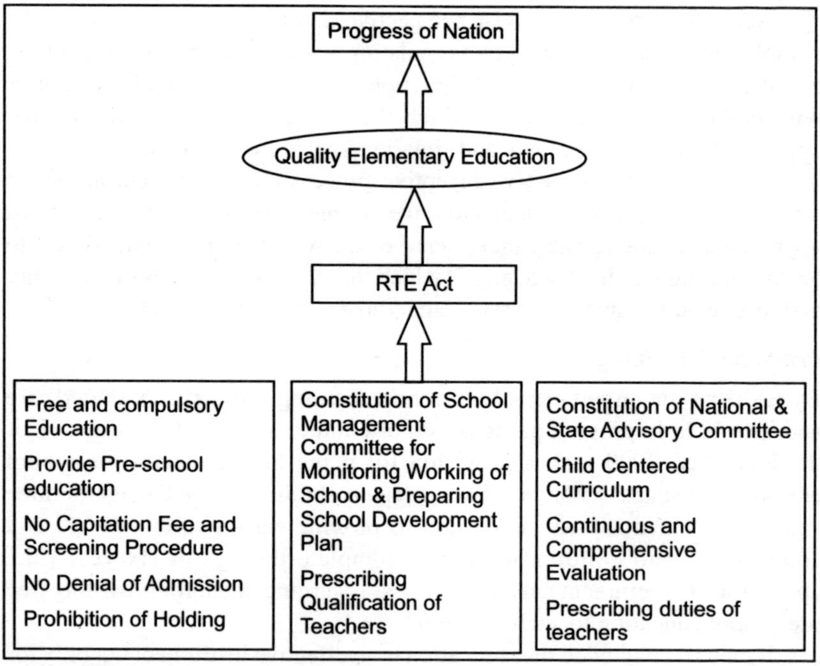

Figure 6.3: The Importance of RTE

References

1. Krishnamacharulu, K. (2006). *Elementary Education*. Hyderabad: Neelkalmal Publications.
2. Manas Ranjan Panigrahi. (2008). *Quality Elementary Education: Researches and Issues*. New Delhi: Mahamaya Publishing House.
3. Mehta, A.C. (2010). *Elementary Education in India*, (Analytical Report 2007-2008). New Delhi: NUEPA
4. Mehta, A.C. (2010). *Elementary Education in Rural India, Where Do We Stand* (Analytical Tables 2008). New Delhi: NUEPA
5. Mehta, A.C. (2010). *Elementary Education in Urban India, Where Do We Stand* (Analytical Tables 2008). New Delhi: NUEPA
6. Ministry of Law and Justice (2009). The Right of Children to Free and Compulsory Education Act, 2009. New Delhi
7. Mohanty, Jagannath. (2002). *Primary and Elementary Education*. New Delhi: Deep & Deep publications
8. Ravindra Babu, J. (2009). *Universalization of Elementary Education: A study of DPEP programme from South India*. UK: Cambridge Scholars Publishing.
9. UNESCO Institute for Statistics (2012). Universal Primary Education. UIS Fact Sheet. UNESCO.
10. UNICEF. (2007). A Human Right Based Approach to Education for All. New York: UNICEF.

7

The RTE Implementation

Some Problems and Concerns

Charu Saini

"If you are planning for a year, sow rice; if you are planning for a decade plant trees; if you are planning for a lifetime, educate people." — Chinese proverb

15 December 2008, seventy one years since Mahatma Gandhi gave the first call for universal education in 1937; sixty one years since independence; fifty eight years since the Constitution, fifteen years since the Supreme Court ruling in 1993 on the right to education; six years after the 86th Constitutional Amendment was passed by the Parliament in 2002 by inserting Article 21A making education a fundamental right for children in the restricted age group of 6 to 14 years; and four years after the Draft Bill was prepared by the CABE (Central Advisory Board of Education) committee, the Right to Free and Compulsory Education Bill was introduced in the Rajya Sabha on 15 December 2008. Though the delay on part of the state was deplorable, the introduction was still welcomed.

The Right to Education Act

The core of right to education relates to its substance, which differs from education itself. Effective and transformative education should be the result of the exercise of the right to education, which is a universal human right. The right is about the entitlement to claim the substance of it; it relates to the possibility of demanding the right to education and making it justifiable. The Right of Children to Free and Compulsory Education Act was passed in 2009 and brought into effect in April 2010. The key features of the Act are as under:

1. Free Elementary Education for All Children in Age Group 6-14 Years in a Neighbourhood School: According to the Act, no financial constraints can "prevent" a child from enrolling, attending and completing elementary education. In other words, if a child lives in a remote area, providing free transportation (or a residential facility or some other facility) will be part of the child's entitlement to education; if a child is disabled and needs crutches to walk to school, then crutches, or some other facility that enables him to go to school will be part of his entitlement under the Act.

2. Compulsory Elementary Education: The word compulsory has implications for the government alone. In other words, while it is the duty of the parents to send their children to school, it is the obligation of the government to ensure not just enrolment, but attendance and completion of elementary education. This implies that the government:

(a) Must identify all children that are out of school or dropped out.
(b) Make sure that they are enrolled in school.
(c) Make sure that they attend school on a regular basis.
(d) Make sure that they complete the elementary cycle of education.
(e) If parents are reluctant to send their children to school, it is the responsibility of the government to find a way of convincing the parents, without use of force/violence/pressure to send their children to school.

3. Age Appropriate Education

(a) This means that children will be enrolled in the class that corresponds to their age. In other words, if a ten year old has not been to school or dropped out earlier, she will be enrolled in class five.
(b) To enable the ten year old child to cope in class five, "special training" will be provided on the premises to bring the child up to the age appropriate level.

4. Quality Norms for all Schools: The Act lays out some basic norms for all schools (government and private):

(a) Pupil-Teacher Ratio (cannot exceed 1:30)
(b) Minimum days of school functioning in a year (200 and 250 for primary and Upper Primary (UP), respectively)
(c) Minimum hours of instruction in school (four and five hours a day for primary and UP)
(d) Minimum working hours for the teacher (45 hours a week)
(e) Separate subject teachers and head-teacher
(f) One room for every teacher
(g) Separate and functional toilets; clean and adequate drinking water
(h) Playground, boundary wall, library, kitchen

5. Qualifications for Teachers

(a) Para Teachers banned
(b) All teachers must subscribe to minimum qualifications and training norms laid out by Academic Authority within five years.
(c) Teacher education and Teacher training institutes to be upgraded to enable fulfilment of quality and qualification norms for teachers.

6. Curriculum in Line with Constitution

(a) This means that curriculum, syllabus and books must conform to the Constitutional values. It implies that communal and harmful agendas cannot be part of the materials used and taught in any school of the country.
(b) Syllabus and Books must also take into account age and learning levels of children.

7. Evaluation System to be based on the Principle of Continuous and Comprehensive Evaluation (CCE)

(a) No failure till completion of elementary cycle.
(b) Evaluation to be done throughout the year and not to be based on an annual exam.
(c) Teachers to maintain PUPIL CUMMULATIVE RECORD (PCR) for every child.
(d) Evaluation to be on "comprehensive" performance of child, reflecting all facets, talents of the child and not to be based on just a few subject areas. The PCR to include music, theatre, leadership skills, social skills, etc. as well.

8. Role of *Panchayati Raj* Institutions (PRIs)

(a) The PRIs are given a wide range of functions related to the implementation of the provisions of the RTE, such as identification of out of school children; neighbourhood-wise school mapping; maintenance of child records (child-tracking); public display of information; education of children from migrant families; participation in School Management Committees (SMCs).
(b) PRIs are also responsible for grievance redressal in matters related to violations of the rights of the child under RTE.

9. Participation of Civil Society

(a) School Management Committees consists largely of parents (75%) and of PRI officials. The civil society partners are given a wide range of functions under the Act, including the preparation of the School Development Plan.

(b) Teachers are accountable to the SMCs.

10. Reservation in Private Schools

(a) All private schools are required to admit in their incoming class 25 per cent children from the weaker sections, and socially disadvantaged groups from their neighbourhood.
(b) Limits of definition to be extended if 25 per cent seats are not being filled within the standard limits of neighbourhood.
(c) Private schools to be reimbursed for these children by the government at the rate of per learner costs of government schools in the state.

11. Separation of Implementation and Monitoring Agency

(a) Implementation responsibilities lie with the education departments in conjunction with the PRIs
(b) Monitoring role has been given to the National Commission for Protection of Child Rights (NCPCR) and the corresponding State Commissions.
(c) This separation is very important and a first in the history of such legislations and allows for independent monitoring of the implementation of the Act.
(d) NCPCR/SCPCR have *quasi-judicial* powers and can function as a civil court. Complaints and grievances can be addressed to them as well.

Some Problems and Concerns

A law in order to be successful has to be in consonance with the society. Any law, which is enacted before its time, is bound to die a slow death. India has witnessed many such situations, especially in the field of education where many important policies failed because of the lack of preparations required before their implementation.

Financial Constraints

While each country must determine its own financial capacity, an examination of countries regarded as having highly successful education systems suggests a figure of five per cent of GDP as a minimum budget target. But it is highly regretful that in the financial year 2012-13, only 3.8 per cent of GDP has been allotted for education.

Shift of Focus from Quality to Quantity

The plan requires total outlay of 2,04,000 crore over the next five years. Also, nearly 13 lakh teachers have to be hired to reach the target of achieving 1:30 teacher-student ratio. Sixty per cent of the schools still do not comply with the teacher-pupil ratio of 1:30 as stipulated in the RTE Act (ASER-2011). The current education programmes have to be reconciled in accordance with the new provisions. The main fear is that like the Sarva Shiksha Abhiyan, the focus might shift from quality to quantity. However, with the operationalization of RTE Act w.e.f. 1 April 2010, the funding pattern in respect of RTE-SSA programme for the period 2010-11 to 2014-15 has been revised as 65:35 for States/Union Territories other than NE States. For the eight North Eastern States, the existing fund sharing pattern of 90:10 between the Centre and States would continue. Hence, at times, it seems that the implementation of RTE is nothing more than a number game in which entire focus is on changing numbers from here to there.

Lack of Basic Infrastructure Facilities in the Schools

According to Annual Status Report of Education 2011, quoted by the union government itself in its Annual Economic Survey 2011-12:

- 56 per cent of the schools in India still have no separate toilets for girls.
- 28.6 per cent of the schools still do not have libraries.
- 28 per cent of the schools have no playground.
- 16.6 per cent of the schools have no provision for drinking water.
- Around 45 per cent of the schools do not have even their own boundary wall.
- More than half of standard two and standard four classes sit together with another class.

Since two years after Right to Education (RTE) Act came into force, more than 95 per cent of schools across India still don't comply with RTE standards for Infrastructure. Most of the Government schools lack in providing basic infrastructure facilities to the students. Even in Delhi, there are schools where the condition of elementary schools is deplorable. They lacks in providing healthy and hygienic environment to the students. Some schools don't have appropriate rooms required for classes. In some schools, the condition of the classrooms and toilets are shockingly bad.

Lack of Awareness

Most well-meaning legislations fail to make significant changes without proper awareness and grassroots pressure. Schools need to be made aware of provisions of the 25 per cent reservations, the role of SMCs and the requirements under the Schedule. The implementation of right to education is not the sole responsibility of the government only; rather we will be able to achieve this aim if we consider it as a collective responsibility. This can be undertaken through mass awareness programmes as well as ensuring proper understanding by stakeholders responsible for its implementation. Since, some schools implemented the Act a couple of years ago, we now have data to show that forcing 25 per cent seats in a classroom to be occupied by students of a particular economic stratum may cause problems. Parents, who pay a high fee to private schools and expect a certain environment within the class, are horrified of students from a different background using abusive language, behaving differently, and not too interested in learning. Teachers find it difficult to teach these uninterested students, school administration is constantly threatened by the parents of these students against any action and the result is that the overall quality of education in the classroom has come down.

School Management Committees (SMCs)

By the Act, SMCs should comprise of mostly parents, and should be responsible for planning and managing the operations of government and aided schools. SMCs will help increase the accountability of government schools, but SMCs for government schools need to be given greater powers over evaluation of teacher competencies and students learning assessment. Members of SMCs are required to volunteer their time and effort. This is an onerous burden for the poor. Payment of some compensation to members of SMCs could help increase the time and focus upon these. Turning to private, but 'aided' schools, the new role of SMCs for private 'aided' schools will lead to a breakdown of the existing management structures.

Teachers' Lack of Preparedness

As we all know effective education depends on the quality of the teachers. Good quality teaching can overcome significant levels of disadvantage in the lives of the students, while poor quality teachers add to the barriers many children face, and can deter them from attending school.

Teachers are generally well versed with the method of chalk and talk. Since this particular Act demands the use of innovative methods by the teachers, hence, it becomes very difficult to retain the students in the schools. They don't find the Teaching-Learning process interesting. Also, Right to Education has banned punishment of any sort, but the teachers in the system don't know how to continue smooth teaching learning process without it's use.

RTE doesn't Follow UN's Child Rights Convention

The Bill needs to bring into its ambit all children in the age group of 3-16 years. It ignores children, who are below six years of age. Also, the fate of children above fourteen years of age has not been discussed seriously.

Absence of Any Strict Law against Child Labour

In passing the 86th Amendment to the Constitution of India, education is a fundamental right. This has implications for fulfilment of the obligation of the State to ensure that every child is in school. Since most children, who do not attend schools, are engaged in some form of work or another, it is essential that there is a comprehensive plan to withdraw children from work and mainstream them into schools. But reality is other way round. Children are engaged in various tasks in both rural and urban areas. Thus, the labour department has a crucial role to abolish child labour in all its forms and ensure that children enjoy their right to education. In most societies, where child labour has been eradicated, multi-pronged strategies were used. Stringent laws were passed, which made child labour illegal. In addition, the educational system was strengthened, so that children removed from work could go to school.

Right to Education for Economically Weaker Sections

The RTE Act directed all schools, including privately-run schools, to reserve 25 per cent of their seats for students from socially and economically backward families. That means, a quarter of students in classes will be from marginalized section of the society. This will change the structure of classes. The present experience of India with mixed or diversified classroom is not encouraging. The children from marginalized sections of society are discriminated in the classroom on the basis of gender, caste, and ethnicity. Despite the Indian Constitution strictly prohibiting discrimination on the basis of caste and other social backgrounds, and making it a punishable act, yet children from marginalized sections are discriminated in schools. How can the discrimination of 'weaker and disadvantaged sections be prevented? There are various theoretical and empirical studies, which have come up observations that children from lower classes are at a back foot in schools in the learning process. They are more vulnerable when enrolled in elite schools. There is nothing in the Act that will prevent unaided private schools from charging students for activities that are not mentioned in the Act. Examples would be laboratory fee, computer fee, building fee, sports fee, fee for stationery, fee for school uniform, fee for extra-curricular activities, such as music, painting, pottery, and so on.

Onerous Regulation Norms to be achieved in a Short Time Span

Then, there is the question of onerous regulation, a ubiquitous problem in India, which still has a largely statist mindset. According to the new law, all private schools must obtain official government recognition within three years or be closed down. Schools must have a certain size of land plot, playground, library, teacher qualifications and salaries. The Act has a timeline of five years. During this period, the schools have to train all their teachers and improve the infrastructure. This in itself is a big challenge. It has been two years since the Act came into existence and presently there are more than seven lakh untrained teachers and more than seven lakh are required. So, more than 14 lakh teachers are required, which is a gigantic task to make up this shortfall and ensure that teachers are well trained within five years. Therefore, all the stakeholders have to get together to implement this because after five years, anyone can take these schools to court for violation of the provisions of the Act. If the schools do not have proper infrastructure and have untrained teachers, the schools will be shut down, what will happen after that? Who will take those children? We have to address these issues, as these are very pressing problems and we are into the third year of the RTE Act implementation.

Private schools for the rich would have little difficulty in meeting these norms. However, budget private schools where the poor go,—those that charge a monthly fee of 70-150 rupees in rural areas, and up to 350 rupees in metro areas—would find it impossible to meet these criteria. It's utopian to demand that a slum school be earthquake resistant when all the houses and buildings in the slum can barely stand up to heavy rains and winds.

Suggestions

For education to be a meaningful right, it must be available, accessible, acceptable, and adaptable. The concept of these 4As was developed by the former UN Special Rapporteur on the Right to Education, Katarina Tomasevski, and it is one of the best ways to assess and act upon the situation. However, it should be noted from the outset that these 4As are not definitive, whilst they are an extremely useful way of explaining the right to education in terms of tangible factors.

The 4As are to be respected, protected and fulfilled by the government as the prime duty-bearer, but there are also duties on other actors in the education process: the child as the privileged subject of the right to education and the bearer of the duty to comply with compulsory-education requirements; the child's parents who are the 'first educators'; and professional educators, namely teachers.

By using a participatory process, this framework of the 4As can become a tool to enable people to think through what the right to education means to them, and compare their current reality to this ideal context.

The 4As can be summarised as follows (*see* Chapter 15 also):

> **Availability**—that education is free and government funded and that there is adequate infrastructure and trained teachers able to support education delivery.
>
> **Accessibility**—that the system is non-discriminatory and accessible to all, and that positive steps are taken to include the most marginalised.

Acceptability—that the content of education is relevant, non-discriminatory and culturally appropriate, and of quality; that the school itself is safe and teachers are professional.

Adaptability—that education can evolve with the changing needs of society and contribute to challenging inequalities, such as gender discrimination, and that it can be adapted locally to suit specific contexts.

Conclusion

In order to meet the challenges and surmount the hurdles that stand in the way of implementing the Right to Education Act, it is needful to concentrate all efforts with full dedication and commitment. Not only the central and state governments, but the nation as a whole should take responsibility in this regard. Community participation and support can make marked difference in achieving this goal. There exists a need for greater coordination amongst different agencies and functionaries involved in this task. To overcome population pressures and budgetary constraints, cost effectiveness and accountability must be ascertained at every level. Efforts should be focused on qualitative improvement of the whole programme.

References

1. Annual Status of Education Report 2011. http://images2.asercentre.org/aserreports/ASER_2011/education_report_card.pdf.
2. Bhargava, P.M. RTE ACT: Some Rights and Wrongs. http://www.thehindu.com/opinion/lead/article533475.ece?homepage=true.
3. Gupta, S. What are the Different Strategies and Approaches to Realize (RTE) Right to Education in India? http://www.right-to-education.org/sites/r2e.gn.apc.org/files/Shantanu_Gupta_RTE%20in%20India.pdf.
4. http://indiabudget.nic.in/ub2012-13/eb/sbe58.pdf.
5. http://www.asercentre.org/ngo-education-india.php?p=Spotlight %3A+ASER+2011.
6. http://www.ncpcr.gov.in/Reports/Abolition_of_Child_Labour_in_India_Strategies_for_11th_Five_Year_Plan_Executive_Summary_to_Planning_Commission.pdf.
7. Nirananjanaradhya and Kashyap Aruna: *The Fundamentals of Fundamental Right to Education in India*, Books for Change, 2006.
8. Right to Education in India. http://right-to-education-india.blogspot.in/2011/05/rte-act-first-anniversary-status-report.html.
9. Sabharwal, M. Right to Education is the wrong thing for the right reason. http://articles.economictimes.indiatimes.com/2012-04 23/news/31387122_1_dysfunctional-government-schools-private-schools-reservation-for-poor-students.

10. Shah. J. Parth. Opening School Doors to India's Poor. http://online.wsj.com/article/SB10001424052702304739104575154582256397118.html.
11. Shah. P. Right to Education: A Critique. http://ajayshahblog.blogspot.in/2010/04/right-to-education-act-critique.html.
12. Sharma, Ram Nath and Sharma, Rajendra Kumar; *Problems of Education in India*; Atlantic Publishers; 2004.
13. Singh, S. (2010). Right to Education and Right to Educate: A Study of the Impact of Right to Education Act on Unrecognized Schools in Delhi, Working Paper No 242, Centre for Civil Society, Delhi. http://ccsindia.org.
14. The Gazette of India, Right to Education Bill 2009.

8

The Right to Education Act 2009

Critical Gaps and Challenges in Its Implementation

Vanita Chopra, Aarti Bhatnagar and *Sonal Chabra*

Education is the most forceful and compelling mechanism for the advancement of human beings. It enlarges, enriches and improves the individual's image of the future. It has been well accepted for long that a man without education is no more than an animal. To put simply, education unfetters the human beings and leads to emancipation from ignorance. According to Pestalozzi, education is a constant process of development of innate powers of man, which are natural, harmonious and progressive. It is said that in the twenty first century, "a nation's ability to convert knowledge into wealth and social good through the process of innovation is going to determine its future," accordingly twenty first century is termed as the century of knowledge. The significance of education was very well explained in case of Brown V Board of Education, in following words: "It is the very foundation of good citizenship. Today, it is the principal instrument in awakening the child to cultural value, in preparing him for later professional training and in helping him to adjust normally to his environment." It is said that child is the future of nation. The quality of education of the child will determine the quality of life in nation. As it is well illustrated in following words: "In ancient shadows and twilights where childhood had strayed, the world's great sorrows were born and its heroes were made. In the lost boyhood of Judas, Christ was betrayed." Both at the national and International levels, efforts are being made to educate more and more people as education contributes in the development of the society, which is consistent with the dignity of the human being.

International cooperation related to what is now called 'the right to education' has a more limited history. A private organisation, the International Bureau of Education, was established in Geneva in 1924 and was transformed into an inter-governmental organization in 1929 as an international coordinating centre for institutions concerned with education. A much broader approach was chosen, however, with the establishment of UNESCO in 1945. United Nations, on 10 December 1998 adopted Universal Declaration of Human Rights. In accordance with the Preamble of UDHR, education should aim at promoting human rights by imparting knowledge and skill to the people of the nation states.

The 86th Constitutional Amendment, which made education a Fundamental Right for all Indian children aged 6-14 years, was passed by the Parliament in 2002. After much dithering for almost seven years subsequent to the 86th Amendment to the Constitution, the RTE Act 2009 received presidential assent on 26 August 2009, taking forward the agenda of free and universal elementary education [Please *see* Chapter 3(2) also].

Passage

Due to a combination of factors including public pressure, a decision was finally taken to introduce a central legislation in the Budget session of Parliament in 2008. Although the redrafted RTE Bill 2008 was not made public or open to consultations, the union cabinet went ahead and cleared the draft Bill on 31 October 2008; with some changes, this got enacted as the RTE Act 2009. The Right of Children to Free and Compulsory Education Act (RTE), a law enabling its implementation, was passed by the Parliament in 2009. Both the Amendment and the law came into effect from 1 April 2010. In this background, elementary education in India aims to imbibe in all children, the qualities essential of the vibrant and dynamic democracy, including value of tolerance, morality and compassion as well as basic abilities of reading, writing, comprehension and reasoning.

It would be very early to comment on whether or not the Right to Education Act (RTE) will achieve its objectives, but for sure, it is going to be an uphill task despite the promising features of the enforced Act. Transformation cannot take place without a beginning. The Act has now become a reality and there is an atmosphere of anticipation, jubilation and enthusiasm all around. It is the first step taken, but more need to be followed to reach anywhere. The road ahead is not going to be an easy one and implementing the Act fairly, poses a major challenge involving creative and sustained efforts. The mere proclamation of a right cannot tantamount to it's fulfilment, and its "actual enjoyment" is possible only when effective institutions are in place to guarantee that right. A right to education is ineffective in the absence of a school to ensure the enrolment of a child and to impart free, elementary education. By taking on the duty to establish a school in every neighbourhood, and stipulating conditions to aid the functioning of such schools, the Government has taken the first step in the right direction.

Problematic Areas

There exist a number of problematic areas, which need redressal in the scheme of this legislation.

Population Explosion

The greatest challenge is posed by the fast growing population and the comparatively slower growing economy. In spite of the fact that there has been a continuous upsurge in the number of schools established at the primary level, thus increasing physical access to schools, large masses of population have remained outside the orbit of the benefits from the public education system in India.

Paucity of Awareness

In spite of the passage of the Bill quite enthusiastically, the teacher, teacher educators, social activities and a common man are not aware of the salient features of this Act. But to bring sustainable changes in the education sector, the pressure has to be laid on creating awareness among the general masses and the intensive attitudinal transformation.

Disabled Left Out of Education Bill

The chances of 20 million children with physical and other disabilities to get the right to education have been jeopardized, as the Right to Education Bill excludes them. Although the earlier draft of the Bill had made specific mention of children with disabilities, the Bill tabled in the Lok Sabha has erased those references, activists say. There are deficiencies in the Act as it was passed in August 2009 in relation to children with disabilities. They should have been included in the definition of disadvantaged groups, but were inadvertently left out. The Act says that their education shall follow the provisions of the Disabilities Act 1996, but that Act has deficiencies in as much that it does not include mental disabilities. The central government has acknowledged these lacunae and promised to bring appropriate amendments in the Budget 2010 session of Parliament, as also to amend the Disabilities Act 1996 appropriately. The proposed Amendments are at Q83.

Activists say that India was one of the first countries to ratify the UN Convention on Rights of Persons with Disabilities, in October 2007, which says, "State parties shall ensure that persons with disabilities are not excluded from the general education system on the basis of disability and that children with disabilities are not excluded from free and compulsory primary education or from secondary education on the basis of disability."

Requirement of Qualified and Trained Teachers

The elementary education part of our system already suffers from shortage of teachers and a fairly large number of teachers of this segment are untrained.

To get trained and qualified teachers within the stipulated period is not only going to prove a Herculean task, but appears to be almost impossible. A gradual and systematic influx of teachers would have been a better approach. Currently, more than 5.23 lakh teacher posts are vacant. To bring the pupil-teacher ratio to 30:1, as prescribed by the RTE Act, 5.1 lakh additional teachers are required. Already, there are 5.1 lakh schools with a pupil-teacher ratio of more than 30:1. On top of that, 5.48 lakh untrained teachers at the primary and 2.25 lakh at upper primary level have to acquire necessary qualification within five years of the RTE Act coming into force. The states with high percentage of untrained teachers and inadequate teacher education capacity are: Assam (55.13% untrained teachers), Bihar (45.5%), Chhattisgarh (31.32%), J&K (43.34%), Jharkhand (32.16%), Uttar Pradesh (25.87%) and West Bengal (32.15%). States like Andhra Pradesh, Delhi, Gujarat, Haryana, Himachal Pradesh, Karnataka, Kerala, Madhya Pradesh, Maharashtra, Punjab, Rajasthan, Tamil Nadu and Uttarakhand have very low percentage of untrained teachers. They also have adequate capacity for teacher education.

No Standard Definition of Teacher Qualification

The existing elementary teacher education programmes (known variously in different parts of the country as JBT, D. Ed., PTC, BSTC, etc.) lack a benchmark and proper definition. Teachers trained for secondary classes (classes IX, X, XI, XII) are considered eligible to teach middle classes (VI, VII, and VIII). But teachers trained to teach the elementary classes are only eligible to teach classes I–V. Even the Supreme Court has accepted this argument. Now, the RTE Act is for the kids in the age group 6-14 studying in classes I–VIII. So, a clear definition of teaching eligibility is required so that a teacher can teach all these eight classes. This will also help administratively as well as keep teachers motivated.

Reservation of Seats in Unaided Private Schools

The Act talks about 25 per cent seat reservation in private/public unaided school for lesser privileged children. The fees of these students will be borne by the state government. The fee will be reimbursed at government rate. There will be a wide gap between the cost of education per child and the reimbursement by the government. Who will bear this deficit portion? Obviously, the remaining 75 per cent of the students. For a certain class of society, who provides education to their kids in these private schools already by stretching their means, this extra burden might prove too much. It's like providing benefit to one at the cost of other. Would improving the standard of the government school be not a better and more justified option?

Automatic Passage to Next Class may be Counter Productive

As per the Act, every student will be passed to the next class. This can promote indolence and insincerity among children towards their studies and carelessness and laxity among the teachers. The Act will create a system with no incentive for students to try to improve themselves, or to behave with a modicum of restraint. It compromises their ability to withstand pressure and compete harder in order to excel. This will create a generation of drifters, who have never tasted hard work or competition. And what happens when the kids turn 14? Leaving aside some notable successes, there will be millions, who have just gone through the system without gaining much – and valuable formative years of life will be wasted.

Status of Poor Kids in the Private Schools

A glaring question is: how interested are the parents of the poor kids to send them to the private schools even if the education is free of cost? The kids will be suddenly exposed to a different living standard. Will they be treated with dignity and equality by their peers and teachers? Will it not be traumatic for the poor kids to cope with that? Moreover, what about the overhead expenses, such as uniform, books, stationery, etc. of attending a private school? The chances are high that the parents themselves would feel intimidated at the thought of sending their kids to private schools.

Input Oriented Act with No Emphasis on Output

The Act is deemed to be excessively input-focused rather than outcome-oriented. The Bill guarantees for the admission of the children, but does not promise the quality of education.

Admission according to Age, but no Facility for Bridge Courses

The Act stipulates that the child should be assigned the class according to age, which is a good step because wasted years can be saved; but no bridge course is suggested that can prepare the child to adjust to the admitted class.

School Recognition

Section 19 of the Act requires all schools except government schools, to meet certain norms and standards relating to infrastructure, pupil-teacher ratio, and teacher salaries on the basis of which they are required to get recognition within three years. This clause penalizes private unrecognized schools, although they provide similar, if not better, teaching services compared to government schools, while spending a much smaller amount. They are susceptible to extinction in three years.

School Management Committee

The Act requires every government and aided school to form a School Management Committee (SMC), which will comprise of parents and will be responsible for planning and managing the operations of the school. SMC members are required to volunteer their time and effort. This can be a burden for the poor parents. And for the aided schools, the SMC rule will lead to a breakdown of their existing management structures.

Lack of Financial Assistance

To make any real impact on the lives of children, the country needs to spend at least ten per cent of GDP on school education and health. Instead of investing in public resources, we as a country are opening up a core sector to private players – a move that goes against both the short and long term interests of children.

What can be done to make the RTE ACT, 2009 A True Reality?

If we want to overcome the above challenges, then it would be necessary to overhaul the entire education system and the following can be suggested for bringing qualitative improvement with respect to RTE Act 2009:

- The right to education can only become real when it gives all children, be it in the 3-6 years age group or out of school children, equal opportunity to realize their fundamental right and should be motivated to learn.
- Only qualified teachers should be appointed for teaching in every part of the country and those not meeting proper qualification criteria should be sacked.
- Children with disabilities should be provided with extra facilities in neighbourhood schools and specially trained teachers should be recruited in every school to realize the dream of RTE.
- Adequate infrastructure should be made available to remove economical, social, cultural, linguistic and disability related barriers.
- Weak students should be identified and remedial classes should be arranged for them apart from the regular classes.
- Performance based evaluation of teachers should be done and innovative teachers should be motivated further through incentives.
- Workshops, seminars and teacher exchange programmes should be encouraged to keep them abreast about the latest development in pedagogical methods.
- Adequate and proper training facilities of teachers and other personnel should be created for the proper implementation of this Act.
- To provide sufficient financial assistance, ten per cent of the development fund should be spent on school education and health of the children.
- Regular and periodic review of elementary curriculum should be followed and necessary changes should be incorporated.
- Awareness should be spread among the rural masses about the importance of education, so that they really feel the need to send their children to schools.

- Certain skill based short term courses should be included in the curriculum to make it interesting for the students and, thus, reducing the drop out ratio.

Summing Up

RTE Act will definitely break the inertia and create a momentum of thoughts in prioritizing the need of elementary education and setting a trend of urgency to evolve ways and means to fulfil well established fundamental need, i.e., the Right to Education.

Obviously, there is no doubt that RTE Act 2009 is expected to be the instrument of change. We are aware of the deep rooted problems prevailing in Government machinery as well as in people at large. Both the stakeholders are deteriorating each other. When the poor governance on the part of government machinery gives rise to the society of ill conceived, ill mannered, incredible, irresponsible and disgusting individuals and, in turn, such degraded society produces and fosters government role players of substandard quality. Consequently, a vicious cycle is created between the government machinery and population reinforcing bad qualities of each other. *However, the RTE Act will function as an apparatus of dialysis for the societies.*

Still, making education a fundamental right is surely a step in the right direction to address the anomalies and disparities of elementary education in India. It gives legislative framework through which we can question and improve the education system. Nevertheless, the proper implementation, monitoring and evaluation of improving quality of public schools, enhanced public-private participation, enhancement of access and adequate quality of education to all children and thereby achieving the goal of Universal Elementary Education has to go a long way.

References

1. Agarwal, Yash (2000). *Public and Private Partnership in Primary Education in India: A study of unrecognized schools in Haryana*, National Institute of Educational Planning and Administration, New Delhi.
2. Bhardwaj, S.; Thareja, V. and Chabra, S. (2011). Awareness of Right to Education Act among the primary school teachers, *Global Researcher*, Vol. 1, No. 2, October 2011.
3. Government of India (2009). *The Right of Children to Free and Compulsory Education Act 2009*, New Delhi: Ministry of Human Resource Development.
4. Walia, J.S. (2005). *Secondary Education and School Management*, New Delhi.
5. www.education.nic.in/Elementary/free%20and%20compulsory.pdf www.scribd.com/doc/26778778/Right-Of-Children-to-Free-and-Compulsory-Education-Act-Model-Rules.

9

The Right to Education and the Common School System

Akthar Parveen

Until the mid-1970s, a sort of common school system existed in India. Most of our distinguished academicians, civil servants and professionals, who dominated the Indian intellectual and social scene during the last quarter of the 20th century received their school education in government or government-aided private schools, which maintained more or less comparable quality and standards.

Subsequently, the state did not invest in the school system the magnitude of resources recommended by the Kothari Commission for building Common School System. This resulted in cumulative neglect of public education system and, hence, a decline in its quality, withdrawal of children by its relatively well to do parents from government schools and turning to private schools. This led to enormous mushrooming of private schools at a fast pace. Today, in government and government aided schools, only the children of the minority groups, who cannot afford the fee charged by the private schools, are pursuing their education.

Origin of the Common School System

The Education Commission (1964-66) recommended a Common School System (CSS) of public education as the basis for building up the national system of education, with a view to bring different social class and groups together and, thus, promote the emergence of an egalitarian and integrated society. The commission warned that if common school system is not followed, it would lead to increase in social segregation and wide class distinction. It further stated that this distinction is bad not only for the poor children, but also for the children of the rich and privileged group as it prevents sharing of the life and experiences of the children, learning experiences of the children and learning realities of life, which makes education "anaemic and incomplete". To eliminate the evil and to make educational system a powerful instrument of national development and promote social and national integration, our education should move toward the goals of a common system of public education.

CSS exists in different forms in nations like USA, France and Scandinavian countries. Recently, the British system of education also moved towards comprehensive school system, which is akin to the CSS. Even Canada and Japan also follows CSS. Based on policy imperative and the emphasis on decentralization along with the necessary flexibility in the school system to be able to respond to the contextual curricular demands, the concept of CSS evolved. But there are wide spread misconceptions about CSS. These are:

- CSS is misperceived as a uniform school system, but on the contrary, the Education Commission itself advocated that each institution should be "intimately involved with the local community that should be regarded as an individual and given academic freedom."
- It is wrongly claimed that CSS will not permit a privately managed schools to retain its non-government and unaided or aided character. Again, on the contrary, the CSS implies that all schools—irrespective of the type of the management, sources of income or affiliating Boards of Examinations—will participate and fulfil their responsibility as part of the National System of Education.

Definition of Common School System

"Common School System means the national system of education that is founded on the principles of equality and social justice as enshrined in the Constitution and provides education of a comparable quality to all children in an equitable manner, irrespective of their caste, creed, language, gender, economic or ethnic background, location or disability (physical or mental), and where in all categories of schools—i.e., government, local body or private, both aided and unaided, or otherwise—will be obliged to fulfil certain minimum infrastructural (including those relating to teachers and other staff), financial, curricular, pedagogic, linguistic and socio-cultural norms and ensure free education to the children in a specified neighbourhood from an age group and up to a stage, as may be prescribed, while having adequate flexibility and academic freedom to explore, innovate and be creative and appropriately reflecting the geo-cultural and linguistic diversity of the country, within the broad policy guidelines and the National Curriculum Framework for school Education as approved by the Central Advisory Board of Education (CABE)."

Important Features of Common School System

The important features of the CSS are listed below:

1. Equitable quality of education for all types of schools, be they government, government-aided, local body or private schools.
2. Minimum physical infrastructure including classrooms, libraries, laboratories, and other facilities.
3. Professional quality of teachers.
4. Optimal teacher and pupil ratio.
5. Provision for performing fine arts and teaching aids.
6. Easy access and other facilities for students suffering from disability.
7. Early childhood care centres and pre-primary schools attached to primary/elementary schools.
8. Diversified and flexible curriculum to reflect the geo-cultural plurality of the country, while emphasizing certain core curricular features of nation-wide significance.
9. A pedagogy, which is holistic and child friendly and has liberating influence on the syllabi.
10. Pedagogy should be designed to derive maximum educational advantage and provide the fullest opportunity for socialization of the children coming from a variety of socio-economic, cultural and other backgrounds, including dalits, tribal, religious and linguistic minorities and physical and mentally challenged children.
11. A decentralized, community controlled school system with adequate autonomy and representation of parents.
12. Apart from gender sensitivity, pedagogic and social empathy for the dalits, tribal, cultural and ethnic minorities and the physically challenged and mental challenged children.
13. A common language policy by adopting Indian languages as media of education at all stages.
14. The concept of neighbourhood school is the central focus of the Common School System

The Ramamurthy Committee (1990) recommends ensuring instructions in the medium of mother tongue at the primary level, particularly for linguist minorities, and active encouragement of teaching in the regional languages at the secondary level. The Indian Parliament has expressed its commitment to the CSS twice in its resolutions on the national policy on education, respectively in 1986 and 1992, and issued as a Cabinet resolution, yet the concept could not be translated into practice because of the following reasons:

- No commitment among the policy makers and political leaders to implement CSS.

- High corruption at all levels from top to bottom.
- Lack of social will to improve the government schools.
- Privatization and commercialization of education.
- Selfish people found escape route to safeguard private schools.

In the year 1988, the CABE appointed a committee on common system, which proposed a ten-year phase-wise programme for the reconstruction of the present school system into a common system.

The Chief Features of Phase-wise Reconstruction Programme of Common School System

The chief features of phase-wise reconstruction programme of CSS are given below:

- Highest political priority for the improvement of both the access and quality of the Government, local body and government-aided schools.
- Decentralization of decision-making and management of schools through the *Panchayati Raj* frame work and making the school entirely accountable to the community it serves.
- Fulfilling the Constitutional obligation of a minimum of eight years of elementary education instead of five years of primary education under Article 45 to all children up to 14 years of age including the early childhood care and pre-primary education groups.
- Allocation of adequate financial resources.
- A pedagogically and socially rationale language policy for the medium of education, not instruction common to all schools, so that language becomes a means of articulation, rather than imposition.
- A carefully constructed programme of incentives, disincentives, persuasion and eventually legislation to gradually bring the private schools into the fold of the Common Schools System.
- Incentives to private schools may include grants for children from low-income groups, such that all children in the neighbourhood have access, disincentives includes gradual withdrawal of all hidden subsidies to private schools, like cheap land, tax-free income and exemption from income tax on donations, teachers trained at public cost, etc.

Need of the Hour

The elite in India have always been dismissive of the concept of common school system by mocking at it as being politically too radical and, therefore, infeasible. In contrast, the poor and the lower middle class have for long internalized the concept as the only means for their empowerment and social justice. It is an irony that such a public system of schooling is followed in some form or the other in European countries, USA and Canada. India's inability to implement CSS is mis-governance and corruption. The seeds of superiority, hierarchy and insensitivity against the people, particularly the poor among them, are sown at an early age in the existing school system and get reflected strongly in governance at each level. The present school system encourages cut-throat competition, privileges and pursuit of self-interest at the cost of the interest of others and is antithetical to fostering spirit of sacrifices, fellow feeling, solidarity and cooperation.

The only historical option left for India for building a cohesive, secular and just society is by implementing the Common School System and making education compulsory to all, by implementing the Right to Education Act.

Right to Education is recognized as a human right and is understood to establish an entitlement to education. It includes the right to free, compulsory, primary education for all. This Act has come into force from 1 April 2010. This is a historic day for the people of India as from this day, the Right to Education will be accorded the same legal status as the fight to life as provided by Article 21A of the Indian Constitution. It also includes a responsibility to provide basic education to individuals, who have not completed primary education by eliminating discrimination at all levels of the educational system, to set minimum standards and to improve the quality.

The Right to Education is enshrined in Article 26 of the Universal Declaration of Human Rights and Article 13 and 14 of the International Covenant on economic, social and cultural rights. It asserts that for education to be a meaningful right, it must be available, accessible, acceptable and adaptable, which is the prime duty of the government. The four "As" framework places duties on the stakeholders in the educational process, such as the child as the privileged subject has the duty to comply with compulsory educational requirements, the parents as the first educators and professional educators are the teachers. These have been already discussed in detail in earlier part of the book.

Levels of Right to Education

There are three levels in the Rights to Education:

1. Primary/elementary/fundamental level of education, which shall be compulsory and free regardless of their nationality, gender, place of birth or any other discrimination.
2. Secondary/elementary/technical and professional education must be generally available and accessible.
3. Higher or university level education should be provided according to the capacity.

It is the chief responsibility of the state to provide education by allocating substantial budgetary resources and regulating the provision of education.

Features

The important features of RTE Act are given below:

1. The cost that prevents a child from accessing school will be borne by the state.
2. It is state's responsibility to enrol the child and ensure attendance and completion of eight years of schooling.
3. No child should be denied admission for want of documents.
4. Admissions must be made throughout the year.
5. There should not be any admission test.
6. Disabled children will also be educated in the mainstream schools.
7. All private schools must enrol children from weaker and disadvantaged communities up to 25 per cent of their enrolment.
8. No such seats must lie vacant.
9. These children are subsidized by the state at the rate of average per learning costs in government schools.
10. All schools must prescribe norms and standards laid out in the Act.
11. All private schools apply for recognition and fulfil standards within three years if not the schools will be penalized rupees one lakh to ten thousand.
12. Norms and standards of teacher qualifications laid down in the Act must be achieved within five years.

Conclusion

It is the responsibility of the civil society, students and teachers, administrators, writers, artists, government legislatures and members of judiciary and all others stakeholders to join hand to work together to build a movement to ensure that every child of this country is in school and is able to get at least eight years of quality of education through CSS as it promotes equality and social justice. It helps in nation building and the creation of social capital, which is essential for sustaining democracy and ensuring economic progress and prosperity. Among all school systems, the CSS is the most conducive to provide good education.

Kothari Commission recommended the transformation of the Indian public education as a common school system with a view to "bring different social classes and groups together and, thus, promote the emergence of an egalitarian and integrated society." The commission asserted that if the educational system is to become powerful instrument of national development in general, and social and national integration in particular, we must move towards a goal of a common system of public education. This is useful to cover the objective of forging and maintaining social cohesion and ensuring the security of the country as India is a country where diversity and heterogeneity exists.

It is the need of the hour for political leaders, policy framers, educationists, philosophers to introspect and peep into the problems of education, because the present system of education is developing cut through competition, which is unhealthy, stress prone, dumping the information into the minds of the tiny tots without any human values. Instead of bringing different classes and groups together, it tends to increase social segregation and class distinctions by widening the gap between classes and masses, which increases the danger of national fragmentation.

Let us hope that the implementation of the Common School System along with compulsory education in our country generates youth with appropriate educational skills, broader mental horizon, and positive attitude, optimistic outlook in life with universe as one family where human values are eternal without any bias, superstitions and psychological restrictions in the name of caste creed, region and religion.

References

1. Ayodhya, P. and Dash, B.N. (2010). *Foundations of Educations*. New Delhi.
2. Dash, B.N. (2007). *Education in the Emerging Indian Society*. New Delhi.
3. *Educational Encyclopaedia* (2009). New Delhi.
4. Government of India, MHRD. National Policy in Education. New Delhi.
5. Naseema, C. (2007). *Human Rights Education*. Shipra Publications, New Delhi.

10

Facets of RTE in Teachers' Perception and Its Impact on the Self Concept of Students Enrolled in Unaided Schools under the RTE Act

Talmeez Fatma Naqvi

The Statement of Objects and Reasons (SOR) attached to the RTE Act reads: "The Right of Children to Free and Compulsory Education Bill, 2008, is anchored in the belief that the values of equality, social justice and democracy and the creation of a just and humane society can be achieved only through the provision of inclusive elementary education to all. Provision of free and compulsory education of satisfactory quality to children from disadvantaged and weaker sections is, therefore, not merely the responsibility of schools run or supported by the appropriate Governments, but also of schools, which are not dependent on Government funds." The SOR as such seeks to bring about "equality, social justice and democracy," create a "just and humane society," by ensuring "inclusive elementary education to *all*" studying in elementary schools. That is precisely why the private (unaided fee-charging) schools, which are not dependent on Government funds, are also included in the RTE Act.

Under the Clause, 12 (1) (c) of the RTE, Act, 2009 mandates private schools to admit a quarter of their class strength from weaker sections and disadvantaged groups of society. The Act under reference directs all schools, including the ones run as private ventures, to reserve 25 per cent of the available seats for students from socially and economically backward families. That means, quarter of students in classes are to be from the marginalized section of society. Pertinently, this may impact social composition of the given classes in schools and lead to structural change therein.

Commenting upon the proposed reservation, Krishna Kumar (2012) has observed that "most ambitious among its objectives is the social engineering it proposes by guaranteeing at least 25 per cent share of enrolment in unaided fee-charging schools to children whose parents cannot afford the fee." Underlining the expected outcome of the provision, he (2012) articulates that "a classroom reflecting life's diversity will benefit children of all strata while enriching teaching experience" and that the "classroom life will now be experientially and linguistically richer. It will be easier to illustrate complex issues with examples drawn from children's own lives." But his argument that classroom diversity will benefit children from weaker section of society may, as of now, be characterized as yet to be substantiated expectation.

In regards to above, Fayaz Bhat's thoughtful observation (2012) is worth taking note of: "School education can't be separated from its social context, those who teach and learn carry with them attitudes, beliefs, habits, customs, orientations, which differ from class to class. The elite schools have their own culture, which suits to children of upper class. The teaching-learning environment at these schools suits children of upper class, while children from weaker section may find themselves alienated from the schools." This, in a way, raises question mark on what Krishna Kumar is hopeful of. While examining the mode of communication of working and middle class, Bernstein (1973) argues that the upper class and weaker section children have different mode of communication and most of the teachers in schools belong to middle class, which gives edge to middle class children in learning. Bourdieu's (1977) empirical research in France brings forth another striking finding that children of upper classes are able to understand contents of knowledge better than their counterparts belonging to marginalized sections of the society.

Fayaz Bhat also articulated that the present experience of India with mixed or diversified classroom is not encouraging. The children from marginalized sections of the society are discriminated in the classroom on the basis of gender, caste, and ethnicity. Despite Indian constitution strictly prohibiting discrimination on the basis of caste and other social backgrounds and making it a punishable act, yet children from marginalized sections are discriminated in schools. How can one prevent discrimination of 'weaker and disadvantaged sections in classrooms?

In addition to above, there are other theoretical and empirical studies, which have come up with the view that children from lower classes are at a back foot in schools in the learning process and that they are more vulnerable when enrolled in elite schools (Blair, A. 2006; Bourdieu, P. 1967; Grimston, J. 2009; Paton, G. 2007).

The present school system – whether government or private – is a far cry from the ideal of school as a site for inclusion. Privately-run, unaided, fee-charging schools and those run by the government or local bodies largely cater to differentiated social categories and economic strata. Consequently, children grow up segregated. The segregation starts as early as the nursery stage, and by the time children are nine or ten years old, many private schools feel reluctant to follow a policy of integrating children from the socio-economically weaker sections of society with those from the better-off strata.

It is widely believed that privately schooled children attain a higher standard of learning. However, learning cannot be understood purely in academic terms, since the aims of education also include the inculcation of values and attitudes consistent with the Constitution's egalitarian framework. Apart from promoting social cohesion, a heterogeneous school population, comprising children across caste, class and gender may provide a multicultural milieu and, ideally speaking, an enriched learning environment.

It is a matter of general perception that learning occurs, not merely from instruction imparted within the four walls of the classroom, but from the classroom ethos and from interactivity between children from different backgrounds—different castes, different religions, different socio-economic backgrounds. Increase in the variability of the backgrounds and culture, thus, enriches the classroom, and expectedly may generate in children respect for difference and diversity, and enhances learning. The classroom culture remains intellectually moribund if it does not acknowledge the diversity and plurality of our people and our country. A school that has only one segment of the wider society represented in it is greatly depleted in terms of human context.

For children of socio-economically weaker backgrounds to feel at home in private schools, it is necessary that they form a substantial proportion or critical mass in the class they join. It is for this reason that the RTE Act provides for admission of 25 per cent children from disadvantaged groups and weaker sections in class I only, not across the whole school. As children admitted to class I move to class II, new children will be admitted to class I, and so on till the completion of eight years of elementary education.

But the teachers, who are used to a selective, homogeneous classroom environment, may hardly be expected to change overnight to meet the implied legal, as also educational requirement for developing required positive attitude and professional skills to deal with a diversified class. The same applies to the children. Children, who have grown up to an age of nine or ten in a homogeneous or segregated environment, have been socialized into a structure of norms and behaviour. It is improbable that they can be transformed on demand. Likewise, the overall school ethos may also not be expected to respond to the requirements of new policy in a positive manner all of a sudden. Education is indeed an act of faith and social engineering—but not quick-fix social engineering. In view of the fact that children take time to socialize and teachers take time to develop new attitudes and pedagogic skills, the RTE Act just provides for admission of disadvantaged and poor children at the entry level, covering pre-school and Class-I.

With these children moving up, and a new cohort of children entering pre-school and Class I in each successive year, the school will gradually have a more diverse population spread across all classes. Progression at this pace will allow children the opportunity to grow up together and create bonds: bonds that can survive social walls. Progression at this pace can allow the school to develop the professional capacity to respond to the intellectual and emotional needs of children from diverse backgrounds. Children, who are younger than eight years of age, are yet to develop a stable social identity. Their values are still forming, and their motivation to derive meaning from experience, both concrete and social, is very strong.

Therefore, it is a valid argument that the policy of mixing children from different socio-economic strata has the best chance of succeeding if it starts from the formative years of nursery/kindergarten and Class-I. Diversity enhances learning and development, while segregation impoverishes the classroom environment of all schools, private or government.

Admission of 25 per cent children from disadvantaged groups and weaker sections in the neighbourhood does not merely seek to provide avenues of quality education to poor and disadvantaged children. The larger objective is to provide a common place where children sit, eat and live together for at least eight years of their lives across caste, class and gender divides in order that it narrows down such divisions in our society. The other objective is that the 75 per cent children, who have been lucky to come from better endowed families, learn through their interaction with the children from families, who have not had similar opportunities, but are rich in knowledge systems allied to trade, craft, farming and other services, and that the pedagogic enrichment of the 75 per cent children is provided by such intermingling. This, of course, necessitates classroom practices, teacher training, etc. to constantly bring out pedagogic practices, rather than merely make children from these two sections sit together. The often voiced concern about how the 25 per cent children from disadvantaged groups and weaker sections can cope in an environment wherein rich children enjoy can be resolved only if the teaching learning process and teachers use these children as sources of knowledge, so that their esteem and recognition goes up and they begin to be treated as equals.

Since people focus attention only on one side of coin that the rich people are not ready to mingle, we tend to ignore how disadvantaged children may feel in a class, where highly rich children are sitting next to them. We hardly consider psychological effect of such intermixing of particularly better off on the children hailing from weaker sections. Krishna Kumar observes: "This is as clear as it can be. Yet, one can understand why private schools are upset and startled. One simple reason is habit. Unaided schools have been used to thinking that they can isolate their children from the poverty, roughness and the pain of daily life that surrounds prosperous Indians. The belief that learning needs withdrawal from the jungle of life belongs to an old, very old tradition. In the history of pedagogic theory, this view was challenged more than a century ago. In Europe and America, experience was recognized as the best teacher at the beginning of the 20th century, and experience meant direct exposure to the reality and diversity of the human condition. Mixed schooling was bitterly debated before it took root, and in the U.S., it had to await the pressure generated by the civil rights movement. Indian private schools, including the elite among them, are startled that they are coming under a law they did not help to formulate."

Involving private schools in the delivery of education for all addresses issues of both access to and quality of education. However, critics challenge this provision on several counts. The first is the government's assumption that it can pass on the responsibility of public education to private institutions. The government rests its claim on the fact that since it grants land rights to schools in prime locations, often in the city centre, it can assert certain rights in exchange.

A question of more immediate relevance to school-based educators is the assimilation of Economically Weaker and Socially Disadvantaged (EWSD) students into the culture of schools that caters to a different social and economic class of students. RTE specifically states that EWSD children "will be treated on par with all the other children in the school," making it imperative for several psycho-social and pedagogic issues to be addressed in order to integrate students from low-income families. In the current exam-driven, competitive ethos that characterize most private schools in India, EWSD students are likely to be first- or second-generation learners, presumably lacking academic support from their families, and may remain low performing. They may suffer by comparison in social markers, such as dress and possessions that could set them apart. For instance, one of the most successful programmes in raising attendance is the mid-day meal scheme in which EWSD students are provided a meal organized by the school. Apart from the practical difficulty of incorporating it into the infrastructure of the private schools, such a programme highlights the gulf between students in terms of 'haves' and 'have-nots', just as free lunch vouchers do in U.S. schools. Practices and expectations like these could acutely affect the self-esteem of underprivileged students. Many private schools may not be inclined or equipped to respond to such specific needs. It is a big and moot question how EWSD students experience in those private schools and how this experience affects them psychologically.

Teacher: A Determining Factor

It does not need to over-emphasize that primary school-age children are in a formative stage. At this stage, teacher's role is central as it is crucial in the overall development of children. The hole at the heart of the RTE is that there is no pipeline of supplies of competent and committed teachers to enable it to work. Teachers are one of the key elements not only in the school system, but they are also among the ones, who influence the lives and personalities of children. Their influence on children goes far beyond the formal academic areas and much more than what can be measured by achievement tests. Researches indicate that in addition to the school and classroom environment, teachers' beliefs, attitude and expectations may have direct bearing even on children's ability to perform (Newman, Rutter and Smith, 1989; Good, 1981).

Very recently, teachers and their problems have been attracting a great deal of attention and concern all over the country. Teachers' efficiency, professional commitment, their perception, attitudes, stress and burnout, and motivations have become the topic of increasing public and professional concern. One of the most recent concerns is the perception of teachers towards educating children coming from deprived and disadvantaged homes. The teachers' overall perception of children coming from low SES, to a large extent, may govern the performance and achievement levels of these children. The teachers' role, therefore, assumes a far greater significance for such children. It is mainly due to their debilitating life circumstances and children stand to benefit the most from supportive teacher—student relationship. A number of researches have shown that.

Some researchers (e.g., Alexander, Entwisle and Thompson, 1987) have suggested that low expectations are a factor in low socio-economic status and minority children's persistently low academic performance. Alexander *et al.* (1987) found that among urban first grades, achievement discrepancies between African-American and White children were greatest in classrooms taught by high socio-economic status teachers and that this effect was stronger for teacher-determined grades than for scores on standardized tests. Other researchers have documented race-based teacher perception of students. For example, Jackson (2002) found that Euro-American elementary teachers' expectations for the causes of school problems differ based on the students' ethnicity. Teachers tended to attribute Euro-American children's problem behaviours to situational factors (e.g., child has problems at home) and African-American and Hispanic children's problem behaviours to within-child factors (i.e. personality and motivation). Previous studies found that teachers are less accurate in rating minority children's academic ability than the ability of Caucasian children and react differently to the same behaviour exhibited by African-American and Caucasian children (Murray, 1996; Partenio and Taylor, 1985). These findings take on increased significance in the light of research indicating that the effects of student-teacher relationship dynamics on achievement are stronger for African American and low SES children than for majority children and higher SES children (Gill & Reynolds, 1999; Jussim *et al.*, 1996).

Teacher-child relationships in the primary grades have the potential to provide children with social support and emotional security. Children with more positive teacher-child relationships appear more able to exploit the learning opportunities available in the classroom (Hoves and Smith 1995), construct positive peer relationship (Howes, Matheson and Hamilton, 1994), and adjust to the demands of formal schooling (Birch and Ladd, 1997; Lynch and Cicchetti, 1992, Pianta and Steinberg 1992). With a few exceptions (see Howes and Hamilton, 1992; Howes *et al.*, 1994, Pianta, Steinberg and Rollins 1997), the research on children's relationship with teachers has been cross sectional rather than longitudinal. Howes, Phillipsen and Feinberg (2000) examined the children's relationship with their teachers in a three-year longitudinal study beginning in their next to last year of pre-school and continuing through kindergarten. Path analysis suggested that the perception of teacher-child relationship quality, particularly conflictual relationship quality, were consistent from pre-school to kindergartens. Children, who enter first grade with below average literacy skills, are at increased risk of low academic performance throughout their school career (Alexander, Entwisle and Horsey, 1997; Entswisle and Alexander, 1988, Finn 1989). Minority and low socio-economic status children often enter school with lower academic competencies as well as social and emotional readiness competencies (Evans, 2004; Stipek, 1997).

It is a matter of general understanding that much of the stress in children and youth emanates from school problems (cf. Spirito, Stark, Grace and Stamoulis, 1991). The researchers have studied effects of stress on children. They have identified short term and long term effects of persistent stress in the context of transactional stress-models (Lazarus, 1966). The researchers formulated indicators for studying effects of stress and took up certain variables, which were depressed or depressive mood, emotional instability, psychosomatic complaints and low or instable self-esteem. From the Kauai longitudinal study, we know aspects and factors of resilience. Besides emotional well-being, emotional support and social integration are the main factors for health. There are then a number of personal resources, such as self-concept, self-esteem and self-efficacy (Taylor, 2003; Werner, 1993; Werner and Smith, 1989). Transactional stress-models consider self-concept as one of the major personal resources in the process of coping with developmental tasks and daily hassles. That applies not only to adults, but increasingly to adolescents and even children. If these resources are not effective, the probability of diseases increases.

Some researchers suggest that dominant discourses of low expectations may 'seep into the consciousnesses of low income residents' (Canvin *et al.*, 2009: 238-242) and make it difficult to build self-esteem and a positive self-narrative (Davidson, 2008: 123).

The Study

With the involvement of private schools in the delivery of education for all, the issues of both access to and quality of education are addressed. The critics challenge this provision on several counts. The first is the government's assumption that it can pass on the responsibility of public education to private institutions. The government rests its claim on the fact that since it grants land rights to schools in prime locations; it can, as a matter of right, assert certain rights in exchange.

Regardless of the right, a question of more instant significance to school-based educators is the assimilation of EWSD students into the culture of private schools that cater to a different social and economic class of students. As mentioned above, the RTE specifically states that EWSD children "will be treated on par with all the other children in the school," making it imperative for several psycho-social and pedagogic issues to be addressed in order to integrate students from low-income families. In the current exam-driven, competitive ethos that characterize most private schools in India, EWSD students are likely to be first- or second-generation learners, probably lacking academic support from their families, and may remain low performing. They may suffer from comparison in social markers, such as dress and possessions that could set them apart. For instance, one of the most successful programmes in raising attendance is the mid-day meal scheme in which EWSD students are provided a meal organized by the school. Apart from the practical difficulty of incorporating it into the infrastructure of the school, such a programme will highlight the distinction between students in terms of 'haves' and 'have-nots', just as free lunch vouchers do elsewhere. Practices and expectations like these might acutely affect the self-esteem of underprivileged students. Many private schools may not be inclined or equipped to respond to such specific requirements.

It is a big and moot question as to what the EWSD students experience in those private schools and how this experience may affect them psychologically. It does not need to be exaggerated that primary school-age children are in a formative stage. At this stage, the teacher's role is central as it is crucial in the overall development of children. The hole at the heart of the RTE is that there is no pipeline of supplies of appropriately competent and committed teachers to enable it to work. Teachers are one of the key elements in the school system as also they are among the ones, who influence the lives and personalities of children. Their influence on children goes far beyond the formal academic areas and much more than what can be measured by achievement tests. Researches indicate that in addition to the school and classroom environment, teachers' beliefs, attitude and expectations may have direct bearing even on children's ability to perform (Newman, Rutter and Smith, 1989; Good, 1981; Smith, 1989).

It is a matter of effective concern for educational psychologist to look into the psychological state of mind or perception of teacher in private schools towards EWSD students and how it affects the psyche of the students – self-concept.

Objectives: The main objectives of the present study were given below:

1 To study the private school teachers' perception of the students enrolled under RTE Act, 2009.

2 To find out the self-concept of Economically Weaker and Socially Disadvantaged students enrolled in private schools under RTE Act, 2009.

3 To find out the impact of teachers perception on self-concept of Economically Weaker and Socially Disadvantaged students.

4 To study the relationship of teachers' perception with students' self-concept.

Methodology: The study was descriptive in nature. The data was collected from the private schools of Bhopal Division after seeking the permission of competent authorities.

***Variables*:** The variables related to the present study were—(i) Independent Variable: Teachers' Perception of the Students Enrolled under RTE Act, 2009. (ii) Dependent Variable: *Self-Concept:* The term self-concept is a general term used to refer to how someone thinks about or perceives himself/herself. The self-concept is how we think about and evaluate ourselves; to be aware of oneself is to have a concept of oneself. Baumeister (1999) puts it as: "the individual's belief about himself or herself, including the person's attributes and who and what the self is."

***Population*:** All the private schools catering to the Economically Weaker and Socially Disadvantaged Students under RTE Act in Bhopal division was the population of study.

***Sample*:** The study was conducted in five private schools catering the EWSD students of Bhopal Division, Madhya Pradesh. As the RTE Act came into force on 1 April 2010, till now only I to III classes are having EWSD students. Only the teachers, who have been involved in teaching the classes having EWSD Students, were interviewed. Ten EWSD students were taken from each class randomly. The sample was 10 teachers from each school and 10 students from each class—standard I, II and III for data collection. In this way, 50 teachers and 150 students were contacted for the study.

***Sampling Technique*:** A stratified random sampling technique was used for selecting the schools, teachers and also students.

Tools of the Study are—1. To measure the teachers' perception: a questionnaire was prepared by the researcher to study the Perception of Teachers towards the children's overall behaviour and aspects of personality.

2. To measure the self-concept: the Piers Harris Children's Self-Concept Scale (2002) was administered.

***Data Collection*:** The data was collected from the five private schools of Bhopal Division catering o EWSD student through stratified random sampling technique. Further, ten teachers from each school and ten students were taken from each class–I, II and III standards for data collection.

***Data Analysis*:** The data collected from teachers and students was analyzed qualitatively and quantitatively.

Results and their Interpretations

In the first phase, the teachers' perception was analyzed qualitatively.

***Phase-I: Qualitative Analysis of Teachers' Perception*:** After conducting the interviews and taking field notes, a number of issues emerged. Amongst them, the prominent one is that the teachers typically have negative perception of and low expectations from the students hailing from marginalised and relatively poor segments of the society. In turn, the teachers' perception affects the nature and quality of their attitude towards students, thus, adversely affecting their overall personality.

The issue of teachers' rather misconceived perception and its impact upon students acquires added significance on two counts. First, the teachers constitute a core group of those, who make schooling what it is. Secondly, India's socio-economic scenario is highly stratified, leaving vast room for the formulations and operation of perceptions emanating from socio-economic determinants.

Teachers asserted that students lack cultural and educational experiences and see this as a detriment to cultivating student interest in the educational process. One teacher commented that "many students come [to school] with specific learning disabilities and it is perhaps for the same reason that they lack prior educational experiences."

As regards parental involvement, teachers usually do not foresee parents as providing comprehensive cultural experiences for their children, as do more economically privileged households. As a teacher very sympathetically explained, "…due to their debilitating economic conditions, these students generally are not exposed to many experiences. During the course of teaching, I realized that they are unable to understand a number of things. Yesterday, I was teaching communication. Most of the students [except those who] are well aware of the modern methods of communication, but those student were not only unable to understand, but also not capable to visualize. At times, I feel bad for them. When I start to explain to them, the rest of 75 per cent students start losing interest in the discussion. When we discuss certain topics, the students know because they have travelled or have been exposed to cultural events. They are aware of certain topics so that when the teacher discusses them, they already know them." Teachers claimed that most of the parents of their students do not present an example of upward social mobility or academic success to their children, but rather they present an example of social stagnation and resignation with their life style. Teachers alluded to the parents' low educational levels and governmental financial assistance as an example of this social stagnation.

Teachers believed that dedication, willingness, support of the family and educational values are an important part of student's academic success. Therefore, if the parents do not get involved in their child's academic life, the student will not obtain academic progress, which the teachers believe is necessary to achieve success. A teacher, who was teaching III standard narrated about a boy, who never paid attention to his studies, was indisciplined and, at times, quarrelsome. She branded him as 'a hopeless boy'.

Teachers do not integrate into the process of acquisition of comprehensive, holistic learning, which takes into consideration student's comprehensive needs. Perception of such teachers may lead students to believe that their teachers do not care about their well-being. Therefore, this could increase the disengagement of students with their education even more and may exacerbate behaviours that teachers identify as uncaring.

The role played by teachers' expectations about the students' academic ability has been an important topic of educational research for almost 30 years. It is now taken for certainty that teachers' expectations can influence their behaviours toward students (Good and Brophy, 2000; Harris and Rosenthal, 1985), and thus students' self-perceptions, motivation, and achievement (e.g., Jussim, 1989; Pelletier and Vallerand, 1996; Trouilloud, Sarrazin, Martinek and Guillet, 2002). This is the concept of Teacher Expectation Effects or TEE (TEE; Good, 1987). TEE occurs when the teacher's expectations about a student affect teacher-student interactions in a manner that leads the student to fulfil the teacher's expectations. Naturalistic studies have repeatedly found support for the presence of TEE in classrooms (*see* Jussim and Harber, 2005; Trouilloud and Sarrazin, 2003, for reviews).

The shaping of students' perceived competence through the TEE process is now relatively well-documented. According to most socio-psychological models (e.g., Darley and Fazio, 1980; Jussim, 1986; Miller and Turnbull, 1986), one of the consequences of a perceiver holding an expectation is that this expectation may lead the target not only to behave consistently with the expectation, but to conclude that he/she is actually that type of person. Thus, if a teacher believes that a particular student is "low" in competence, this student, after numerous interactions with the teacher, may conclude that he or she is actually "low" in competence, and therefore, have a low perceived competence. Indeed, teachers' early expectations for their students' ability had been shown to influence students' later self-concept of ability in various contexts, such as mathematics (e.g., Jussim, 1989; Parsons, Kaczala and Meece, 1982; Madon, *et al.*, 2001), reading (e.g., Brattesani, Weinstein and Marshall, 1984) and physical education classes (Trouilloud *et al.*, 2002). For example, Jussim (1989) showed that teachers' expectations of students' performance in October significantly predicted changes in students' self-concept of math ability in the spring, even after controlling the students' previous achievement and perceived ability. Moreover, students' perceived competence seems to be one important mediator of TEE on students' achievement (Jussim, 1986); that is, the influence of teachers' expectations on students' perceived competence may impact students' achievement (Trouilloud *et al.*, 2002).

The desire for a positive evaluation of self affects a person's feelings, actions, and aspirations throughout life. In the course of childhood and adolescence, school experiences play an important role in the development of self-perceptions and can have powerful and long-term effects on a child's self-esteem. So, it is pertinent to discern the self-concept of disadvantaged group of student, who enrolled under the RTE mandate.

***Phase-II: Quantitative Analysis of Students' Self Concept*:** In the second phase of the analysis, the data obtained from the primary class students was analyzed quantitatively. Piers-Harris Children's Self-Concept Scale (second edition) was administered to identify the self-concept in the students, who got admission under the RTE mandate. Scoring was done as mentioned in manual, one score was tabulated for each response that was keyed in the direction of a positive self-concept. Thus, the total score had a possible range of 0 to 60. The cluster scores were tabulated based on the number of items that belonged to each dimension. Hence, cluster scores had a possible range of 0 to 16. The arithmetic mean was calculated of the raw scores of the participant. For the purpose of interpreting participants' self-concepts, raw scores were converted into Z-scores and transformed into T-scores.

Table 10.1: Mean Raw Scores, T Scores and Range of the Dimensions and Total Score of Self Concept

	Behavioural Adjustment (BEH)	*Intellectual and School Status (INT)*	*Physical Appearance and Attributes (PHY)*	*Freedom From Anxiety (FRE)*	*Popularity (POP)*	*Happiness and Satisfaction (HAP)*	*Total Score (TOT)*
Mean Raw Score	3	5	7	12	7	10	33
T-score	30	34	45	54	44	59	39
Range	Low	Low	Average	Average	Below Average	Above Average	Low

The self-concept scales include the Total (TOT) score and the six domain scales. The six domain scales determine specific aspects of self-concept. They can also be used to evaluate strengths and weaknesses in self-image. On all scales, higher scores designate favourable self-concept (i.e., high degree of self-esteem or self-regard), whereas lower scores are associated with more negative self-concept.

Self-Concept Total Score (TOT)

The TOT score is a measure of general self-concept. It is based on responses to all 60 Piers-Harris items. The average total scores of students are 33 and the T score of 39*T* is in the Low range. It was found that students expressed serious doubts about their own self-worth. They likely had negative self-appraisals in several specific areas of functioning, which can be clarified by examining the domain scale scores and item responses. TOT scores in this range are frequently associated with disturbances in mood and behaviour.

Behavioural Adjustment (BEH)

The Behavioural Adjustment scale measures admission or denial of problematic behaviours in home and school settings. The student's BEH score of 29*T* is in the Very Low range. The students endorsed persistent negative feelings about their own behaviour. They somehow feel that they repeatedly cause trouble, act aggressively, and are unable to comply with the standards of conduct set by their teachers. Very low BEH scores can be associated with a variety of psychological syndromes, especially disruptive behaviour disorders, such as conduct disorder, oppositional defiant disorder, and attention-deficit/hyperactivity disorder.

Intellectual and School Status (INT)

The Intellectual and School Status scale represents a youngster's self-assessment of intellectual abilities and academic performance. The items also cover the satisfaction with school and future prospect about achievement. The students' INT score of 34*T* is in the Low range. They accepted copious apparent difficulties in school-related tasks. Depending on the item responses, these problems may be academic and/or behavioural in nature. They have a general sense that they somehow are unable to adjust at school and do not have the necessary "smartness" to succeed in their schoolwork. A low INT score may have varying significance depending on the student's prior history of academic achievement. In youngsters with a record of low academic achievement or a history of learning or behavioural problems in school, a low INT score may reflect an internalization of the disappointment of parents, teachers, and other authority figures.

Physical Appearance and Attributes (PHY)

The Physical Appearance and Attributes scale measures a student's consideration of his/her physical appearance, as well as attributes such as leadership and the ability to express ideas. The students' PHY score of 45*T* is in the Average range. They seem to have relatively balanced feelings about their physical appearance and strength.

Freedom from Anxiety (FRE)

The Freedom from Anxiety scale assesses anxiety and dysphoric mood. Individual items tap a variety of specific emotions, including worry, nervousness, shyness, sadness, and fear. The students' FRE score of 54*T* is in the Average range. They usually appeared in positive mood states, but acknowledged a few negative feelings as well.

Popularity (POP)

The Popularity scale symbolizes students' evaluation of their social functioning. The items tap perceived popularity, ability to make friends, and inclusion in activities, such as games and sports. The students' POP score of 44*T* is in the Low Average range. It gives a mixture of positive and negative feelings with regard to their peer relationships.

Happiness and Satisfaction (HAP)

The Happiness and Satisfaction scale assesses general feelings of happiness and satisfaction with life. The students' HAP score of 59*T* is in the Above Average range. It was found that they evaluated themselves and their life circumstances in a generally positive way. They reported an overall sense of wellbeing. They would tend to describe themselves as cheerful, satisfied, lucky, and able to get along well with others.

Findings of the Study

This study builds the argument that teacher perception may influence students' self-concept or self-perceptions. In a review of research, Brophy (1981) concluded that some students are better able to get more praise from teachers, usually students with "personal qualities, such as confidence, sociability, and extraversion" (p. 12). Pintrich and Blumenfeld (1985) found a positive correlation between perceptions of competence and teacher praise for academic work. Stipek and Daniels (1988) concluded that the daily feedback from teachers had a greater effect on self-perception than other forms of feedback (e.g., summary reports sent to parents). In a review of research, Wittrock (1986) came to the same conclusion, suggesting that teacher feedback can influence a student's perceptions of ability in future school performances.

The results indicate that students of economically weaker and socially disadvantaged sections of society face somehow negative perception and low expectations from their teachers. These students are suffering from low self-concept, which might be the result of teachers' negative perception. All the more painful is the fact that while interacting with the students, the teachers plainly told them that they were incompetent and hopeless and were not liked at all. As such, they developed negative self-concept about themselves. It is worth emphasizing that when we make a negative self-assigned status, such as I think that I am "unlovable", "inadequate", "irrational", "incompetent", "worthless" or just "inferior", we can see that we have already resigned ourselves ineligible to participate in life (Bergner, 2000 p. 2). If we find ourselves unlovable, then there remains no hope at all in participating in this life, because we think nobody can love us. If we think that we are inadequate, then we feel we will never measure up. If we think that we are incompetent, we never gain the confidence to do anything worthwhile. Tragically, this can become the case. "Along with restricting the behavioural possibilities of people, the self-concept has important implications that will show how a person will deem appropriate to act" (Bergner, 2000). Burnett's findings (1999, 2003) exhibited the importance of teachers' verbal statements and indicated teachers' positive feedback was more beneficial than negative feedback to academic self-concept.

Conclusion

The perception of teachers is considered a significant aspect in the teaching-learning process in the classroom. Their attitude is linked with students' attitude, which, in turn, is associated with her/his achievement and personality dimensions. Students may also feel out of place in the school environment. If teachers do not understand the behaviour of the student, they may inadvertently make the student feel unimportant and alienated. A number of researches maintain that teachers form differential perceptions and have varying expectations for student behaviour and achievement early in the school year, and behave differently towards various students. This treatment demands students as to how they were to behave in the classroom and perform in academic tasks. If the teacher treatment is consistent over time and if students do not actively resist or change it, it will likely affect their self-concepts, achievement motivations, levels of aspirations, classroom conducts, and interactions with the teacher. These effects generally complement and reinforce the teacher's perception and expectations, so much so that the students come to develop a mindset, which is confirmatory to these perceptions. Ultimately, this affects the student's achievements and other outcomes. Positively perceived, the students will be led to achieve better according to their potential, but negatively perceived students will not gain as much as they could have gained if taught differently.

It is important that teachers and teacher education programmes place additional emphasis on the role of positive self-fulfilling prophecies for students and high expectations for teachers. Teacher education institutions, practicing teachers and families need to work collaboratively to ensure that students remain optimistic, motivated and successful within the schooling environment. In this way, every child will have the opportunity to thrive and reach his or her potential in a classroom environment that is supportive, constructive, encouraging and caring.

References

1. Alexander, Karl; Doris, Entwisle and Carrie, Horsey. (1997). From First Grade Forward: Early Foundations of High School Dropout. *Sociology of Education* 70 (April): 87-107.
2. Alexender, K.L.; Entwistle, D.R., and Thomspson, M.S. (1987). School Performance, Status Relation and the Structure of Sentiments: Bringing the teacher back in *American Sociological Review,* 52 (October) 665-682.
3. Annual Status of Educational Report (2010). "Annual Status of Educational Report (Rural), assessed 21 April 2012: http://www.pratham.org/aser08/ASER_2010_Report.pdf.
4. Baumeister, R.F. and Stack, A.D. (1999). Catharsis, Aggression, and Persuasive Influence: Self-fulfilling or self-defeating prophecies? *Journal of Personality and Social Psychology.*
5. Bergner, R. and Holmes, J. (2000). Self-concepts and Self-concept Change: A status dynamic approach. *Psychotherapy: Theory, Research, Practice, Training.* 37, 1-5.
6. Bernstein, B. (1973). *Class Codes and Control: Applied Studies towards a Sociology of Language*, London: Routledge Kegan Paul.
7. Birch, S.H. and Ladd, G.W. (1997). The teacher-child relationship and children's early school adjustment.
8. Blair, A. (2006). 'Fewer Students from Poor Families at Top Universities', *The Times*, 20 July.
9. Bourdieu, P. (1967). 'Systems of Education and Systems of Thought', *Social Science Information* 14: 338-58.
10. Bourdieu, P. (1977). "Cultural Reproduction and Social Reproduction", In Karabel, J. and A.H., Halsey, (ed), *Power and Ideology in Education.* Oxford University Press, New York, pp. 487-511.
11. Brattesani, K.A.; Weinstein, R.S. and Marshall, H.H. (1984). Student perceptions of differential teacher treatment as moderators of teacher expectation effects. *Journal of Educational Psychology*, 76, 236-247.
12. Canvin, K.; Marttila, A.; Burstrom, B. and Whitehead, M. (2009). Tales of the unexpected? Hidden resilience in poor households in Britain, *Social Science and Medicine*, 69, pp. 238-245.

13. Darley, J. M., and Fazio, R.H. (1980). Expectancy-confirmation processes arising in the social interaction sequence. *American Psychologist*, 35, 867-881.
14. Davidson, R. (2008). More than Just Coping: The Antecedents and Dynamics of Resilience in a Qualitative Longitudinal Study. *Social Policy and Society* 8 (1), pp. 115-125.
15. Entwisle, D.R. and Alexander, K.L. (1988). Factors affecting achievement test scores and marks of Black and White first graders. *Elementary School Journal* 88:449-471.
16. Evans, G.W. (2004, February/March). The environment of childhood poverty. *American Psychologist. 59*(2), 77-92.
17. Fayaz Bhat's thoughtful observation (2012). is
18. Finn, J.D. (1989). Withdrawing from school. *Review of Educational Research, 59,* 117-142.
19. Gill, S., and Reynolds, A.J. (1999). Educational expectations and school achievement of urban African American children. *Journal of School Psychology,* 37, 403-424.
20. Good, T.L. (1981). Teacher expectations and student perceptions: A decade of research. *Educational Leadership,* 38(5), 415-422.
21. Good, T.L. and Brophy, J.E. (2003). *Looking in classrooms* (9th ed.). Boston, MA: Allyn and Bacon.
22. Good, T. and Brophy, J. (2000). *Looking in classrooms* (8th ed.). New York, NY: Longman.
23. Grimston, J. (2009). 'Universities Fail to Woo Poor Students', *The Sunday Times*, 4 January.
24. Harris, M.J. and Rosenthal, R. (1985). Mediation of interpersonal expectancy effects: 31 meta-analyses. *Psychological Bulletin*, 97, 363-386.
25. Howes, C. and Hamilton, C.E. (1992). Children's relationships with caregivers: Mothers and child care teachers. *Child Development,* 63(4), 859-866. EJ 450 556.
26. Howes, C. and Smith, E. (1995). Relations Among Child Care Quality, Teacher Behaviour, Children's Play Activities, Emotional Security, and Cognitive Activity in Child Care. *Early Childhood Research Quarterly*, 10, 381-404.
27. Howes, C.; Matheson C.C. and Hanilton, C.E ((1994) Maternal, teacher and child care history: correlates of children's relationship with peers. *Child Development*, 65, 264-273.
28. Howes, C.; Phillpsen, L.C.; and Peisner-Feinberg, E. (2000). The consistency of perceived teacher-child relationships between preschool and kindergarten. *Journal of School Psychology,* 38, 113-132.
29. Jackson, SA. A study of teachers' perceptions of youth problems. *Journal of Youth Behaviour*. 2002; 5:313-322.
30. Jussim (1989). Teacher expectations: Self-fulfilling prophecies, perceptual biases, and accuracy. *Journal of Personality and Social Psychology,* 57, 469-480.
31. Jussim, L. and Harber, K.D. (2005). Teacher Expectation and self-fulfilling prophecies: Known and Unknown resolved and unresolved controversies. *Personality and social psychology review*, 9, 131-155.
32. Jussim, L. (1986). Self Fulfilling Prophecies: A theoretical and Integrative Review. *Psychological Review.* 93 429-445.

33. Jussim, L.; Eccles, J. and Madon, S. (1996). Social perception, social stereotypes, and teacher expectations: Accuracy and the quest for the powerful self-fulfilling prophecy. In M.P. Zanna (Ed.), *Advances in Experimental Social Psychology* (Vol. 28, pp. 281-388). San Diego, CA: Academic Press.
34. Jussim, L.; Eccles, J. and Madon, S.J. (1996). Social perception, social stereotypes, and teacher expectations: Accuracy and the quest for the powerful self-fulfilling prophecy. *Advances in Experimental Social Psychology,* 29, 281-388.
35. Jussim, L.; Smith, A.; Madon, S. and Palumbo, P. (1998). Teacher expectations. In J.E. Brophy (Ed.), *Advances in research on teaching: Expectations in the classroom* (Vol. 7, pp. 1-48). Greenwich, Connecticut: JAI Press.
36. Jussim, Lee and Harber, Kent D. (2005). Teacher Expectations and Self-Fulfilling Prophecies: Knowns and Unknowns, Resolved and Unresolved Controversies; *Personality and Social Psychology*; *Review* 9; 131.
37. Kumar, Krishna (2012). "Let a hundred children blossom: A classroom reflecting life's diversity will benefit children of all strata while enriching teaching experience." *The Hindu*, Delhi, 20 April 2012.
38. Lazarus, R. (1991). *Emotion and Adaption.* New York: Oxford University Press.
39. Lazarus, R.S. (1966). *Psychological Stress and the Coping Process.* New York: McGraw-Hill.
40. Lynch, M. and Cicchetti, D. (1997). Children's relationships with adults and peers: An examination of elementary and junior high school students. *Journal of School Psychology,* 35(1), 81-99.
41. Madon, S.; Smith, A.; Jussim, L.; Russell, D.W.; Walkiewicz, M.; Eccles, J.S. and Palumbo, P. (2001). Am I as you see me or do you see me as I am? Self-fulfilling prophecies and self-verification. *Personality and Social Psychology Bulletin*, 27, 1214-1224.
42. Miller, D.T. and Turnbull, W. (1986). Expectancies and interpersonal processes. *Annual Review of Psychology*, 37, 233-256.
43. Murray C.B. (1996). Estimating achievement performance: A confirmation bias. *Journal of Black Psychology*. 1996; 22:67-85.
44. Newman, P.N.; Rutter, R.A.; and Smith M.S. (1989). Organizational Factors that Affect School Sense of Efficacy, Community and Expectations, *Sociology of Education.* 62 (4), 221-238.
45. Parsons, J.E.; Kaczala, C.M.; Meece, J.L. (1982). Socialization of achievement attitudes and beliefs: Classroom influences. *Child Development*, 53, 322-339.
46. Partenio, I. and Taylor R.L. The relationship of teacher ratings and IQ: A question of bias? *School Psychology Review*. 1985; 14:79-83.
47. Paton, G. (2007) 'Education Apartheid as Private Schools Flood Elite Universities', *The Daily Telegraph*, 27 November, p. 1.
48. Pianta, R.C. and Steinberg, M. (1992). Teacher-child relationships and the process of adjusting to school. *New Directions for Child Development,* 57(1), 61-80.
49. Pianta, R.; Steinberg, M. and Rollins, K. (1995). The first two years of school: Teacher-child relationships and deflections in children's classroom adjustment. *Development of Psychology*, 7, 295-312.
50. Pintrich, P.R. and Blumenfeld, P.C. (1985). Classroom experience and children's self-perceptions of ability, effort and conduct. Journal of Educational Psychology, 77, 646-657 *School Psychology,* 35(1), 61-79.

51. Sibal, Kapil (2012): Admitting kids from weaker sections, while not lowering quality of teaching will be difficult for private schools, but it can be done: RTE can be a Model for the World *The Times of India*, New Delhi, 20 April.
52. Spirito, A.; Stark, L.J.; Grace, N. and Stamoulis, D. (1991). Common problems and coping strategies reported in childhood and early adolescence. Journal of Youth and Adolescence, 20, 531-544.
53. Stipek, D. (1997) Success in school—for a head start in life. In: Luthar, S.S.; Burack, J.A.; Cicchetti, D.; Weisz, J.R. (editors) *Developmental Psychopathology.* Cambridge University Press; New York: pp. 75-91.
54. Stipek, D. and Daniels, D. H. (1988). Declining perceptions of competence: A consequence of changes in the child or in the educational environment. *Journal of Educational Psychology*, 80, 352-356.
55. Trouilloud, D.; Sarrazin, P.; Martinek, T. and Guillet, E. (2002). The influence of teacher expectations on students' achievement in physical education classes: Pygmalion revisited. *European Journal of Social Psychology*, 32, 1-17.
56. Wittrock, M. (1986). Students' thought processes. In M. Wittrock (Ed.), *Handbook of research on teaching* (3rd Ed.) (pp. 297-314). New York: MacMillan & Co.

11

Responsibilities of Teacher Education Institutions for Preparing Effective Teachers for Implementing the Right to Education (RTE) Act

Sajid Jamal

The crucial role of Universal Elementary Education for strengthening the social fabric of democracy through the provision of equal opportunities to all has been accepted since the inception of our Republic. The original Article 45 in the Directive Principles of State Policy in the Constitution mandated the State to endeavour to provide free and compulsory education to all children up to age fourteen in a period of ten years. The National Policy on Education (NPE), 1986/92, which stands as a major landmark in the country's journey towards Universal Elementary Education (UEE) states: "*In our national perception, education is essentially for all…Education has an acculturating role. It refines sensitivities and perceptions that contribute to national cohesion, a scientific temper and independence of mind and spirit – thus furthering the goals of socialism, secularism and democracy enshrined in our Constitution.*"

With the formulation of NPE, India initiated a wide range of programmes for achieving the goal of UEE. These efforts were intensified in the 1980s and 1990s through several schematic and programme interventions, such as the Operation Black Board (OBB), Shiksha Karmi Project (SKP), Andhra Pradesh Primary Education Project (APPEP), Bihar Education Project (BEP), UP Basic Education Project (UPBEP), Mahila Samakhya (MS), Lok Jumbish Project (LJP), and Teacher Education, which put in place a decentralised system of teacher support through District Institutes of Education and Training, and District Primary Education Programme (DPEP). Currently, Sarva Shiksha Abhiyan (SSA) is implemented as one of India's flagship programmes for universalising elementary education. Its overall goals include universal access and retention, bridging of gender and social category gaps in education and enhancement of learning levels of children. SSA provides for a variety of interventions, including *inter alia,* opening of new schools and alternate schooling facilities, construction of schools and additional classrooms, toilets and drinking water, provisioning of teachers, periodic teacher training and academic resource support, textbooks and support for learning achievement. Over the years, there has been significant spatial and numerical expansion of elementary schools in the country, yet the goal of universal elementary education continues to elude us. The number of children, particularly children from disadvantaged groups and weaker sections, who drop out of school before completing elementary education, remains high. The quality of learning achievement is not always entirely satisfactory even in the case of children, who complete elementary education.

The Constitution (Eighty-Sixth Amendment) Act, 2002 inserted Article 21-A in the Constitution of India to provide free and compulsory education to all children in the age group of six to fourteen years as a Fundamental Right in such manner as the State may, by law, determine. The Right of Children to Free and Compulsory Education (RTE) Act, 2009, which represents the consequential legislation envisaged under Article 21-A, means that every child has a right to full time elementary education of satisfactory and equitable quality in a formal school, which satisfies certain essential norms and standards. 'Compulsory education' casts an obligation on the appropriate Government to provide and ensure admission, attendance and completion of elementary education. 'Free education' means that no child, other than a child, who has been admitted by his or her parents to a school, which is not supported by the appropriate Government, shall be liable to pay any kind of fee or charges or expenses, which may prevent him or her from pursuing and completing elementary education.

The RTE Act, 2009 has become a reality, and guarantees every child the most basic fundamental right—the right to education. The RTE Act, along with Article 21-A inserted in the Fundamental Rights of the Constitution of India, became operational on 1st April 2010. The new Act provides a justifiable legal framework that entitles all children between the ages of 6-14 years free and compulsory admission, attendance and completion of elementary education. It provides for children's right to an education of reasonable quality, based on the principles of equity and non-discrimination. Most importantly, it provides for children's right to an education that is free from fear, stress and anxiety.

Significance of the RTE Act

In its barest outline, the RTE Act has three goals: (1) bringing children of marginalized sections of our society into the ambit of school education, (2) ensuring that all schools and their teachers meet certain specified norms, and (3) ensuring that all children receive schooling of reasonable quality, free from any form of discrimination. Hence, in several educational quarters, the Act has been hailed as great landmark legislation in the history of education in India. It is expected that its implementation will provide not only for free and compulsory education to every child between the age of 6 and 14 years of age, but also help in raising the standard of education. The present Act specifies the duties of various stakeholders in education, i.e., the Central Government, the State Government, Local Authorities, the Parents and Teachers, etc.

With RTE, India can emerge as a global leader in achieving the Millennium Development Goal of ensuring that all children complete their primary schooling by 2015. If the provisions made in the Act are successfully and wilfully implemented, then, India can take its rightful leadership role in education on the global stage. RTE will propel this great nation to even higher heights of prosperity and productivity by guaranteeing all children their right to a quality education and a brighter future. The RTE Act attaches immense significance to the role of teachers in reforming elementary education and highlights the need for making available professionally trained teachers for the school system.

Responsibilities of Schools and Teachers Fixed by the RTE Act, 2009

1. The Act lays out some basic norms for all schools (both government and private) as following:
   a) Pupil-Teacher Ratio (PTR) cannot exceed 1:30.
   b) Minimum days of school functioning in a year (200 and 250 for primary and Upper Primary, respectively).
   c) Minimum hours of instruction in school (four and five hours a day for primary and upper primary).
   d) Minimum working hours for the teacher (45 hours a week)
   e) Separate subject teachers and head-teacher
   f) One room for every teacher
   g) Separate and functional toilets; clean and adequate drinking water
   h) Playground, boundary wall, library, kitchen
2. The Act sets qualification and following working norms for teachers in all schools:
   a) Para Teachers banned
   b) All teachers must subscribe to minimum qualifications and training norms laid out by Academic Authority within five years.
   c) Teacher education and Teacher training institutes to be upgraded to enable fulfilment of quality and qualification norms for teachers.

d) Qualification for appointment of teachers to be laid down by academic authority authorised by the Central Government.
e) Lays down academic responsibilities of teachers
f) Prohibits private tuition by teachers
g) Prohibits deployment of teachers for non-education purpose, except decennial census, disaster relief and elections.

3. The Act fixes the responsibilities of the schools as following:
a) Guidelines about the pupil-teacher ratio (PTR):
   - Requirement of additional teachers to maintain PTR – within six months at primary level
   - Admitted children Up to 60 – Two teachers
   - Between 61 to 90 – Three teachers
   - Between 91 to 120 – Four teachers
   - Between 121 to 200 – Five teachers
   - Above 150 – 5 teachers + one Head teacher
   - Above 200 – Pupil-Teacher Ratio 1:40 (excluding Head teacher)

PTR at upper primary level: (1) At least one teacher per class so that there shall be at least one teacher each for – (i) Science and Mathematics; (ii) Social Studies; (iii) Languages. (2) At least one teacher for every thirty-five children. (3) In those schools, where admission of children is above one hundred – (i) a full time head-teacher; and (ii) part time instructors for – (A) Art Education; (B) Health and Physical Education; (C) Work Education.

b) Guidelines about the infrastructure:
All-weather building consisting of – (i) at least one class-room for every teacher and an office-cum-store-cum-Head teacher's room; (ii) barrier-free access; (iii) separate toilets for boys and girls; (iv) safe and adequate drinking water facility to all children; (v) a kitchen where mid-day meal is cooked in the school; (vi) Playground; vii) arrangements for securing the school building by boundary wall or fencing.

c) Guidelines about the minimum number of working days:
Working Days in an academic year (i) Class 1 to 5 – 200 days (ii) Class 6 to 8–220 days in an academic year (iii) Class 1 to 5–800 hours (iv) Class 6 to 8 – 1000 hours (v) Minimum number of working hours per week for the teacher: 45 teaching plus preparation hours. (vi) Teaching learning equipment shall be provided to each class as required.

d) Instructions about the library and play material:
There shall be a library in each school providing newspaper, magazines and books on all subjects, including story-books and

play material, games/sports equipment shall be provided to each class as required.

4. Instructions for the schools:
   a) No capitation fees will be charged by the schools.
   b) In case of capitation fees, a fine up to 10 times the capitation fees may be charged.
   c) No screening for admission will be conducted by the schools.
   d) In case the school is found to conduct screening for admission, a fine of ₹ 25,000 may be charged for 1st contravention and ₹ 50,000 for each subsequent contravention.
   e) No school will be allowed to run without recognition.
   f) In case of running the school without recognition, a fine of ₹ one lakh may be charged; in case of continuing contravention, penalty of ₹ 10,000 per day may be charged.
   g) No recognition will be granted to the schools without fulfilling norms and standards.
   h) Three years initial grace period will be provided to fulfil norms. However, the PTR has to be ensured within six months in every school.
5. The Act mandates curriculum in all schools to be in consonance with constitutional values. This means that:
   a) The curriculum, syllabus and books must conform to Constitutional values. It implies that communal and harmful agendas cannot be part of the materials used and taught in any school of the country.
   b) Syllabus and Books must also take into account age and learning levels of children.

   Make child free from fear, trauma and anxiety.
   c) Child centred, child friendly; provide for learning through activities, discovery and exploration.
   e) Medium of instruction will be child's mother tongue to the extent possible.
   f) Comprehensive and continuous evaluation has to be conducted.
   g) No Board examinations till completion of elementary education.
6. The Act enhances the role of *Panchayati Raj* Institutions (PRIs) in implementation as well as grievance redressal. Role of *Panchayati Raj* Institutions will be as follows:
   a) The PRIs have been given a wide range of functions related to the implementation of the provisions of the RTE, such as identification of out of school children; neighbourhood-wise school mapping; maintenance of child records (child-tracking); public display of information; education of children from migrant

families; participation in School Management Committees (SMCs)

b) PRIs have also been made responsible for grievance redressal in matters related to the violation of the rights of the child under RTE.

7. The Act mandates the participation of civil society in the management of schools; makes teachers accountable to parents and the community. In this context:

a) The School Management Committees consisting largely of parents (75%) and of PRIs officialst: and civil society partners have been given a wide range of functions under the Act, including the preparation of the School Development Plan.

b) Teachers have been made accountable to the SMCs.

8. The Act democratizes education delivery in the country by mandating 25 per cent reservation for children from weaker sections in private schools. According to the Act:

a) All private schools are required to admit in their incoming class 25 per cent children from weaker sections and socially disadvantaged groups from their neighbourhood.

b) Limits of definition to be extended if 25 per cent seats are not being filled within the standard limits of neighbourhood.

c) Private schools to be reimbursed for these children by the government at the rate of per learner costs of government schools in the state.

Responsibilities of Teacher Education Institutions for Preparing Effective Teachers for Implementing RTE Act, 2009

The successful implementation of the RTE Act, 2009 depends on well qualified and well informed teachers. Their will power and ability to perform will decide the future of this Act. The responsibility of making them able and competent mainly lies on the shoulders of the teacher education institutions of our country. In this context, the teacher education institutions have to discharge the following responsibilities:

1) *Responsibility of Ensuring Optimum Infrastructure in the Teacher Education Institutions:* Most of the teacher education institutions in India suffer from lack of adequate facilities, and they do not adhere to the norms regarding physical facilities or provision of adequate staff. These institutions are generally understaffed or the staff is under qualified. Many private colleges have sprung up and in a number of degree colleges, teacher education courses have been instituted without ensuring the availability of suitable facilities and qualified staff. However, one of the salient features of the RTE Act, 2009 is

that it ensures the minimum infrastructure in the schools regarding the number of minimum teachers, number of the rooms, playground, furniture and other teaching learning equipments. Unless and until those institutions, who impart training to the prospective teachers itself will have the minimum infrastructure, the prospective teachers will not be made aware about the importance of optimum infrastructure in the schools. Hence, the teacher education institutions should ensure optimum infrastructure according to the needs of the teacher trainees.

2) *Responsibility of Providing Proper Exposure to the Prospective Teachers:* Teachers directly contribute to the social and material growth of the country. Their noble profession lifts the society from misery to progress. They aim at preparing the students for active and responsible participation in the society. They equip the students with life coping skills and are responsible for the all-round growth of the students and, thus, increase the excellence of the achievement of the human mind and spirit. Besides that, they are also primarily responsible to restore our cultural heritage. In this regard, RTE Act, 2009 fixes some additional responsibilities on their shoulders for nation building. Hence, the teachers should be made aware of the vital contribution they make to the society. For this, proper exposure should be given to the prospective teachers about the roles that they have to play in the future and about the provisions of the RTE Act, 2009 and various children's rights mentioned in the Act. For this, they should be informed in the classroom about various provisions of the RTE Act, 2009 and how these may be materialised. The trainees should also be given a chance to go through various provisions of the Act in the Library and discuss it with their class fellows, their teachers and various educationists in this regard. It will give an insight to them regarding various merits and demerits of the Act in detail.

In this context, it will not be out of place to mention that the time and attention being paid to the actual practice of teaching is not sufficient. The trainees are required to complete 40-60 lessons and only a small portion of that is supervised. It is a common knowledge that the examiners appointed to test their skills are able to view the lessons for a few moments, because they do not find enough time to evaluate the trainees comprehensively. Hence, in the first place, the prevailing isolation between the Teacher Education Institutions and schools must end. The preparation of a teacher must be regarded as a joint responsibility of the cooperating school and the Teacher Education Institution. There must be a constant dialogue between these institutions and schools so that the programmes are developed together and any misgivings that might arise are removed. School teachers should also be invited to Teacher Education Institutions to give demonstration lessons and share their rich practical experiences with the young trainees. Besides that, the trainees are expected to gain such experiences during practice teaching, which may help them in organising various co-curricular activities and working with the community.

3) *Responsibility of Training the Prospective Teachers in an Effective Manner*: From the conventional concept of mastery of the content and the inherent authority, the objectives of preparing teachers have expanded. Nowadays, the focus is on the acquisition of competencies and nurturing of qualities of every individual teacher to make him/her fit so that he/she may discharge his/her responsibilities in the emerging India, where the social justice and equity could apparently be the visible and desirable components of all the future social processes. In this context, a good teacher may be the one, who:

a) Is liked and loved by the children, appreciated by the community and endeared by the peers.
b) Is modest and has the necessary self-confidence and self-image of being a partner in the nation building process.
c) Is aware of the impact of the knowledge explosion, population explosion and explosion of the rising expectations from education.
d) Knows how to collect information from the right sources and process it for the teaching learning strategies.
e) Is willing to renew his/her approach, methodology and techniques in consonance with the changing times.
f) Is confident, willing and skilled to achieve professional upgradation, particularly through self-directed learning.
g) Realises his/her position as a role model for the children and as a communicator of new developments to the community.
h) Has the capacity, as a socializing agent, to interact with all those, who could help enhance institutional efficiency and contribute to the growth, relevance and utility of education.

Hence, the teacher education institutions should assure that they are training the prospective teachers in such a way that they are well aware about the above mentioned characteristics of a good teacher. Orientation to the prospective teachers must also include knowledge about their future responsibilities and how well they will discharge those responsibilities, particularly about:

a) How to complete the entire curriculum in the specified period.
b) How to assess the learning abilities of each child and accordingly supplement additional instructions, if any, as required.
c) How to hold regular meetings with the parents and guardians and apprise them about the ability to learn, progress made in learning and any other relevant information about the child.

4) *Responsibility of Making the Curriculum of Teacher Education Institutions Inclusive in Nature*: In the RTE Act 2009, equity means equal opportunity for all children to complete elementary education irrespective of their gender, religion, caste, socio-economic, cultural, or linguistic background and geographical location. It cuts across the components of access, enrolment, retention and participation. While the RTE Act provides a legal entitlement for children belonging to disadvantaged groups and communities and weaker sections, their actual participation will require innovative and sustained measures integrated with mainstream interventions to ensure meaningful progress on equity. In order to pursue these measures, the teacher education institutions, teacher educators, educationists, NGOs and Central and State Government authorities collectively should strive to find newer ways of breaking the barriers that prevent the participation of children from these backgrounds. Hence, a multi-pronged strategy that includes advocacy, teacher training, curricular reform as well as community sensitization must be chalked out. So for as the curriculum reform of the teacher education institutions is concerned, it must be changed and it should be made more inclusive in nature. Particularly, the needs and aspirations of the downtrodden sections of the society, first generation learners, physically challenged persons and minorities must be included in the curriculum. Their characteristics, strength and weaknesses, etc. must be discussed in detail. The prospective teachers must also be sensitized about the needs of the inclusion and their constitutional responsibilities and obligations in this regard.

5) *Responsibility of Equipping the Prospective Teachers in Modern Teaching Methodologies*: The problem of Universalization of Elementary Education (UEE) lies less with enrolment and much more with retention. This is where a teacher has direct and active role to play. There are many factors, several of which lie outside the realm of the teacher and school, which result in drop outs. But a motivated teacher can do much to retain a student by establishing better relationship with the student, by establishing communication with parents and helping them see the value of educating their children, by providing remedial help and encouragement where needed, and above all, by making his/her own teaching interesting, relevant and effective. At this juncture of time, the teaching methodology has changed. New concepts, teaching models and strategies are in abundance. All these must be discussed with the prospective teachers in detail. The method of teaching that is being taught to the prospective teachers must be made more inclusive. Particularly, they must be trained in how to handle the slow learners, how to control the class through democratic means and how to maintain the discipline in a class of diverse population belonging to different religions, caste, socio-economic status, etc. in order to fulfil the requirements of the RTE Act. The teachers must also be trained to help each child to express his/her views freely and confidently.

6) *Responsibility of Giving Training to the Prospective Teachers to Organise Teaching Learning in the Natural Environment of the Child:* Nowadays, learning theories are focusing more on social environment/context from which learners and teachers come, because the social climate of the school and the classroom exert a deep impact on the process of learning. Learning is to be appreciated as occurring in shared social and everyday contexts. While on the subject of reading, it is important to point out that in preparing instructional materials for the primary school child, particularly at the early stages, every care must be taken to use words, which are close to the child's own linguistic background and environment. In this context, it is worthwhile to mention that a research project conducted by Homi Bhabha Centre for Science Education revealed that simplifying the language of exposition of science texts improved considerably the performance of the students and led to a much better teacher-pupil interaction in the classroom. Similarly, NCERT-UNESCO sponsored programme of Comprehensive Access to Primary Education (CAPE) has been designed in such a manner that it provides a method and approach to make education situational and contextual, so that it relates better to the needs and realities of the students.

Given these, there is need to provide a major shift from an overwhelming emphasis on the psychological characteristics of the individual learner to his/her social, cultural, political and economic context. All these concepts must be discussed in teacher training institutions in detail with the prospective teachers to provide them an insight into their required teaching behaviour in the classrooms. The teacher education programmes need to provide the space for engagement with issues and concerns of contemporary Indian society, its pluralistic nature and issues of identity, gender, equity and poverty. This can help the prospective teachers to contextualize education and evolve a deeper understanding of the purpose of education and its relationship with society. This will also help them in providing quality education to the students, which is one of the important goals of the RTE Act.

7) *Responsibility of Inculcating Values in the Prospective Teachers*: The RTE Act, 2009 demands some special qualities from the teachers and for this, the trainees must inculcate some values from the teacher educators, for example, order and punctuality, hard work and discipline, consideration for others, co-operation and team spirit, concern for the weak and disadvantaged and care for children. Qualities of responsibility and initiative are imbibed when opportunities are provided to them to act responsibly in situations and organize competently. For this, camps, excursions, various outdoor activities and exposure to various seminars, conferences, symposia, etc. must be provided to them by the teacher educators.

Furthermore, new textual materials and reference books concerning various provisions, implications and challenges of RTE Act, 2009, specially in the Indian languages, need to be produced by the teacher educators. Existing reading lists have to be updated to include the educational thought of contemporary Indian thinkers and the special nature of Indian society and the aspirations of her people. Discussions, tutorials, seminars, projects etc. should also be encouraged to stimulate thinking of the trainees.

8) *Responsibility of Maintaining Quality of the Teacher Education Programmes*: It is observed that some of the teacher education institutions charge capitation fees, thereby commercializing teacher education. The teachers, who have gone through this polluting mill and profited by it, can hardly be expected to stand for high principles of rectitude and correct behaviour. Moreover, majority of our teacher education institutions are woefully inadequate in the context of changing needs of India today. The minimum requirement of teachers' training programme is that it should enable the trainee to acquire the basic skills and competencies of a good teacher, such as; to communicate ideas logically and with clarity; to use the technology available to make teaching effective; to organize educative experiences outside of class and to learn to work with the community and help the students to do so.

Apart from these normal expectations, the RTE Act expects from tomorrow's teacher that they will translate the national goals into educational actions. The teacher has to communicate to his/her pupils the importance of and the feeling for national integrity and unity; the need for a scientific attitude; a commitment to excellence in standards of work and a concern for the society. At a global level, he/she should have an understanding of population explosion, environmental pollution, climate change, bio diversity, extinction of flora and fauna, need of sustainable development, the threat of a nuclear holocaust and the quest for world peace. UGC, NCERT, NCTE and other Central and State Government institutions must ensure that the teacher education institutions are delivering quality to the teacher education programmes by imbibing in the teachers the right attitudes and values besides making them proficient in the skills related to teaching.

9) *Responsibility of Maintaining a Close Link with the Schools*: The teacher education institutions send their students in the schools for practice teaching, which lasts only for one month or forty days. Unless and until there is a close link between these institutions and the schools, the prospective teachers will be unable to know various requirements of the schools in the context of the RTE Act. For this, the trainees must be sent for internship. They must be there in the schools for the full working day and should observe the functioning of the schools very minutely. In this regard, the observation of the Education Commission (Kothari Commission) (1964-66) may be very relevant even today, which says, "Make student-teaching a comprehensive internship in which trainees are able to observe the entire work of the school and to participate actively in all the professional activities of a teacher, both

in and out of the class room. Such comprehensive and fruitful internship will be possible only when there is a systematic collaboration and cooperation between the schools and the training institutions and when student-teaching is regarded as the joint responsibility of the training institutions and the schools."

10) *Responsibility of Maintaining a Close Link with the Society*: It is a bitter truth that the vast majority of our children come to school from those homes that are illiterate and poor and the case for schooling and learning preparedness for those children needs no special advocacy. Moreover, it is also known that the first five or six years of schooling forms the most crucial period for the all round development of the child and he/she must be helped to awaken his/her senses and open his/her mind to the world around him/her and learn to relate to nature, to people, and to the environment and be socially and emotionally integrated. The target set for the notion of education for all in the RTE Act, 2009 can be achieved only when the resources of the community and of the society are mobilized to the full extent and there is a mass movement and the creation of a national fervour for education among all sections of the people. Hence, the teacher training institutions must develop a close link with the society (either directly or through the schools) and sought the help of various trade unions, kisan sabhas, political outfits, philanthropist organizations, non-governmental organizations, media and industries. Only in that situation, they will be able to develop a kind of awareness among the masses about the various provisions of the RTE Act, 2009.

11) *Responsibility of Giving Training to the Prospective Teachers to Coordinate Properly with Various Members of School Management Committee:* The constitution of School Management Committee (SMC) in each school for planning, monitoring and implementation of Sarva Shiksha Abhiyan schemes is one of the most important features of the RTE Act, 2009. According to the Act, seventy five percent of the strength of the School Management Committee shall be from amongst parents or guardians of children provided fifty percent of committee shall be women and proportionate representation shall be given to the parents or guardians of children belonging to disadvantaged groups and weaker sections. To manage its affairs, the School Management Committee shall elect a Chairperson and Vice Chairperson from among the parent members. The Head teacher of the school or where the school does not have a head teacher, the senior most teacher of the school shall be the ex-officio Member-Convener of the School Management Committee. The School Management Committee shall meet at least once a month and the minutes and decisions of the meetings shall be properly recorded and made available to the public. The important functions of School Management Committee will be as following:

a) To ensure regularity and punctuality in attendance by teachers of the school.
b) To assess the learning ability of each child and accordingly supplement additional instructions, if any required.
c) To ensure the enrolment and continued attendance of all the children from the neighbourhood of the school.
d) To bring to the notice of the Local Education Authority any deviation from the rights of the child, in particular, mental and physical harassment of the children, denial of admission and timely provision of free entitlements.
e) To communicate in simple and creative ways to the population in the neighbourhood of the school, the rights of the child as enunciated in the Act as also the duties of the appropriate government, local authority, school, parents and guardian.
f) To ensure that no child shall be liable to pay any kind of fee or charges or expenses, which may prevent him or her from pursuing and completing the elementary education.
g) To identify the needs, prepare a plan, and monitor the implementation of the provisions, where a child above six years of age has not been admitted in any school or though admitted, could not complete his or her elementary education, then, he or she shall be admitted in a class appropriate to his or her age.
h) To monitor the identification and enrolment of Children with Special Needs (CWSN) and mobilize facilities for education of children with disability, as per Persons with Disabilities Act, 1995 and ensure their participation in and completion of elementary education.
i) To list out specifications for equitable quality of education in a school.
j) To monitor the implementation of the mid-day meal scheme in the school.
k) To ensure that no teacher shall engage himself or herself in private tuitions or private teaching activities.
l) The School Management Committee shall prepare a School Development Plan at least three months before the end of the financial year in which it is first constituted under the Act.
m) Monitor that teachers are not burdened with non-academic duties other than those specified in Section 27. No teacher shall be deployed for any non-educational purposes other than the decennial population census, disaster relief duties or duties related to elections to the local authority or the state legislatures or parliament, as the case may be.
n) Assess financial requirements and needs of the RTE Act 2009, including for providing special training facility specified in Section 4. Entitlements of children, such as free text books and uniforms,

and any other additional requirement for fulfilling the responsibilities of the school under the Act.

o) Monitoring of utilisation of the grants received from the appropriate Government or Local authority or any other source.

Keeping in mind the importance and functions of the SMC and the diverse background of its members, it is inevitable that if the teachers are not trained properly to manage a balance with other members of the SMC, then a tussle and tug of war may occur and the progress of the school will be hampered. Hence, it is the sacred duty of the teacher education institutions to give the training to the prospective teachers, so that the SMC may perform its duties smoothly as is required by the RTE Act, 2009.

12) *Responsibility of Giving Training to the Prospective Teachers for Conducting Internal Evaluation Properly*: The Act mandates a system of evaluation that is free of the oppression of annual exams and is based on the principle of Continuous and Comprehensive Evaluation (CCE), which means:

a) No failure till completion of elementary education.
b) Evaluation to be done throughout the year and not to be based on an annual exam.
c) Teachers to maintain Pupil Cummulative: Record (PCR) for every child.
d) Evaluation to be on "comprehensive" performance of child, reflecting all facets, talents of the child and not to be based on just a few subject areas. The PCR needs to include music, theatre, leadership skills, social skills etc., as well.

In this context, it is the responsibility of the teacher education institutions to train the prospective teachers in conducting the comprehensive and continuous internal evaluation. The prospective teachers must be properly trained on how to maintain Pupil Cummulative: Record (PCR) for every child as well as how to conduct the evaluation on the "comprehensive" performance of child, reflecting all facets, talents of the child and not to be based on just a few subject areas. How the performance in music, theatre, leadership skills, social skills, etc., will be maintained in PCR has also be told to the prospective teachers.

13) *Responsibility of Ensuring No Denial of Admission to the Children Belonging to the Poor Section of the Society by the Private Schools*: The RTE Act, 2009 ensures at least 25 per cent admission of the poor section of the society in private schools. If the private schools fail to ensure this, then, legal action can be taken against them. What action and consequences will be there, this must be very clear in the mind of the prospective teachers. Hence, a kind of awareness about this must be developed in the mind of the prospective

teachers in the teacher education institutions. It may happen that a few of these teachers may teach in the private schools, and then, they will be able to convince their management to follow the norms of the Act in this regard.

14) *Responsibility of Ensuring Minimum Level of Learning*: The RTE Act, 2009 ensures that no child will be held back in the same class, i.e., each and every child has to be promoted to the next class whether he/she clears the exams or not. This requires a lot of hard work on the part of the teachers, as they have to ensure that the child has received minimum level of learning (MLL), necessary to be comfortable in the next class. The teacher education institutions should train the prospective teachers for that. Before going to the practicing schools, they should be very clearly told what the meaning of MLL is and what steps have to be taken to ensure MLL in a particular class/course.

15) *Responsibility of Conducting Various Action Researches*: The teacher education institutions should conduct various action researches as to how to successfully implement various provisions of the RTE Act, 2009. The teacher educators and the pupil teachers should visit the schools in the vicinity of the teacher education institutions regularly and conduct action research to suggest solutions to the problems faced by the schools in this context. They must also provide extension services to the schools as opined by the Education Commission (Kothari Commission) (1964-66), "Every training institution should be required to guide neighbourhood schools and their staff in planning their work and in using improved methods of teaching. Such extension work is needed as much for the improvement of schools as for the improvement of the training programme itself."

16) *Responsibility of Training the Prospective Teachers in the Constructivist Approach of Learning*: Now-a-days, much focus is on constructive approach of learning and NCF, 2005 also recommends it. According to this approach, the teacher will be a facilitator of learning and not simply the presenter of facts and transmitter of knowledge to the passive recipients. The teacher has to work towards creating a variety of learning experiences in and out of classroom that enable the children to construct knowledge from activities and experiences in day to day life. The teacher has to make personal interaction between him/her and the students. If the teachers want to apply this theory in their classrooms, then, the most important quality they have to develop among the students is sincerity and good habits of thinking and imagination. His/her curiosity must neither be postponed nor must he/she be scolded. The teacher should ensure that the student gradually begins to become aware of his/her deeper self and that with his/her growing awareness, he/she is able to harmonise and resolve his/her inner conflicts. Thus, research projects must be carried out by the teacher education institutions on constructive approach of learning, which could help in the modification of

methodology according to the need of the students and would help to create a healthy environment in the schools as expected in the Act.

17) *Responsibility of Training the Prospective Teachers in Utilising ICT Resources*: ICT has a lot of scope in fulfilling various provisions of the RTE Act, 2009. Particularly, it may be helpful in the following situations:

a) Helping the teachers through flexible models of reaching curricular goals;
b) Enabling the teachers to access various sources of knowledge and to create knowledge; and
c) Making the teaching and learning effective and interesting and, hence ensuring the retention.

Hence, it becomes necessary for every teacher education institution to ensure that every prospective teacher is well versed in handling various instruments related with ICT and a proper training in ICT is a prerequisite. Particularly, the prospective teachers should be trained to:

a) Use computer as a presentation tool
b) Use computer as a tutor
c) Use computer as a cognitive tool
d) Plan and conduct a computer based lesson (CBL), and
e) Prepare slides for power point presentations

18) *Responsibility of Ensuring the Selection of Suitable Candidates for the Teaching Profession*: If the teacher education institutions could find some methods to attract persons of ability and of character to the teaching profession, prevent the recruitment of the unsuitable, and purge the profession of the incompetent, the standards of education in this country would improve very rapidly. Hence, in the context of the RTE Act, the teacher education institutions must ensure that they are selecting those teachers, who love teaching, enjoy the company of children and are motivated to work for the welfare of the children and are willing to teach. For this, the selection procedure has to be modified and the following characteristics have to be looked for while selecting a teacher for the teacher training courses:

a) A good physique,
b) Linguistic ability and communication skills,
c) A fair degree of general mental ability,
d) General awareness of the world,
e) A positive outlook on life, and
f) A capacity for good human relationship.

A few of these can be tested objectively through tests and rating scales, but there are others that require well-designed interviews by a body chosen for their vision, impartiality and expertise in the field. Small group discussions may also prove to be a useful technique in judging the capacity for listening to others, articulation, adaptability and leadership. The procedure suggested for the selection of the candidates for the teacher training courses may take time, but it would be well worthwhile.

19) *Responsibility of Refreshing the Skills of In-Service Teachers*: The teacher training institutions must refresh the skills of in-service teachers by organizing various training courses, workshops, seminars, conferences and symposia for them. These institutions must create a system of lifelong professional development and support the headmasters, teachers and principals. They should focus on ICT literacy; shaping communication, problem solving and trade skills in the desired manner; organizing group discussions; to be responsible for the learning and enhancing creativity in educational work.

20) *Responsibility of Coordinating Properly with the Private Schools*: The teacher education institutions should take the cooperation of those private schools, which have a proven track record in providing sound education and have the potential for playing a significant role in enabling shifts in the government education system towards a more child-friendly and teacher-friendly education system. Particularly, their cooperation must be sought in:

a) Preparing an age-appropriate curriculum with a significant amount of local content that children, teachers and parents can relate to.
b) Organising the curriculum as a learning continuum that is mapped out in accordance with progressively organised learning goals in various curricular areas.
c) Preparing teaching-learning materials for smaller, sequential curricular units, and participation of teachers in selecting and/or constructing appropriate teaching-learning materials.
d) Preparing assessment strategies that are both diagnostic and suggestive of remedial steps.
e) Making a shift in the teacher's role as a facilitator of each student's learning, which implies a shift in the relationship between teachers and students to one of cooperation and support. This would enhance the quality of the learning in government schools and make the overall education system more receptive to the implementation of the RTE Act.
f) Supporting practical components in teacher training because the task of preparing a large number of trained teachers in the next five years, as well as re-orienting and motivating existing teachers, as envisaged by the RTE Act, is indeed a huge one. It would, thus, be a desirable step to identify and take support from the selected private schools,

which have sound curricular and pedagogic practices, to set up facilities for conducting teacher enrichment programmes.

g) Making the inclusion of children of the poor in mainstream education possible. To let it happen, school managements should be convinced to work towards some basic shifts in their orientation and structuring of support for culturally diverse sets of children. Alongside this, a shift in sensibilities of teachers, other students and their parents will be needed, if underprivileged students are to have a worthwhile educational experience in private schools. Teacher education institutions can do this in the best possible manner if they establish a close link with private schools.

References

1. Comprehensive Access to Primary Education (CAPE). www.ncert.nic.in/rightside/links/pdf/./annual_report_10-11.pdf.
2. Government of India (1966). Education and National Development: Report of Education Commission. New Delhi: Ministry of Education.
3. Government of India (1986). National Policy on Education. New Delhi: Ministry of Human Resource Development.
4. Government of India (1992). Programme of Action. New Delhi: Ministry of Human Resource Development.
5. Government of India (1996). The Persons with Disabilities (Equal Opportunities, Protection of Rights and Full Participation) Act, 1995. New Delhi: Ministry of Law and Justice.
6. Homi Bhabha Centre for Science Education, Tata Institute of Fundamental Research, Mumbai. www.hbsce.tifr.res.in.
7. Millennium Development Goals. www.un.org/millenniumgoals/.
8. National Curriculum Framework, 2005. New Delhi: National Council of Educational Research and Training, Publication Department.
9. Right of Children to Free and Compulsory Education Act, 2009. MHRD, New Delhi. www.delta.org.in/form/rte.pdf.

12

The Perception of Teachers

An Important Factor in Determining the Success of RTE

Manju Negi, Sonal Chabra and *Ravneet Gaur*

Education is a power, which imbibes the values of tolerance, solidarity and cooperation. Modern education reforms are increasingly driven by a growing understanding of what works in education and how to go about successfully improving teaching and learning in schools. Every citizen of India has the right to education. Some of the basic principles, which guide us, are—education shall be free, at least in the elementary and fundamental stages; elementary education shall be compulsory; technical and professional education shall be made generally available and higher education shall be equally accessible to all on the basis of merit. Social justice and equity are by themselves a strong argument for providing basic education for all. It is an established fact that basic education improves the level of human well-being, especially with regard to life expectancy, infant mortality, nutritional status of children, etc. Studies have shown that universal basic education significantly contributes to economic growth. Elementary education in India means eight years of schooling from the age of six. Elementary education is the foundation on which the development of every citizen and the nation as a whole is built on. In recent past, India has made huge progress in terms of increasing primary education enrolment, retention, regular attendance rate and expanding literacy to approximately two thirds of the population. India's improved education system is often cited as one of the main contributors to the economic development of India. At the same time, the quality of elementary education in India has also been a major concern.

The present educational system of India is an implantation of British rulers. Wood's Dispatch of 1854 laid the foundation of present system of education in India. This was followed by efforts made by Maharaja of Baroda (now known as Vadodara) when he introduced compulsory education for boys in Amreli Taluk in 1893 and later extended it to the whole state by passing an

Act in 1906. Later in 1917, Shri Vithalbhai Patel was successful in getting the Bill on compulsory education passed. This Act was first of its kind and is popularly known as the Patel Act. This was followed by several Compulsory Education Acts in the country; however, the Hartog Committee's (1930) recommendation for better quality education hindered the further spread and development of primary education, for some years, just before independence.

The present RTE Act has its history in the drafting of the Indian Constitution at the time of Independence, but more specifically to the Constitutional Amendment that included Article 21A in the Indian Constitution making education a fundamental right. The Supreme Court in the case *Unnikrishnan vs. State of Andhra Pradesh* (1993) ruled that the Right to Education is a fundamental right that flow from the Right to Life in Article 21 of the Indian Constitution. Following this ruling, the 86th Constitutional Amendment Act 2002 added Article 21A stating, "The State shall provide free and compulsory education to all children of the age of six to fourteen years in such manner as the State may, by law, determine." The 86th Amendment also modified Article 45, which now reads as "The State shall endeavour to provide early childhood care and education for all children until they complete the age of 16 years." The rough draft of the Bill was composed in year 2005. It received much opposition due to its mandatory provision to provide 25 per cent reservation for disadvantaged children in private schools.

The sub-committee of the Central Advisory Board of Education, which prepared the draft Bill, held this provision as a significant prerequisite for creating a democratic and egalitarian society. The Indian Law Commission had initially proposed 50 per cent reservation for disadvantaged students in private schools. The Bill was approved by the Parliament *http://en.wikipedia.org/wiki/Union_Council_of_Ministers_of_India* on 2 July 2009 and on 4 August 2009; it received the Presidential assent and was notified as law on 3 September 2009 as The Children's Right to Free and Compulsory Education Act. The law came into effect in the whole of India except the state of Jammu and Kashmir from 1 April 2010, the first time in the history of India a law was brought into force by a speech by the Prime Minister. The Right of Children to Free and Compulsory Education Act has come into force from 1 April 2010. This is a historic day for the people of India as from this day, the Right to Education will be accorded the same legal status as the Right to Life as provided by Article 21A of the Indian Constitution. Every child in the age group of 6-14 years will be provided eight years of elementary education in an age appropriate classroom in the vicinity of his/her neighbourhood.

The UN Children's Fund (UNICEF) estimates that there are eight million children in this age group, mostly girls, who are out-of-school in India. "Tens of millions of children will benefit from this initiative ensuring quality education with equity," said UNICEF Representative in India, Karin Hulshof.

The Right to Education Act will "propel India to even greater heights of prosperity and productivity for all, guaranteeing children their right to a quality education and a brighter future," she added. UNICEF pointed out in a news release that without India, the world cannot reach the Millennium Development Goal (MDG) of having every child complete primary school by 2015. "This Act is an essential step towards improving each child's accessibility to secondary and higher education, bringing India closer to achieving national educational development goals, as well as the MDGs and Education for All (EFA)," said UNESCO New Delhi Director, Armoogum Parsuramen.

The Study

Education has always been an issue in India even before India got independence questions were being raised to educate the masses. The reformers of late 18th century always felt that only education would break the shackles of poverty, superstition, casteism, practice of sati, child marriage, dowry and other such evil prevalent in the Indian society, but the change could be only brought about in the higher section of the society. When Indian Constitution was drafted, one of the Directive Principle of the State was to protect the right of the people to live with dignity when he is educated. Article 45 of the Directive Principles of State Policy effectively stated, "The State shall endeavour to provide, within a period of ten years from the commencement of this Constitution, for free and compulsory education for all children until they complete the age of fourteen years." Policy level changes are definitely needed to improve the educational status of any country and especially for a nation like India, which is rich in diversity and is inclusive at the same time. It needs to be appreciated here that these policy level changes in books and papers alone cannot bring the much desired change until developments happen at the grassroots level. At the most basic level, it is the teachers, who are ultimately working for the cause. Thus, it becomes essential to ascertain the opinion of the teachers regarding the concerned right.

In the discussed study, the researchers studied the background, legal provisions, need, importance and implementation of Right to Education Act with a focus on the view of teachers towards the status of free and compulsory education in India, role of private schools in providing free and compulsory education, need, importance and success of the Children's Right to Free and Compulsory Education Act.

Objectives: The main objectives of the study are as follows:

- To study the perception of teachers toward free and compulsory education in India.
- To study the perception of teachers towards the role of private schools in free and compulsory education.

- To study the perception of teachers towards the need of Right of Education Act.
- To study the perception of teachers towards the importance of Right to Education Act.
- To study the perception of teachers towards the success of Right to Education Act.

Methodology: For the present study, the researchers used the Descriptive Survey Method to ascertain the opinion of the teachers.

***Sample and Sampling Technique*:** A sample of 100 teachers teaching elementary classes was purposively selected from ten privately managed schools of Delhi.

***Tools*:** As the RTE is relatively a newer research area, the researchers were unable to find a standardized tool related to the perception of teacher towards RTE. Therefore, a self-made questionnaire was used for collecting the data. The questionnaire consists of 25 questions and each question had five responses, i.e., strongly agree, agree, disagree, strongly disagree and can't say.

***Data Analysis*:** The responses of the teachers to all the 25 questions were analyzed.

Results and Findings

The main findings from the research have been encapsulated under the following points for better comprehensibility of the readers.

- About 50 per cent teachers strongly agree that Right to Free and Compulsory Education will improve the quality of education, which will definitely improve the quality of life. 61 per cent teachers were in favour that RTE will help in the reduction of child labour. It is possible only when there will be awareness among the people about RTE, specially parents are forced to send the children to school.
- Teachers believed that it is financially viable for weak parents. Parents of weaker section can finally realize their dream of providing elementary education to their children without any financial strain.
- Majority of teachers believed that the proper implementation of provisions of RTE will improve educational services and incidence of private tuitions and coaching can be limited. 41 per cent teachers strongly agreed to it, 37 per cent teachers agreed that RTE will help in prohibiting private tuitions.
- Sixty-two per cent teachers strongly agreed and 21 per cent teachers agreed that readmission of out of school children will make teachers' task challenging. Further, maximum (76%) teachers were of the opinion that because of lack of formal and systematic education, it is very difficult for a non-enrolled child to be admitted in the age

appropriate grade to cope with rest of the class. The provision for special training of school drop-outs to bring them at par with students of the same age is not an easy task.

- Eighty-nine per cent teachers collectively agreed that without examination system, the quality of education will be definitely affected. Further, 44 per cent teachers strongly agreed, 33 per cent teachers agreed that Continuous and Comprehensive Evaluation (CCE) provides ample opportunity for the child's development. However, they held that CCE does not treat academically bright students and weak students at par. 83 per cent teachers were in favour that distribution of weightage of assignments and projects is not a fair treatment with bright students. Since most projects are group based and if assignments are not done in strictly controlled environment, then, it is not fair to academically sincere students.
- Seventy-seven per cent of teachers opined that CCE gives the child an opportunity to grow despite of his learning abilities or disabilities. It will definitely help in enhancing the all-round development of the students.
- More than 50 per cent teachers believed that there should be penal provisions for parents not sending their children to school. The RTE Act is the first legislation in the world that puts the responsibility of ensuring enrolment, attendance and completion on the Government. It is the parents' responsibility to send the children to schools and the collective efforts of all the beneficiaries involved can bring it to success.
- Maximum (74%) teachers said that Ban on Corporal punishment will help in emotional development of the child. It will definitely prove helpful in enhancing the all-round development of the students. However, 61 per cent teachers were of the opinion that prohibition on punishment will make the child more undisciplined.
- Very few teachers were in favour of inclusive education. Bringing the children with special needs in mainstream education is not fair for academically bright students. It makes the teachers' task very difficult to deal with the needs of special children as well as normal children.
- Seventy per cent teachers were of the opinion that lack of proper implementation of RTE cannot realize the dream. Proper implementation of RTE is a must for its success. The cooperation of all the people involved in the education process is required to make it successful.

Educational Implications of the Study

The implications of the present study are as follows:

- There is need of awareness and acceptance among the people about RTE, as majority of people are living below the poverty line and look upon their children as the ones, who can be relied upon to bring the much needed extra income. RTE will ensure that every child between the ages of six to fourteen years has the right to free and compulsory education in a school. It will improve the quality of education, which will definitely improve the quality of life of people. It is possible only when there will be awareness among the people about RTE, specially parents are forced to send the children to school.
- It requires all private schools to reserve 25 per cent of seats for children from poor families. It also prohibits all unrecognized schools to continue and makes provisions for no donation or capitation fees and no interview of the child or parent at the time of admission.
- Teachers were of opinion that because of lack of formal and systematic education, it is very difficult for a non-enrolled child to be admitted in the age appropriate grade to cope with the rest of the class. The sincere efforts should be taken by the concerned authority for special training of school drop-outs to bring them at par with students of the same age. The most serious efforts of teachers are needed to make it successful.

Majority of teachers were of opinion that lack of proper implementation of RTE cannot realize the dream. Proper implementation of RTE is a must for its success. The cooperation of all the people involved in the education process is required to make it successful.

Conclusion

"Constitutional mechanisms play an essential role in protecting and enforcing the right to education as an entitlement. The enforcement of legal mechanisms guaranteeing equality of opportunity in education is crucial in safeguarding such entitlement. In India, jurisprudence also underlines State obligations relating to the right to education and the equality of educational opportunities. Teachers and administrators concerned have been facing various problems during implementation of RTE" (Bhardwaj, Thareja and Chabra, 2011). RTE has been enforced, however, historical evidence suggests that what brought about universal basic education in the developed world, were not legal measures, but a persistent social movement viewing basic education as an integral component of establishing a democratic social policy. Similarly, *the challenge in RTE implementation is changing the mindsets of teachers, parents and the school management.* In conclusion, it may be stated that the solution lies in enhanced social mobilization and focused advocacy.

References

1. Bhardwaj, S.; Thareja, V. and Chabra, S. (2011). Awareness of Right to Education Act Among the Primary School Teachers, *Global Researcher*, Vol. 1, No. 2, October 2011.
2. Desai, D.M. (1995). *Universal, Compulsory and Free Primary Education in India*. Bombay: Indian Institute of Education.
3. Devan, K. (2011). Development of the Right to Education in India, *Indian Journal of Adult Education*, Vol. 72 (2), 93-98.
4. Juneja, Nalini (1996). *Compulsory Education in India: The Policy in Practice*. New Delhi: National Institute of Educational Planning and Administration.
5. Naik, J.P. (1995). *Equality, Quality and Quantity: The Elusive Triangle in Indian Education*. New Delhi: Allied publishers.
6. Sadgopal, Anil (2006). *Dilution, Distortion and Diversion: A Post-Jomtien Reflection on the Educational Policy*. In Kumar, Ravi (ed.) New Delhi: Sage publications.
7. Tomasevski, K. (2003) *Education Denied: Costs and Remedies*. London: Zed Books.

13

The Right to Education and Scheduled Castes and Scheduled Tribes

Surveying the Landscape from Below

Talmeez Fatma Naqvi

We are in the era of knowledge society and knowledge economy, which indeed is marked by singular importance of Education as being the most important event of the individual and national development in terms of social and economic aspects. Taking cognizance of this fact, the World Bank underlines the importance of education in unequivocal terms by asserting that it is "important determinant of individual's income, health (and that of their children) and capacity to interact and communicate with others. Inequality in education, thus, contributes to inequality in other important dimensions of wellbeing. Measuring inequality in education is not an easy task" (World Bank—Equity and Development, World Development Report, 2006). In view of above, the Education for All has become a global phenomenon. India is no exception.

India has made a concrete effort to address the issue of providing free and compulsory quality education by amending its Constitution to make quality elementary education the right of every child, thereby strengthening the legal framework for providing free and compulsory quality elementary education for all the country's children.

The Vision

It is worth recalling that Education for All movement is a global commitment to provide quality basic education for all children, youth and adults. The movement was launched at the *World Conference on Education for All (EFA)* in 1990 in Jomtien, Thailand, when representatives of the international community agreed to universalize primary education and massively reduce illiteracy by the end of the decade. From this conference, the *World Declaration on Education for All* was adopted, which stressed that education is a fundamental human right and, therefore, asked countries to strengthen their efforts to improve education in order to ensure the basic learning needs for all were met. The international community affirmed its commitment again in 2000, in Dakar, Senegal, to achieve Education for All by the year 2015. The reaffirmation was necessitated by the fact that despite the efforts since Jomtien, the global situation of education remained unsatisfactory: Worldwide, there were then 113 million children, 60 per cent of them girls, who were not going to school. At least 880 million adults were illiterate, two-thirds of them women. Since education is a fundamental human right, this is unacceptable. With this in mind, 164 nations, including India agreed at the Dakar conference to the Dakar Framework for Action, which set six goals for EFA. The target devoted to primary education sought to ensure that by 2015, all children, particularly girls, children in difficult circumstances, and those belonging to ethnic minorities, have access to and complete free and compulsory primary education of good quality. However, in spite of all the commitments made by the member nations in Dakar, millions of children still remained deprived of educational opportunities, especially free and compulsory quality basic education.

By declaring education a fundamental right enshrined in its Constitution, India has taken the right step in the right direction to ensure what the global community has mandated to achieve. The question, however, remains if the country has been able to take the benefits of the provision to the oppressed and poor sections of society in letter and spirit and, if not, why.

India's visionary academicians and politicians flatter themselves in the political mirror with high words, "We have created a near political utopia where there are these wonderful rights – right to work, education and food. We are proud of the caring and sensitive state we are building." Of course, the significance of social access in universalising elementary education needs no emphasis any further.

The Scenario

It is an undeniable fact also that India is a multi-cultural society marked by numerous regional and local variants. Here, the hierarchies based on caste, economic status and gender are prominent features, which deeply influence children's access to education. As per the egalitarian framework of our Constitution, the state as well as schools are required to respect India's diversity and plurality, and appreciate differences arising out of uneven social and economic development. Among these variants, the caste system is the foremost facet of the Indian society, observes Dr. K.S. Ingole. Ingole's critical study of social exclusion and its implication underlines the fact that caste not only reflects in social life of Indian people, but the economic and political behaviours of people are also governed by the caste system.

The caste system is the backbone of the Hindu society. A person can change his religion, class and, now even gender, but not caste. Dr. B.R. Ambedkar observed: by the Hindu social system, the communities are placed in an ascending scale of reverence and a descending scale of contempt. The Hindu caste system is a pyramid like social structure in which majority of the lowest castes are forcibly kept at the bottom of the pyramid, condemned to manual professions and forced to serve the castes above them. According to him, Brahmins were the originators of this unnatural institution founded and maintained through unnatural means. The Government of India's Anthropological Survey of India (ASI), undertaken under the leadership of K.S. Singh, brought out a series of publications, titled '*The People of India*'. This project identified 2800 castes including 450 SC, 461 ST and 766 OBC. It concludes that the caste continues to be the basic building brick of Indian society. This historic verdict of the ASI project did not get any publicity in India's press because the ruling class is shy of admitting this fact, which has made them the rulers (Rajshekar 2002). Dalit Vice Editor, Mr. V.T.Rajshekar says, "Almost all political party leaders be they nationalists, socialists, communists and Hindu Nazi, have uniform opinion on caste, 'caste is bad and hence it has to be destroyed. Indian scholars and researchers have produced considerable literature to prove that caste is non-existent'. They believed and made others believe that with economic development, the superficial "caste" could be eradicated. Based on this belief, our planners and rulers introduced hundreds of welfare schemes and invested thousands of crore of rupees on these schemes. All these economic programs proved an utter failure" (Rajshekar 2002). What Mr. Rajshekar says is true because, caste system yet persists in India and functions in a well-organized manner.

Discrimination is an inseparable ingredient that is the spring-board of caste system. Though the Indian constitution provides some preferential schemes designed to stop discrimination against the Scheduled Castes/ Scheduled Tribes hitherto, mayhem against them continue unabated. The provision in the Constitution resolves, "The state shall not discriminate against any citizen on grounds of religion, race, caste, place and birth or any form." In the Directive Principles, it adds that the "state shall promote with special care the educational and economic interest of the Scheduled Castes/Tribes and shall protect them from social injustice and all forms of exploitation."

The Right of Children to Free and Compulsory Education (RTE) Act, 2009, which has come into force with effect from 1 April 2010, prohibits 'physical punishment' and 'mental harassment' under Section 17(1) and makes it a punishable offence under Section 17(2). These provisions read as follows:

- Prohibition of physical punishment and mental harassment to child—(1) No child shall be subjected to physical punishment or mental harassment. (2) Whoever contravenes the provisions of Sub-section (1) shall be liable to disciplinary action under the service rules applicable to such person.

- Sections 8 and 9 of the RTE Act place a duty on the appropriate Government and the local authority to "ensure that the child belonging to weaker section and the child belonging to disadvantaged group are not discriminated against and prevented from pursuing and completing elementary education on any grounds."
- The RTE Act does not preclude the application of other legislation that relates to the violation of the rights of the child, for example, booking the offenses under the IPC and the SC and ST.

Prevention of Atrocities Act of 1989

- As required under Section 32(1) of the RTE Act, State Governments and UT Administrations should designate appropriate 'local authority' and notify the same to all concerned for the purpose of redressing the grievances relating to corporal punishment and discrimination. Such 'local authority' should be a member of the District Child Protection Society (DCPS), which exists under the Integrated Child Protection Scheme (ICPS) and is headed by the District Collector/ Magistrate/Deputy Commissioner.
- The DCPS should function as the District Level Committee for the purpose of corporal punishment under the Chairpersonship of the District Collector/Magistrate/Deputy Commissioner and the concerned.
- Sub-divisional Magistrate (SDM) should be its ex officio Member Secretary/Convener. The District Collector/Magistrate/Deputy Commissioner should receive the complaints of physical punishment, mental harassment and discrimination in schools and get these redressed within a reasonable timeframe.

Caste-based Obstinacy

But and despite all these provisions, caste based discrimination still continues, notes K.S. Ingole. The question arises as to why the constitutional provisions have not been appropriately and effectively translated into action. It is presumably because the depressed castes are not in the capacity to implement the provisions made in the Constitution. The crucial political, social and economic powers are vested in the hands of upper caste Hindus. As upper caste Hindus did enjoy power by virtue of the caste system, they do not want to implement the Constitutional provisions for serving their own vested interests. What Dr. Babasaheb Ambedkar, the champion of human rights, once said is largely true even today. He said: "Millions of people living in the midst of civilization are still in a savage state and are leading the life of hereditary criminals. But the Hindus have never felt ashamed of it. This is a phenomenon, which in my view is quite unparalleled." Consequently, the law-enforcement machinery and the political class have united to put off the depressed castes from utilizing programmes designed for them. The statistics speak for themselves.

Caste discrimination not only hinders SC/ST children from attending school, but also affects the quality of education they receive. Available data shows that the progress of schooling among Dalit children between the ages of 6-14 has been low and drop-out rate among them is very high as compared to that of the general population. The overall literacy rate for Scheduled Castes increased from a mere 2.3 per cent in 1941 to 54.7 per cent in 2001. Despite this impressive increase in the literacy in 2001, it remained less than the corresponding general literacy rate of the country (65.6%) as a whole. The perpetuation of inequalities even in terms of basic ability to read and write is alarmingly high. A look into the basic statistical information shows that the drop-out rates of the Scheduled Caste children are still high. The drop-out rate for the Scheduled Caste children was 30.09 per cent in the classes I-V, but it is very high at 52.47 per cent, if the classes I-VIII are taken together. It is still higher, (68.42), if it is taken for classes I-X. There is a higher drop-out rate in the higher classes (Table 13.1). The report, prepared by the National University of Educational Planning and Administration (NUEPA) said that enrolment rate among SC decreased to 19.06 per cent in 2010-11 as compared to 19.81 during 2009-10. Enrolment rate among ST also dipped to 10.70 per cent in 2010-11 from 10.93 per cent in 2009-10, said the report, which tracks the progress of states towards providing universal elementary education. It said among the OBCs, the enrolment at primary level was 40.09 per cent in 2010-11 as compared to 42.15 in 2009-10, underpinning a concerted effort from the government to address the issue (NUEPA, 2013).

According to the same report, Muslim enrolment at the primary level stood at 13.04 per cent (2013), down from 13.48 per cent registered in 2009-10.

Table 13.1: Drop-out Rates of General Population and Scheduled Castes in India

Classes	*General Population*			*Scheduled Castes*		
	Boys	*Girls*	*Total*	*Boys*	*Girls*	*Total*
I–V	25.70	24.41	25.09	34.37	24.52	30.09
I–VIII	43.72	41.34	42.68	53.56	51.12	52.47
I–X	56.55	57.33	56.71	68.05	68.90	68.42

Source: Selected Educational Statistics, 2007-08.

However, it said overall enrolment in schools between class I and V showed a marked improvement (18,02,476) standing at 13,52,07,057 in 2010-11 as compared to 13,34,05,581 in 2009-10. Similarly, enrolment in classes VI-VIII rose by 33,77,527 as it stood at 5,78,44,942 in 2010-11 as against 5,44,67,415 in 2009-10, the report said. The study was based on the data received from as many as 1.36 million schools spread over 637 districts across 35 states.

Prejudiced Self-conceit

Do the down trodden, oppressed, the poor or the SCs and STs and ethnic minorities have inferior brain structure or lower average intelligence? The opinion that there are differences in the brain structures or sizes of different racial and ethnic groups was widely held and studied during the 19th and early 20th centuries. During these centuries, research on race and intelligence was often used to claim that one race was superior to another, justifying the poor status and treatment of the "inferior" race. The writings of Sir Francis Galton, a psycho-metrician and Polymath (1822-1911) spurred interest in the study of mental abilities, particularly as they relate to heredity and eugenics. Galton claimed that the African people were significantly below Anglo-Saxons' position in the normal frequency distribution of general mental ability; these claims continue to spark a good deal of controversy in academia even today.

The most controversial and most publicized part of the debate is whether group IQ differences also reflect a genetic component. Hereditarianism hypothesizes that a genetic contribution to intelligence could include genes linked to neuron structure or function, brain size or metabolism, or other physiological differences, which could vary with bio-geographic ancestry.

The book *Inequality by Design: Cracking the Bell Curve Myth* claims that it is not lower average intelligence that leads to the lower status of ethnic minorities; it is, instead, their lower status that leads to their lower average intelligence test scores. The following Table 13.2 from the same work compares social status or caste position to test scores and school success in nations around the world.

Despite a century of heated debate, psychologists are no closer to an agreed conception of the nature of intelligence (Sternberg and Detterman, 1986). Nevertheless, throughout this century, standardised intelligence tests have been influential in shaping the perceptions of educators regarding the nature of intelligence. Schools have readily embraced the "one-shot instantiation" (Bruner, 1986, p. 51) of so-called objective measures, such as IQ tests in determining the abilities of the students. Such tests, however, consistently fail to identify children from non-mainstream groups (including low socio-economic and ethnic minority groups) as possessing high cognitive abilities (Gould, 1981; Staples, 1986). Research has clearly demonstrated

Table 13.2: Group Differences around the World

Country	Status or class position		Test Scores, School Success	
	High	Low	High	Low
United States	Whites	Blacks	Whites	Blacks
	Asians	Latinos	Asians	Latinos
	Whites	American Indians	Whites	American Indians
Great Britain	English	Irish, Scottish	English	Irish, Scottish
Northern Island	Protestants	Catholics	Protestants	Catholics
Australia	Whites	Aborigines	Whites	Aborigines
New Zealand	Whites	Maoris	Whites	Maoris
South Africa	English	Afrikaners	English	Afrikaners
Belgium	Flemish	French	Flemish	French
Israel	Jews	Arabs	Jews	Arabs
	Western Jews	Eastern Jews	Western Jews	Eastern Jews
India	Non Tribals	Tribals	Non Tribals	Tribals
	Brahmins	Dalits	Brahmins	Dalits
	High castes	Low Castes	High castes	Low Castes
Czechoslovakia	Slovakes	Gypsies	Slovakes	Gypsies

Source: Fischer *et al.* (1996) p. 192

that stereotypical attitudes toward race, for example, have adversely affected the educational attainments of children with minority status (McAdoo and McAdoo, 1985).

SC/ST Students—Victims of Prejudiced Attitude

Dalit bias runs deeper and deeper even in 21st century, not only among the uneducated people, but also among highly educated modern people. In view of pre-conceived notion about academic calibre of the SC/STs students, they are labelled 'academically backward'. A number of cases are reported wherein biased treatment was meted out to scheduled caste students in the schools. Several such facts have been revealed in the *'Indian Education Report'*. Upper caste teachers refuse to touch scheduled castes students. At the same time, they make these children special targets of verbal abuse and physical punishment (*Times of India*, 27 February 2002).

According to another news item, 'SC students face discrimination when it comes to mid-day meals' dated 25 June 2012 (Radheshyam Jadhav, TNN): "Children from the schedule caste (SC) are discriminated against in the implementation of government sponsored mid-day meal scheme and segregation is practiced in seating arrangements and in eating mid-day meals," said a report released recently by the Working Group on Human Rights in India and the UN (WGHR). According to another news item, "SC students face discrimination when it comes to mid-day meals" dated 25 June 2012 (Radheshyam Jadhav, TNN). The *Times of India* (dated 9 September 2012) likewise quoted the same report released by the Working Group on Human Rights in India and the UN (WGHR).

On 26 November 2012 *Indian Express* reported that more than 180 schools serving the mid-day meal (MDM) across five states have allowed caste or gender based discrimination over the last two years, quoting a status report of discrimination in schools. As per the news item, forty-one independent monitoring institutes (MI) submitted reports to the Union Human Resource Development Ministry about instances of discrimination and untouchability in 186 schools across Rajasthan, Madhya Pradesh, Orissa, Uttar Pradesh and Gujarat. It was noted that Children from the SC/ST categories were routinely segregated from other children, made to sit and eat separately; food cooked by SC/ST cooks is often refused by many children or their parents. There were also cases where Dalit students were served from a distance, and several students bringing their own plates for fear of utensils being touched by Dalit classmates. There are instances of gender discrimination as well with only girls being made to serve meals in some schools, the reports revealed. As per a report published in the *Hindustan Times*, the Government report accepts that dalit students, cooks faced discrimination. It was suspected that discrimination was practiced, but the report makes it official. For the first time, a government report accepted that dalit students and cooks were subjected to untouchability during mid-day meal distribution in schools. An internal inspection report of department of *panchayat* and rural development mentioned the fact in the context of Bhishampur Primary School in Satna district.

Such behaviour of teachers adversely affects the educational desire among the scheduled caste children. According to a news item dated 25 June 2012 (Radheshyam Jadhav, TNN): "Caste bias manifests itself also in higher educational institutions, where there have been reports of teachers ignoring SC students and unjustly failing them in exams; social exclusion and physical abuse; and the unwillingness of university administrations to assist SC students and support them. Between 2008 and 2011, the number of SC students in higher educational institutions that committed suicide was 18 across India. This number only represents official statistics without counting all the SC students whose families did not protest against the incessant discrimination that eventually led to their suicide," states the report.

While in college the identity of SC/ST students is manipulated as they are characterized 'reserved quota' students. Thus, in spite of academic competence, comments like 'these reserved chaps will never be as good as us' are passed. Another issue is the non-admission of 'merit' students in the 'open' category, despite a central direction that they must be. It is always thought why enrol an extra low caste student when we already have to admit a certain number of them? This follows two consequences, it brands a brilliant student as one coming from the reserved category and it deprives another needy SC/ST student of a seat. Their contribution is not recognized in any area; they are always put in an environment, which hampers their personal development and performance. Constant attempts are made to destroy their 'self'. In educational institutions and even at work places, discussions are held on reservation policy. The major objective of such discussion is not to find out the ideology behind the measure, but to create hatred among the students and employees in organizations. The worth of SC/STs is not prized at work place, though they have potentials. No one can deny that backwardness arises, rather very substantially, from lack of access to economic resources and facilities like quality education and employment opportunities. However, the two aspects are conveniently overlooked by upper castes Hindus. An interesting thing may be mentioned here is that caste is not uniquely Indian. The Vedas define the structure of a Hindu community to consist of the Brahmans, Kshatriyas, Vaishnavas, and Sudras. This classification is similar to what was followed in Europe along with the guild system. They had the nobles, priests, soldiers and serfs. Serfs were the labourers and servants, who worked for the other classes. But that was back in the 10th century. So what has made their societies move on? The founding of America and the occurrences of French Revolution, the Industrial Revolution and Renaissance have all played their role in the development of the European society. But in India, caste based stratification is still a hard reality. Still, with the inception of constitutional democracy, the democratic India opened up various new avenues, making it possible for them to move up the socio-economic ladder, as equality of opportunity and social justice have come to be recognized as the guiding principles of development planning in independent India. With the constitutional safeguards and protection as well as better educational and economic facilities acting as motivating factors for upward social mobility, these safeguards made it possible for members of the Scheduled Castes and Scheduled Tribes to be at par with non-scheduled population and enabled them to enter into mainstream of national life (Uplaonkar; 1982). The governments have, likewise, endeavoured to provide many opportunities to these categories so that they can utilize the benefits and overcome oppression.

In reality, says Uplaonkar (1982), only a small proportion of Scheduled Caste students have been able to reap the benefits of higher education and consequently, the benefits of reservations in organized labour market, for which educational qualifications are major considerations. Some of the studies (Kumar, *et al.*, 2000) also showed positive indications of improvement in literacy and development of Scheduled Caste children. Some of the states have significantly improved their performance and have been successful in reducing the drop-out and wastage of children in schools, making considerable improvement in terms of their enrolment and participation. Kulkarni (2000) in his study in the States of Bihar, Rajasthan and Uttar Pradesh found that there is a widening disparity between other castes and Dalits in terms of school completion, while it is narrowing in literacy and school completion rates between other castes and Dalits in some of the states, such as Himachal Pradesh, Kerala and Tamil Nadu.

While Anitha (2000) also showed positive impact in the school, if there is a good relationship between the school, the community and the teachers, on the other hand, there is evidence enough to show that the teachers in India are predominantly upper caste and bring their own understandings of the legitimacy of caste relations into the classroom.

Scheduled Caste children are assumed to run errands and assigned menial tasks, such as sweeping and cleaning the classrooms. Besides, it was also found that "higher rates of teacher absenteeism were reported when children were mainly from the Scheduled Caste communities" (Govinda, R. and Varghese, N.V., 1993; Kabeer, 2006). Be that as it may, the inherent fear of the disadvantaged children towards the teacher, and their ability to establish communication link with the teacher was also reflected in low attendance. The micro-level evidence (NUEPA Occasional Papers) on high drop-out rates (Sujatha, 1998) shows that initiatives, such as mid-day meals, self-help women's groups, environment building programmes, appointment of local community teachers, developing partnership between school and village communities in school management have helped the disadvantaged groups to realize the importance of education and adopt positive attitude towards girls' education (Sujatha, 2002).

Another study conducted by Kumar, Arora, Huria and Daya (2000) found that mid-day meals, free uniform, free textbooks, scholarships for attendance are widely availed of by children of disadvantaged groups, but there is lack of satisfactory community participation through PTA and VEC.

Lackadaisical Reforms

Considering the socio-economic backwardness of the Scheduled Castes, the Constitution of India envisaged special measures for their socio-economic uplift, especially their educational development. Several policies and programmes have been adopted by the central and state governments for their educational development. There have been a variety of schemes, such as scholarships, free uniforms, free books, free coaching, free boarding, free lodging and many other incentives in order to promote their welfare.

Apparently a number of efforts are being made on the front of policy making and implementation, but still some hurdles obstruct in achieving the desired goals. Content of curriculum, pedagogic methods, assessment and evaluation are among the key issues that need to be addressed. In the Brahmanic

India, curriculum and the content of education have been central to the processes of reproduction of caste, class, cultural and patriarchal domination-subordination. Brahmanisation of curriculum and curricular processes have been evident in the emphasis on (1) 'pure' language, (2) literature and knowledge of the civilization and culture, narration of past, polity and religion that is produced by the higher castes, which reflect Brahmanical world view and experiences and Brahmanical perspectives on Indian society, history and culture, and (3) high caste cultural and religious symbols, linguistic and social competencies, modes of life and behaviour. Furthermore, the overarching stress has been on praising to the skies mental as against manual labour. There is almost no place for dialects, cultures, traditions, and folklore of dalits and adivasis as also of peasantry.

The above mentioned gulf stemming from the differences of language and culture is epitomized in a play produced by black and white students. Interacting with her teacher, an adolescent black girl argues: My way of communicating may be different from yours, but it fills my adaptive and emotional needs as I perform it. Why should my 'at home' way of talking be 'wrong' and your standard version be 'right'? ... Show me... that by adding a fluency in standard dialect, you are adding something to my language and not taking something away from me. Help me retain my identity and self-respect while learning to talk 'your' way (Heath, 1983, p. 271).

Yvonne Haig and Rhonda Oliver observed that there were differences in the number and nature of the problems teachers identified in the speech of students in low SES schools compared to those in high SES schools. The teachers identified many aspects of pronunciation, vocabulary, grammar and language use in low SES schools. But many of the features of student speech criticized by the teachers were forms other than those usually designated as standard, but in common use. The causes teachers ascribed to the speech problems differed according to students' socio-economic stratum and, thus, denominated attitudinal duality. The teachers described the low SES students' as the 'victims' of poor home and community language models, 'restricted' life experiences, chronic parental unemployment and negative peer influences. On the other hand, the high SES students' problems were perceived to be mainly developmental, related to school curriculum demands, the result of adolescent rebellion or due to generally deteriorating standards in society. Perceptible difference in the ways of perceiving the cause of one and the same problem denominates the difference in the teachers' attitude towards the two sets of children.

The cause of low SES students' use of non-standard forms is also attributed to their 'restricted' language and 'limited' vocabulary; this problem is commonly associated with working class speech (Creber, 1972; Hughes, 1992) and with dialect speakers (Van Calcar *et al.*, 1989). From the way the primary teachers described the situation, it would seem that the vocabulary valued at school does not match that of the children's homes, essentially because they come from a different social and cultural background. This would imply that the cultural capital (Bourdieu, 1974, 1991), in the form of lexical knowledge, which children bring to school, is neither recognized nor valued.

Midatala Rani (2000) observed that the dominating languages exhibit features like numerical majority, medium of education, communication and administration, vehicles of regional development and prestige. Speakers are monolingual. The dominated tribal language speakers are bi-lingual or multilingual depending on the local linguistic situation. They are invaded by outsiders in various spheres, viz., socio-economic and cultural, though they are locally in numerical majority, but they are turned into a minority under the regional pressures. They are discriminated against by non-recognition of their languages and cultural traits. The attitude of dominant ethnic groups towards tribal languages consists of outright rejection of a tribal language in a bilingual context and ridiculing the tribal for using their mother tongue in a public place. The attitude of tribals towards the majority languages is total recognition and learning it for inter-group communication and acceptance as a language of social mobility, economic emancipation and status. The tribals identify themselves with majority language of their area. The tribal child is not unique or deficient. A tribal child is born into a culture, which uses a language different from others. Like any other culture, the tribal child also uses language, grammar and dialect in the same manner as others do. Tribal education is not opposed to mainstream education.

The monolingual child faces cognitive and communicative problems where the instruction is in the major regional language as, for instance, the Kuvi and Santhali children attending the Oriya or Bengali Medium schools in Orissa˜ or West Bengal. In a situation like this, the content of the primers is also alien and new. Writing about "Aliens in their own Home", Sudhir Shukla (*The Hindu*, 14 March 1993) writes: On his first day in a remote village school in Madhya Pradesh, six year old Bishnoo asks his friend Surta to "*Ingey vaita*" (Gondi for "Come here"). But what follows is a scream from the teacher, "*chup baith, ganwar kahin ka*" (Shut up, you village idiot). Shukla further writes: "cowed down, little Bishnoo does not know whether he was wrong in using Gondi in the classroom, which invited his teacher's wrath. But within a few months, he learns that speaking his native tongue in the classroom is an offence. Though Bishnoo cannot understand Hindi of the teacher or of the textbooks, he realises that the only language he knows has no place in the school."

There are several Bishnoos all over the country and such children suffer for speaking in their mother tongue and not being able to speak the school language. They neither understand the language of the text nor of the teacher. As the teacher does not know the language of the learner and the parents neither know the language of the textbook nor that of the teacher, the break is almost complete. The education is, therefore, merely symbolic.

The subsequent significant element of the curriculum and functioning of school is forbidding the dalits is its 'colonial' character, which privileged western modernization. The defining features of the structure are: full time attendance of age specific groups in teacher supervised classrooms for the study of graded curricula. Full day schools, compulsory attendance, unconducive long time span of classes and vacations, served as deterrents, being ill suited to educating SC/ST children, especially in the initial years when access was just being opened up and availed. Most of the students in village school do not turn up during sowing and harvesting time. We are giving them vacations in summer and winter aping the colonial way. our school organisation and curricula have not been sensitive as yet to fundamentally different economic situations, life aims and social circumstances of children belonging to poorer strata households or communities in the shaping of the school structure. Furthermore, the curriculum itself as a tool of cultural dominance and hegemony has an alienating and intimidating impact (Velaskar, 2005).

Paradigm Shift

The ongoing problem demands paradigm shift. If our nation is providing education as a fundamental right, then, there must be a clear understanding of the very essence of rights. If we interpret the phrase "education is a right", then we must take "Education" in a bit broad sense. There is a lot of literature on the meaning of the word 'right', but let us keep it simple and just look at what "right" means in terms of its common usage. Here, it seems to mean something, which is universally applicable—it is not just available to some section of society, and it is something that we are entitled to no strings attached, no costs incurred. Hence, it looks like education being a "right" is supposed to mean that we have a universal entitlement to it without incurring a personal cost.

It is a well-accepted fact that education is the path to a number of personal strengths—awareness, understanding, confidence, safety, resilience and so on. Free education terrifies dictators, bullies, extremists and those who would control the thinking of others. It is their chief enemy. Ignorance, after all, as Orwell aptly wrote, is strength. Around the world, in every country where there is political and religious strife, education is not seen as a right and children suffer in extreme ways. These events not only should make those of us, in richer, stable countries, angry and committed to ending injustice and cruelty in those places, they should also remind us that we have a responsibility to ensure that we provide *all* our children with the best education possible—and freely—as a right.

Conclusion

The expansion of government schooling has undeniably represented a shift from mass exclusion to mass inclusion, but it is also a well accepted fact that it has been an incredibly delayed, weak and highly discriminatory inclusion. Disgustingly uneven provision, accompanied by an alienating curriculum, ruling class language and disinterested and biased and bigoted teaching learning process seem to have kept alive the traditional Brahmanical principle of closure. SC/ST children are largely "cooled out" at the primary level itself. There occurs an effective physical exclusion of SC/ST children or they achieve low levels of schooling, which do not necessarily reflect learning.

Whether we like to admit it or not, in India education is treated as a privilege, one that belongs to the rich more than the poor. The trend towards 'user pays' and 'if you pay more, you get more,' mentalities, attitudes that have always been ghosts in the education machine, driven historically by the privileged rich, continues to fuel government versus private debates (and mythologies) and enables governments to partially allay their responsibilities to provide free and equitable education to all children.

Its most obvious product is the ongoing glaring disparity between rich, privileged private schools and poor government schools. We all know that student success later in life is largely determined by parent's means and the school attended. The poor section of our society (read SC and ST) is in the hand of upper class hostile teachers and alien curriculum and poor fellows do not understand and take it as a right. Now our government only gave the right to be literate to the poor section of the society, not the right to education. It is the reality.

References

1. Anitha, B.K. (2000): *Village, Caste and Education*, Rawat Publications, Jaipur and New Delhi.
2. Bourdieu, P. (1974). The school as a conservative force: Scholastic and cultural inequities. In J. Eagleston (ed.) *Contemporary Research in the Sociology of Education*, pp. 32-46. London: Methuen.
3. Bourdieu, P. (1991). *Language and Symbolic Power*. Oxford: Polity Press.
4. Bruner, J. (1986). *Actual minds, possible worlds.* Cambridge, MA: Harvard University Press.
5. Creber, J.W.P. (1972). *Lost for Words: Language and Educational Failure.* Harmondsworth: Penguin.

6. Fischer, Claude S. Michael Hout, Martín Sánchez Jankowski, Samuel R. Lucas, Ann Swidler and Kim Vos (1996). Inequality by Design: Cracking the Bell Curve Myth. NJ Princeton: Princeton University Press.
7. Gould, S. (1981). *The Mismeasure of Man.* New York: W.W. Norton & Company.
8. Govinda, R. and Varghese, N.V. (1993). *Quality of Primary Schooling in India A Case Study of Madhya Pradesh,* New Delhi: IEP, NIEPA
9. Heath, S.B. (1983). *Ways with words: Language, life, and work in communities and classrooms.* Cambridge: Cambridge University Press.
10. Hughes, S.E. (1992). Expletives of lower working class women. *Language in Society* 21, 291-303.
11. Ingole, K.S. (n.d) Social Exclusion and Its Implication. *StudyMode.com.* Retrieved 03, 2013, from http://www.studymode.com/essays/Social-Exclusion-And-Its-Implication-1478839.html.
12. Jadhav R., Union government expresses concern about manual scavenging, TNN June 25, 2012.
13. Kabeer, Naila (2006). "Social Exclusion and the MDGs: The Challenge of 'Durable Inequalities' in the Asian Context", Institute of Development Studies, paper presented at the Asia 2015 Conference.
14. Kulkarni, P.M. (2000). '*Inter-State Variations in Human Development Differentials among Social Groups in India.*' National Council of Applied Economic Research, New Delhi.(Unpublished).
15. Kumar, Y., and Arrora R.P., Hurai A.R., Daya Kishan (2000). *Mid-Term Assessment Survey—DPEP*, Haryana.
16. Kumar, Y., Arora R.P. and Chaudhary, Mamta (2000). *A Study of Incidence and Factors Responsible for Dropping Out of Girl Students from GPS Rampur*, Baralyawali and Dhanur Villages of Sirsa District, Haryana.
17. McAdoo, H.P. and McAdoo, J.L. (1985). *Black Children.* Beverly Hills: Sage.
18. Mukul, A. (2012). Report on Caste Bias in Midday Meal Stirs Row. *Times of India* Sep. 9, 2012.
19. NUEPA, (2013). *Elementary Education in India: Progress towards UEE.* New Delhi: National University of Educational Planning and Administration.
20. Rajshekar, V.T. (2002). *Caste: A Nation within the Nation*, Bangalore: Books for Change.
21. Rani M. (2000). Tribal Languages and Tribal Education, *Social Action,* Vol. 50, October December.
22. Singh, K.S. (1994). *People of India: Anthropological Survey of India.* New Delhi: Manohar Publishers.
23. Staples, R. (1986). *The Black Family: Essays and Studies.* Third Edition. Belmont, CA: Wadsworth Publishing Company, Inc.
24. Sternberg, R.J. and Detterman, D.K. (1986). *What is intelligence? Contemporary viewpoints on its nature and definition.* Norwood, NJ: Ablex Publishing.
25. Sudhir Shukla (1993). Aliens in their own Home, *The Hindu*, March 14.
26. Sujatha, K. (2002). *Education among Scheduled Tribes*, in Govinda, R., India

Education Report: A Profile of Basic Education, New Delhi: Oxford University Press.

27. *Times of India*, February 27, 2002).
28. Uplaonkar, Ambrao T. (1982). Social Background and Occupational Aspirations of College Students: A Case of SC *vis-à-vis* Non-SC Students in Higher Education. *Journal of Higher Education*, Vol. 8 (1).
29. Van Calcar, C., Van Calcar, W. and De Jonge, C. (1989). Language in the classroom: The Amsterdam and Groningen Projects. In J. Cheshire, V. Edwards, H. Münstermann and B. Weltens (eds) *Dialect and Education: Some European Perspectives*, pp. 256-68. Clevedon: Multilingual Matters.
30. Velaskar, P. (2005). Educational Stratification, Dominant Ideology and the Reproduction of Disadvantage in India, in Dahiwale, S.M. (ed.) *Understanding Indian Society: The Non-Brahmanic Perspective*. Delhi: Rawat Publication, pp. 196-220.
31. Vishnoi, A. (2012). Report Says Caste, Gender Discrimination Rampant, *Indian Express*. New Delhi, Monday, 26 November 2012.

14

A Study of the Awareness of Elementary Teachers towards the RTE Act, 2009

Shabana Ashraf

The purpose of any educational system is to provide good standard of living for learners. In this regard, our preamble also reflects that every human being is entitled to enjoy every right, irrespective of religion, race, caste, sex, nationality, etc. Human rights are necessary for human survival, well being, dignity, respect for humanity and equality and liberty of human beings. Human rights are broadly classified into eight types of rights: they are civil rights, cultural rights, economic rights, educational rights, legal rights, political rights, social rights and international rights. Educational rights have been specified as one of the fundamental human rights in Article 26 of the universal declaration of human rights. The right to education has been universally recognised since the Universal Declaration of Human Rights in 1948 (though referred to by the ILO as early as the 1920s) and has since been enshrined in various international conventions, national constitutions and development plans. In the constitution of India, Article 21-A was inserted in eighty-sixth Amendment Act 2002 to provide free and compulsory education to all children in the age group of six to fourteen years as a Fundamental Right in such a manner as the State may, by law, determine. The Right of Children to Free and Compulsory Education (RTE) Act, 2009, which represents the consequential legislation envisaged under Article 21-A, means that every child has a right to take full time elementary education of satisfactory and equitable quality in a formal school, which satisfies certain essential norms and standards.

In the RTE Act, 'Free education' means that no child, other than a child, who has been admitted by his or her parents to a school, which is not supported by the appropriate Government, shall be liable to pay any kind of fee or charges or expenses, which may prevent him or her from pursuing and completing elementary education. 'Compulsory education' casts an obligation on the appropriate Government and local authorities to provide and ensure admission, attendance and completion of elementary education by all children in the 6-14 age group. With this, India has moved forward to a rights based framework that casts a legal obligation on the Central and State Governments to implement this fundamental child right as enshrined in the Article 21-A of the Constitution, in accordance with the provisions of the RTE Act.

According to NCFTE (2009), School education has seen significant development over the decades since independence. According to the Government of India estimates, 82 per cent of the 20 crore children of the 5-14 age group were in school as per enrolment figures, nearly 50 per cent of these children drop out before completing class VIII. One finds the situation on the ground ridden with difficulties. Regional, social, and gender disparities continue to pose new challenges. This reality increases the challenge of implementing the Right of Children to Free and Compulsory Education Act and, in particular, the role and place of the school teacher. The teacher must be equipped not only to teach, but also to understand the students and the community of parents, so that children are regular in schools and they should learn. The Act mandates that the teacher should refrain from inflicting corporal punishment, complete the entire curriculum within the given time, assess students, hold parent's meetings and apprise them and as part of the school management committee, organize the overall running of the school. The above para indicates the need of awareness and knowledge of RTE Act among teachers of elementary level. So, the researcher wants to know the level of awareness of RTE Act among elementary teachers of Bhopal district. For that, the researcher selected the sample of elementary teachers of government and private schools of rural and urban locality of Bhopal district and formulated the following objectives.

Objectives: The main objectives of the present study were:

1. To study the level of awareness of RTE Act among elementary teachers.
2. To study the comparison of level of awareness of RTE Act in respect of type, locality of school and gender of the teachers.

Hypothesis Formulated: The following hypotheses were formulated:

1. There is average level of awareness of RTE Act among elementary teachers.
2. There is no significant difference between the level of awareness of RTE Act among government and private elementary teachers.
3. There is no significant difference between the level of awareness of RTE Act among rural and urban elementary teachers.
4. There is no significant difference between the level of awareness of RTE Act among male and female elementary teachers.

Design of the study: To conduct the study, the design of the study was prepared and it was as follows:

Sample: For the present study, the survey type descriptive research method was adopted. Two hundred elementary teachers of government and private schools of rural and urban locality of Bhopal District of Madhya Pradesh State were the sample of this study. They were selected through stratified random sampling on the basis of equal allocation. The study involves comparison between, rural and urban, government and private as well as male and female elementary teachers. One hundred teachers were selected from rural locality including (50 from government and 50 from private schools) and 100 teachers were selected from urban locality including (50 from government and 50 from private schools) of Bhopal District. The gender of the elementary teachers was considered as the second strata. Two hundred elementary teachers (100 male and 100 female students) are taken as a sample. In short, the size of the sample was 200 elementary teachers, which included government and private, urban and rural and male and female elementary teachers.

Tool: For measuring the level of awareness of RTE Act among elementary teachers, a self-prepared tool, of Right to Education Act Awareness Scale (RTEAS) based on four dimensions, was used by the researcher, which was standardized by the researcher by calculating validity and reliability. This tool contains of a total of 45 items, each item has two alternative answers, out of which one is correct.

Statistical Technique: The obtained data was analyzed with the help of '*t*' test.

Results Obtained

The following results were obtained:

I. RTE Act Awareness among Government and Private School Elementary Teachers

Table 14.1: The level of RTE Act Awareness among Government and Private School Elementary Teachers

S. No.	*Categories*	*Range*	*Government*	*%*	*Private*	*%*
1.	High	30-45	10	10.00	23	23.00
2.	Average	15-30	68	68.00	67	67.00
3.	Low	00-15	22	22.00	10	10.00
Total			100		100	100

On the basis of the observation of Table 14.1, we can infer that ten per cent elementary teachers of government schools have high level of RTE Act awareness, while 23 per cent elementary teachers of private schools have high level of RTE Act awareness. Further, 68 per cent government school elementary teachers, 67 per cent private school elementary teachers possess average level of RTE Act awareness, while 22 per cent elementary teachers of government schools and ten per cent elementary teachers of private schools have low category of RTE Act awareness. Overall, 135 elementary teachers have average level of RTE Act awareness. Therefore, we can infer that there is average level of RTE Act awareness among elementary teachers.

Table 14.2: The level of RTE Act Awareness among Rural and Urban Elementary Teachers

S. No	*Categories*	*Range*	*Rural*	*%*	*Urban*	*%*
1.	High	30-45	07	07.00	23	23.00
2.	Average	15-30	47	47.00	56	56.00
3.	Low	00-15	46	46.00	21	21.00
Total			100		100	

From Table 14.2, we can infer that seven per cent elementary teachers of schools of rural locality have high level of RTE Act awareness, while 23 per cent elementary teachers of schools of urban locality have high level of RTE Act awareness. Fourty-seven per cent elementary teachers of rural area, 56 per cent elementary teachers of urban locality possess average level of RTE Act awareness, while 46 per cent elementary teachers of schools of rural and 21 per cent elementary teachers of schools of urban locality have low category of RTE Act awareness. Overall, 93 elementary teachers have average level of RTE Act awareness. Therefore, we can infer that there is average level of RTE Act awareness among elementary teachers.

Table 14.3: The level of RTE Act Awareness among Male and Female Elementary School Teachers

S. No	*Categories*	*Range*	*Male*	*%*	*Female*	*%*
1.	High	30-45	33	33.00	20	20.00
2.	Average	15-30	56	56.00	47	47.00
3.	Low	00-15	11	11.00	33	33.00
Total			100		100	

Table 14.3 shows that 33 per cent male elementary teachers have high level of RTE Act awareness, while 20 per cent female elementary teachers have high level of RTE Act awareness; 56 per cent male elementary teachers, 47 per cent female elementary teachers possesses average level of RTE Act awareness, while eleven per cent male elementary teachers and 33 per cent female elementary teachers have low category of RTE Act awareness. Overall, 103 male and female elementary teachers have average level of RTE Act awareness. Hence, we can infer that there is average level of RTE Act awareness among elementary teachers.

Table 14.4: Mean, SD and '*t*' value of the Level of Awareness of RTE Act among Government and Private School Elementary Teachers

Category	*Mean*	*S.D*	*N*	*df*	*'t'*
Government School Elementary Teachers	30.50	4.72	100	198	5.48**
Private School Elementary Teachers	34.23	5.00	100		

The value of '*t*' is 5.48, which is found to be significant and the hypothesis is not accepted. Thus, it is concluded that there is significant difference between the level of awareness of RTE Act among government and private elementary teachers. It is observed that private school elementary teachers (34.23) possess higher level of awareness of RTE Act than government school elementary teachers (30.50). It may be inferred that in private schools, elementary teachers are more aware than elementary teachers of government schools.

Table 14.5: Mean, SD and '*t*' value of the Level of Awareness of Right to Education Act among Rural and Urban Elementary Teachers

Category	*Mean*	*S.D*	*N*	*df*	*'t'*
Rural Elementary Teachers	32.33	5.23	100	198	6.53**
Urban Elementary Teachers	37.23	5.46	100		

The value of '*t*' is 6.53, which is found to be significant at 0.01 and 0.05 level of significance, so the hypothesis is not accepted. Thus, it is concluded that there is significant difference between the level of awareness of Right to Education Act among rural and urban elementary teachers. It is found that urban elementary teachers (37.23) are superior to rural elementary teachers (32.33) in respect of RTE Act awareness. The urban elementary teachers possess more favourable RTE Act awareness than the rural elementary teachers. It may be inferred that locality influences the level of awareness of RTE Act. This supremacy of urban locality may be due to the reason that they have more media exposure. May be, this is the reason behind differential levels of awareness about the Right to Education Act among rural and urban elementary teachers.

Table 14.6: Mean, SD and '*t*' value of the Level of Awareness of Right to Education Act among Male and Female Elementary Teachers

Category	*Mean*	*SD*	*N*	*df*	*'t'*
Male	35.72	4.38	100	198	5.44**
Female	32.13	5.00	100		

The value of '*t*' is 5.44 and it is found to be significant at 0.01 and 0.05 levels of significance, so the hypothesis is not accepted. Thus, it is concluded that there is significant difference between the level of awareness of the Right to Education Act among male and female elementary teachers. It is further found that male (35.72) elementary teachers are superior to female elementary teachers (32.13) in respect of RTE Act awareness. The male elementary teachers possess more favourable RTE Act awareness than the female elementary teachers. It may be inferred that gender do influence the level of RTE Act awareness, supremacy of male may be due to the reason that they have more exposure outside the home and they have more interaction in society. May be, this is the reason of males being more aware about the Act in comparison to females.

Results and Discussion

The results of the study can be summarized as:

1. There is average level of RTE Act awareness among elementary teachers of Government and private schools of rural and urban locality.
2. Significant difference was found between the level of RTE Act awareness among Government and private school elementary teachers.
3. Significant difference was found between the level of RTE Act awareness among rural and urban elementary teachers.
4. Significant difference was found between the level of RTE Act awareness among male and female elementary teachers.

Conclusion and Suggestions

The results of this study show that awaréness level of RTE Act is of average level in elementary teachers. Elementary teachers of urban locality and private schools have more awareness than their counterparts from rural locality and government schools. Similarly, male teachers also have more level of awareness of RTE Act than their counterpart female teachers. This indicates that there is serious need to increase the level of awareness and knowledge of RTE Act among teachers at elementary level of government schools and schools in rural locality. In this regard, the Government of India launched the Sarva Shiksha Abhiyan (SSA) in 2002 and the financial commitment and education cess to augment the universalization of elementary education mission have underscored the need to prepare the teachers adequately to address the growing demand for quality education.

Decline in the quality of education in the school system, commercialization of schools and increasing competition is forcing children into unprecedented situation. This RTE Act will play a major role to overcome this situation, but it is possible when teachers are aware of the Act, because this Act emphasizes areas like all round development of child, learning through activities, discovery and exploration in a friendly and stress free environment. So, the teachers should be equipped to understand the need of growing demand of quality education. They should be able to act as a facilitator of knowledge to their learners; they must act as mediating agents through whom curriculum is transacted and knowledge is co-constructed along with the learners. They should connect the learners with knowledge beyond the boundaries of classroom and enrich the curriculum with familiar or local experiences by making it less textbook centred.

References

1. Best W. John, Kahn (2007): *Research in Education*, Ninth edition, Pearson education, Delhi.
2. Garrett, E. Henry (2005): *Statistics in Psychology and Education*, twelfth Indian Reprint, Paragon International Publishers. pp. 212-215.
3. Lord Henry Peter Brougham in http://en.wikipedia.org/wiki/right to education
4. Mayer, J. and Salovey, P. (1997) in Mangal, S.K. (2007). *Essentials of Educational Psychology*, Prentice – Hall of India, New Delhi. p. 104.
5. Mangal, S.K. (2007). *Essentials of Educational Psychology*, Prentice-Hall, India, New Delhi. pp. 90-111.
6. Preamble to the Universal Declaration of Human Rights, 1948 in http://en.wikipedia.org/wiki/rights to education.

Webliography

http://en.wikipedia.org/wiki/human rights
http://en.wikipedia.org/wiki/rights to edu

15

Making the Right to Education Meaningful

The 4As Framework

Noushad Husain

The right to education has been universally recognized since the Universal Declaration of Human Rights and has since been enshrined in various international conventions, national constitutions and development plans. However, while the vast majority of countries have signed up to and ratified international conventions (such as the Universal Declaration of Human Rights and the UN Convention on the Rights of the Child), far fewer have integrated these rights in their national constitutions or provided the legislative and administrative framework to ensure that these rights are realized in practice. In some cases, the right exists along with the assumption that the user should pay for this right, undermining the very concept of a right. In others, the right exists in theory, but there is no capacity to implement this right in practice. Inevitably, a lack of government support for the right to education hits the poorest the hardest. Today, the right to education is still denied to millions around the world.

As well as being a right in itself, the right to education is also an enabling right. Education *'creates the "voice" through which rights can be claimed and protected'* (Watkins, K; 2000) and without education, people lack the capacity '*to achieve valuable functioning as part of the living*' (Sen, A.; 1993). If people have access to education, they can develop the skills, capacity and confidence to secure other rights. Education gives people the ability to access information detailing the range of rights that they hold and the government's obligations. It supports people to develop communication skills to demand these rights, the confidence to speak in a variety of forums and the ability to negotiate with a wide range of government officials and power holders.

In this chapter, the author has sought to clarify the 4As framework for the right to education. After discussing the core elements of right to education, the author clarifies the concepts of rights and obligations. The author explains deeply that to check the fulfilment of right to education, the 4As framework can be used satisfactorily. The chapter is meant to sum up the analysis of the RTE Act, 2009 in the light of the 4As framework.

Understanding the Right to Education

Education is both a human right in itself and an indispensable means of realizing other human rights. Education is essential for the development of human potential, the enjoyment of full range of human rights and respect for the rights of others.

It is the primary vehicle by which economically and socially marginalized adults and children can lift themselves out of poverty and obtain the means to participate fully in their communities. Throughout the world, education is seen as one of the best financial investments that a State can make. The importance of education is not just practical. A well-educated, enlightened and active mind that is able to wander freely and widely is one of the joys and rewards of human existence (UN Economic and Social Council, 1999).

The right to education is a human right. A right is something, which one is entitled to and which one can claim. Having a right means that someone else has an obligation. If someone has the right to free education, then the government or school cannot demand one to pay to access education.

In addition to being a human right in itself, the right to education is often considered as an enabling right. It brings better health and employment opportunities, enhanced national growth, democracy, respect for human rights and equality. Because of its enabling quality, there are many other human rights, which are linked to the right to education – such as the right to freedom from forced labour, the right to work and the right to participate in decision-making. There is no absolute agreement as to how to define the right to education, but the aims and objectives of education, as defined in the international covenants and treaties, include the following:

- The development of human personality, a sense of dignity of individual talent, and mental and physical ability.
- Respect for human rights and fundamental freedoms, as well as cultural identity, language and values.
- Enable people to participate effectively in a free society.
- The promotion of understanding, tolerance, friendship among all groups, and to maintain peace.
- To promote gender equality and respect for the environment.

Core Elements of the Right to Education (RTE)

The right to education straddles civil and political rights, and economic, social and cultural rights. Core elements of the right to education, as specified in international treaties, include:

- Entitlement to free and compulsory primary education.
- Availability of different forms of secondary education.
- Access to higher education on the basis of capacity and on non-discriminatory terms.
- Availability of accessible educational and vocational information.
- Measures developed by the State to ensure full participation in education.
- Availability of some form of basic education for those, who may not have received or completed primary education.
- Protection and improvement of conditions for teachers.
- Respect for the right of parents/legal guardians to choose for their children schools other than those established and funded by the State, and to ensure that the religious and moral education of their children conforms to their own convictions.
- Respect for academic freedom and institutional autonomy. This includes the freedom of and the accompanying obligations on individuals to express opinions about the institution or system in which they work, to fulfil their functions without discrimination or fear of sanction, and to participate in professional or representative academic bodies.

Rights and Obligations

Primary education should be available, accessible, acceptable and adaptable and Article 13 (2) (a) of the ICESCR asserts that primary education must be compulsory and available free to all. The 1993 World Conference on Human Rights reaffirmed that States are duty-bound to ensure that education is aimed at strengthening the respect of human rights and fundamental freedoms' and the ICESCR guarantees that the right to education will be exercised without discrimination of any kind. There is also a clear obligation on the part of the international community to support the right to education, as interpreted by the committee to the ICESCR (who are the authoritative body, charged with monitoring legislation related to the covenant). Finally, if free primary education, which meets the 4As standards, exists, there are obligations on the part of parents and guardians to ensure that their children are in school.

Grounding the Right to Education Locally

The right to education is an abstract concept and although the right itself may be enshrined in a series of national laws and international conventions, this is meaningless for people, who have never experienced the right and may not know that the right even exists for them. They are likely to be unaware of their constitution or how it can be legally enforced. Grounding the right to education locally means transforming the abstract concept into a concrete reality; it means looking at current provisions for the right to education and exploring what local people need to make their right to education a reality. The real meaning of right to education can be understood with the help of Figure 15.1 given below:

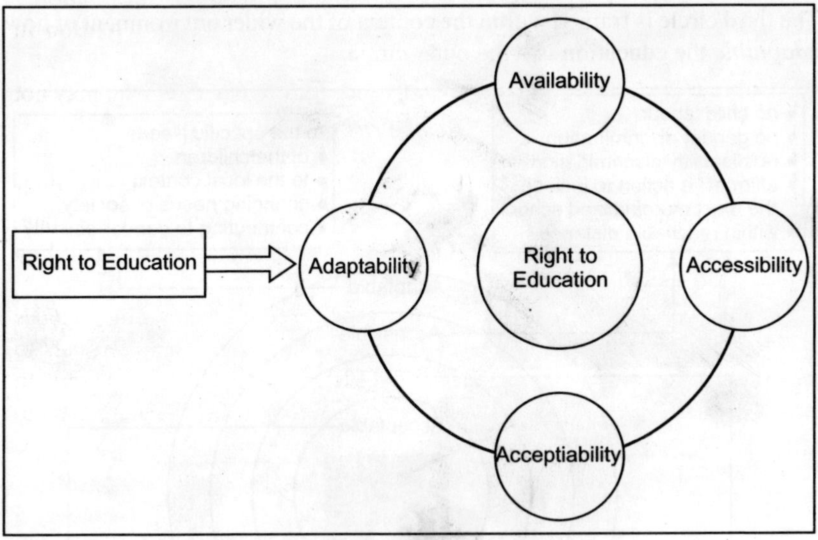

Figure 15.1: The Real Meaning of Right to Education

A framework of '4As' has been developed by Katarina Tomasevski to help people think through different dimensions of the right to education. By using a participatory process, this framework can become a tool to enable people to think through what the right to education means to them, and compare their current reality to this ideal context.

Visualizing the 4As

Using an Education Rights Circle Diagram, you can use the 4As to analyse local education provision and work with the local group to identify specific criteria by which education could be evaluated. The four circles show different aspects of the right to education.

First Circle or Inner Circle

The inner circle shows issues that will make education *acceptable* to the individual or group.

Second Circle

The second circle identifies the 'ingredients', which would make education *available*.

Third Circle

The third circle refers to the ingredients that would make education *accessible.*

Fourth Circle or Outer Circle

The third circle is framed within the context of the wider environment of how *adaptable* the education is—the outer circle.

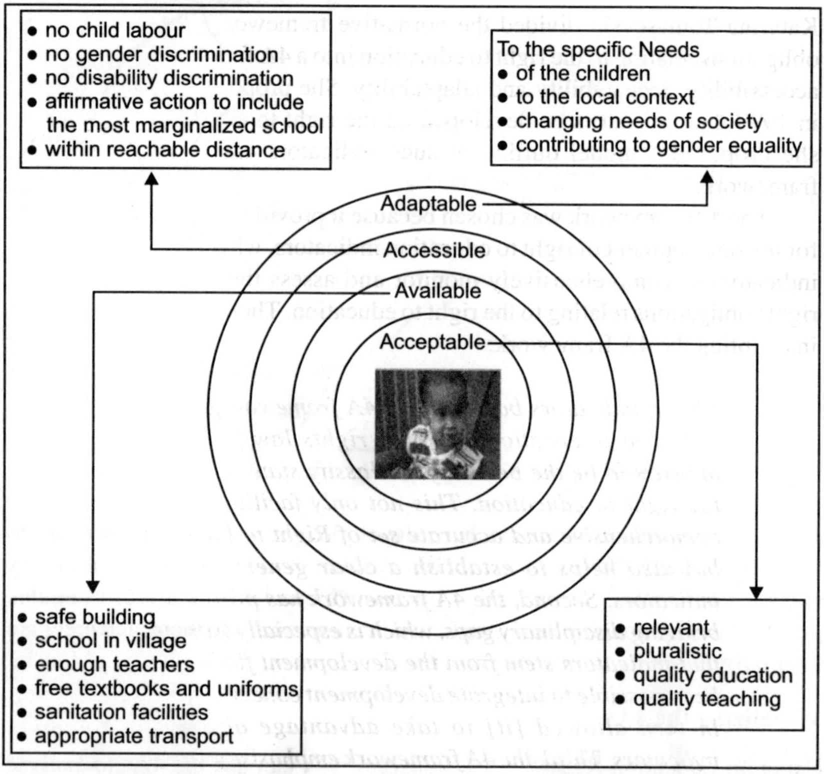

Figure 15.2: Education Rights Circle Diagram

For the outer circle, the group should consider issues in relation to their current reality, which impact education (these may have a negative impact on education and the challenge will be to think through what needs to be put in place to facilitate education rights). Once the diagram is generated, the group could compare their lived reality to this ideal context. This involves looking at where the differences and similarities are, analysing why these differences occur and developing strategies for action.

Analysis Based on the 4As

By using an 'Education Rights Circle Diagram', one can use the 4As to analyses local education provision and work with the local group to identify specific criteria by which education could be evaluated. The four circles show different aspects of the right to education.

Why the 4As?

Katarina Tomaševski divided the normative framework and corresponding obligations relating to the right to education into a 4A framework: availability, accessibility, acceptability and adaptability. She proposed in her first report in 1999 that indicators be developed on the right to education and in 2002, she proposed a model outline of such indicators on the basis of the 4A framework.

The 4A framework was chosen because it provides a systematic structure for the development of right to education indicators, which goes beyond other indicators to comprehensively monitor and assess the full range of human rights obligations relating to the right to education. There are three advantages in adopting the 4A framework:

> *"First, indicators based on the 4A framework are the most closely linked to international human rights law, since this framework appears to be the best way to classify state obligations relating to the right to education. This not only facilitates the creation of a comprehensive and accurate set of Right to Education Indicators, but also helps to establish a clear general structure for these indicators. Second, the 4A framework has proven to be effective in bridging disciplinary gaps, which is especially important considering that indicators stem from the development field. As a result, it has been possible to integrate development concerns into the 4As, which in turn allowed [it] to take advantage of existing education indicators. Third, the 4A framework emphasises both the quantitative and qualitative aspects of the right to education, by measuring not only the right to education, but also rights in education and rights through education. In view of this, in contrast to the Right to Education Indicators of the OHCHR, the Right to Education Indicators based on the 4A framework rely not only on quantitative, but also on qualitative data."*

Assessment of Fulfilment of Right to Education in the Light of 4As Framework

The fulfilment of the right to education can be assessed using the 4As framework, which asserts that for education to be a meaningful and right, it must be available, accessible, acceptable and adaptable. The 4As framework was developed by the former UN Special Rapporteur on the Right to Education, Katarina Tomasevski.

The 4As framework proposes that governments, as the prime duty-bearers, have to respect, protect and fulfil the right to education by making education available, accessible, acceptable and adaptable. The framework also places duties on other stakeholders in the education process: the child, who as the privileged subject of the right to education has the duty to comply with compulsory education requirements, the parents as the 'first educators' and professional educators, namely teachers. The 4As have been further elaborated as follows:

Availability

Educational institutions and programs should be sufficient in number. The physical facilities should be properly kept up and equipped with electricity, running water, sanitary facilities (separately for boys and girls) etc. Teachers, duly trained, should receive a salary that is competitive at the national level. The number of students per class should not be excessively high. The teaching material should be adequate, including—where appropriate—a library, computers and information technology.

In this regard, it is worth recalling Article 13.2.e of the International Covenant on Economic, Social and Cultural Rights:

> *"The development of a system of schools at all levels shall be actively pursued, an adequate fellowship system shall be established, and the material conditions of teaching staff shall be continuously improved."*

Availability includes safe buildings; school in the village; sufficient number of teachers; free textbooks and uniforms; sanitation facilities; and appropriate transport. Funded by the governments, education is universal, free and compulsory. There should be proper infrastructure and facilities in place with adequate books and materials for students. Buildings should meet both safety and sanitation standards, such as having clean drinking water. Active recruitment, proper training and appropriate retention methods should ensure that enough qualified staff is available at each school.

Accessibility

Educational institutions and programmes should be accessible to everybody, without discrimination (sex, language, religion, nationality, etc.). The teaching should take place in a reasonably accessible place (for example in a neighbourhood school) or by means of modern technology (for long-distance education). The *Convention on the Rights of Persons with Disabilities* requires that the governments take the necessary measures to ensure that "reasonable accommodation of the individual's requirements is provided" (Article 24.2.c).

Accessible means no child labour; no gender discrimination; no disability discrimination; affirmative action to include the most marginalized in school; and schools within reachable distance. All children should have equal access to school services regardless of gender, race, religion, ethnicity or socio-economic status. Efforts should be made to ensure the inclusion of marginalized groups including children of refugees, the homeless or those with disabilities. There should be no form of segregation or denial of access to any student. This includes ensuring that proper laws are in place against any child labour or exploitation to prevent children from obtaining primary or secondary education. Schools must be within a reasonable distance for children within the community, otherwise, transportation should be provided to students, particularly to those, who might live in rural areas, to ensure that the ways to school are safe and convenient. Education should be affordable to all, with textbooks, supplies and uniforms provided to students at no additional costs.

Acceptability

Acceptable means providing quality education and quality teaching that is relevant and pluralistic. The quality of education provided should be free of discrimination, relevant and culturally appropriate for all students. Students should not be expected to conform to any specific religious or ideological views. Methods of teaching should be objective and unbiased and materials available should reflect a wide array of ideas and beliefs. Health and safety should be emphasized within schools including the elimination of any forms of corporal punishment. Professionalism of staff and teachers should be maintained.

In line with this, the Committee on the Rights of the Child states: "The education to which every child has a right is one designed to provide the child with life skills, to strengthen the child's capacity to enjoy the full range of human rights. Human rights education should be a comprehensive, life-long process and start with the reflection of human rights values in the daily life and experiences of children." Article 29.1 of the *Convention on the Rights of the Child*, cited above, is unequivocal in this respect.

One can add to all this UNESCO's recommendation on Education for International Understanding, Co-operation and Peace and Education relating to Human Rights and Fundamental Freedoms:

> *"Combining learning, training, information and action, international education should further the appropriate intellectual and emotional*

development of the individual. It should develop a sense of social responsibility and of solidarity with less privileged groups and should lead to the observance of the principles of equality in everyday conduct. It should also help to develop qualities, aptitudes and abilities, which enable the individual to acquire a critical understanding of problems at the national and the international levels; to understand and explain facts, opinions and ideas; to work in a group; to accept and participate in free discussions; to observe the elementary rules of procedure applicable to any discussion; and to base value judgments and decisions on a rational analysis of relevant facts and factors.

"Education should stress the inadmissibility of recourse to war for purposes of expansion, aggression and domination, or of the use of force and violence for purposes of repression, and should bring every person to understand and assume his or her responsibilities for the maintenance of peace. It should contribute to international understanding and strengthening of world peace and to the activities in the struggle against colonialism and neo-colonialism in all their forms and manifestations, and against all forms and varieties of racialism, fascism, and apartheid as well as other ideologies which breed national and racial hatred and which are contrary to the purposes of this recommendation."

Adaptability

Adaptable includes meeting the specific needs of the children in the local context; meeting the changing needs of society; and contributing to gender equality. Educational programmes should be flexible and able to adjust according to societal changes and the needs of the community. Observance of religious or cultural holidays should be respected by schools in order to accommodate students, along with providing adequate care to those students with disabilities.

Possible Questions Regarding the 4As

It is clear from the analysis of the framework of 4As given above that for the purpose of assessment of right to education, there are several possible questions that can take place in the mind and we must explore the satisfactory answers to these questions. These possible questions related to each aspect of 4As, i.e., Availability, Accessibility, Acceptability and Adaptability can be shown in Figure 15.3.

Availability

- Is primary education free and compulsory?
- If not, is there a government plan to achieve free and compulsory primary education, with a reasonable time frame and budget?
- Is sufficient money allocated for all children to receive primary education?
- Is the state making concrete steps towards achieving free secondary and higher education?
- Are teachers well trained, and do they receive domestically competitive salaries, do they have appropriate working conditions, teaching materials and the right to organize?
- Are school buildings safe, do sanitation facilities exist, is there safe drinking water, a library, ICT resources?

Accessibility

- Is education accessible to all, without discrimination on any grounds for example race, colour, ethnicity, sex, language, religion, economic or social status? Are positive actions made to reach the most vulnerable? Are there any laws, such as preventing child labour laws, which need to be enforced to ensure accessibility?
- Is education within safe physical reach? Are there appropriate transport facilities?
- Is education affordable for all this includes indirect costs such as textbooks and uniforms?
- Have all legal and administrative obstacles, such as the need for a birth certificate, been abolished?

RTE

Acceptability

- Is education pluralistic? Is it free from religious (or other) indoctrination? Are the curriculum and texts open and tolerant towards a range of different (religious, political, etc.) belief systems?
- Is education non-discriminatory? Are texts and curriculum nonbiased and objective? Is the education relevant and culturally appropriate?
- Are there minimum standards for education (numbers of text books, methods of instruction, etc.), which are monitored and enforced by government (in both the private and public school systems)?
- Is the school safe? Is violence condemned? Are minimum health standards in place?
- Are there sufficient teachers? Are they trained to an appropriate standard? Are they properly supported and supervised?

Adaptability

- Is the school able to adapt education provision to the specific needs of their pupils and local children? E.g. are religious and cultural holidays recognized, are students with disabilities catered for etc.?
- Can education adapt to the changing needs of societies and communities? E.g. Is there adequate provision for linguistic and cultural minorities balancing learning national language and culture with preserving their own? Is education adapting to respond to the HIV pandemic etc.?
- Is there a link between school leaving age and minimum age for employment, marriage, military, criminal responsibility etc.? What happens to young people if there is a mismatch of ages?
- Does schooling protect and enhance children's rights e.g. does it prevent them from child labour or forced marriages, does it enhance their employability, increase gender equality etc.?

Figure 15.3: Possible Questions Regarding Availability, Accessibility, Acceptability and Adaptability

Analysis of RTE Act, 2009 in the Light of 4As Framework

As discussed earlier in the paper that every country should make the elementary education system serve the needs of the learners. It should be available, accessible, acceptable and adaptable to the learners as mentioned in the 4As framework. In order to know if the RTE Act, 2009 of India has the core elements of 4As framework, an analysis was done and in this analysis, those sections of the RTE Act, 2009 were identified that can be categorized into the four fold framework of 4As. In other words, those sections of the RTE Act, 2009 were identified that make the elementary education system of India available, accessible, acceptable and adaptable to the learners.

A. Availability

1. Right of Child to Free and Compulsory Education [Sections 3(1), 3(2)]

Section 3 (1) of the RTE Act provides the right of free and compulsory education to every child in the six to fourteen years age group. Under the Act, this education will be provided in a neighbourhood school till the completion of elementary education. Section 3(2) expressly states that no child will be liable to pay any kind of fee or charges, which may prevent him or her from pursuing elementary education.

Under the provisions of the Act, a school established by the Government or local authority will provide free and compulsory elementary education to all admitted children. Moreover, all unaided schools are required to provide free education to at least 25 per cent of children from weaker sections of society residing in their neighbourhood.

2. Standards for Recognition of Schools [Sections (18(1), 19(2)]

The RTE Act prescribes norms and standards (appended in the schedule to the Act) for a school, highlighting the key parameters such as:

- The ideal pupil-teacher ratio
- Guidelines related to school building
- Minimum number of working days
- Instructional hours in an academic year
- Minimum number of working hours per week for teachers
- Library facility
- Guidelines on teaching or play material

Moreover, under Section 18 (1) of the RTE Act, no school will be able to operate without obtaining a certificate of recognition from a competent local authority, subject to conformity with Section 19 of the Act. If a school is found in contravention of the conditions of recognition, the authority will withdraw recognition.

Section 19 (2) of the Act requires schools, established before the commencement of the Act and which do not conform to the norms and standards specified in the Schedule, to undertake steps to fulfil such norms and standards at their own expense within a period of three years from the commencement of the Act.

3. Establishment of Additional Schools [Sections 6, 7 (1), 7 (2)]

Section six of the RTE Act requires establishment of a school in areas/ neighbourhood, where any such provision is non-existent, within a stipulated period from commencement of the Act. According to Section 7 (1), both the Central Government and the state governments will have concurrent financial responsibilities for undertaking the provisions of the Act. As per Section 7(2), the Central Government will prepare estimates of capital and recurring expenditure required for the implementation of the Act.

4. Appointment of Qualified Teachers [Sections 23(1), 23(2)]

Section 23(1) of the RTE Act states that any person with minimum qualifications as laid down by the academic authority authorized by the Central Government will be eligible for appointment as a teacher. Section 23(2) also enables the Central Government to relax minimum qualifications (for a period not exceeding five years) for appointment as a teacher in states that do not have adequate number of institutions offering courses of training in teachers' education. Moreover, Section 23(2) allows teachers, who do not have the minimum qualification required at the time of commencement of the Act, to acquire this within a period of five years.

B. Accessibility

1. Disallowing Capitation Fees and Screening Procedure [Sections 13(1), 2(o)]

Section 13(1) of the RTE Act expressly disallows any school or person from collecting any capitation fee and subjecting a child or his/her parents or guardian to any screening procedure. Moreover, Section 2(o) calls for the use of only random procedures for admitting a child to a school. Under the random procedure, a lottery system is to be used to fill the seats if the number of children applying to a particular school exceeds the available seats.

2. Provision for Special Training (Section 4)

The RTE Act (Section 4) also requires admission of a child above six years, who has neither been admitted to any school nor has been able to complete his or her elementary education to an age-appropriate class. It specifies that any such child will also have the right to receive special training.

3. Admission of Students Belonging to Weaker and Disadvantaged Groups [Sections 12(1c), 12(2)]

Under Section 12(1c), private unaided schools will have to admit students belonging to weaker and disadvantaged groups to the extent of at least 25 per cent of their class strength. Section 12(2) of the RTE Act states that private unaided schools will be reimbursed their expenditure to the extent of the lesser of either per-child expenditure incurred by the Government or the actual amount charged for the child.

4. Balanced Representation on the School Management Committee [Section 21(1)]

Under Section 21(1) of the RTE Act, schools are required to constitute a School Management Committee (SMC) consisting of elected representatives from the local authority, parents or guardians of children admitted and teachers. It further states that three-fourths of the members of such a committee will be parents or guardians, with proportionate representation given to the parents or guardians of children belonging to disadvantaged groups and weaker sections of society. Moreover, it states that 50 per cent of the members of any such committee will be women. This section of the Act is not applicable to an unaided school, which is not receiving any aid or grants from the Government or local authority.

C. Acceptability

1. Development of National Curriculum [Sections 7(6a), 29(2)]

Under Section 7(6a) of the RTE Act, the Central Government is expected to develop the framework of a national curriculum with the help of academic authorities appointed by the state governments. In a notification dated 31 March 2010, the Central Government authorized the National Council of Educational Research and Training (NCERT) as the academic authority under Section 29 of the RTE Act that would lay down the curriculum and evaluation procedure for elementary education. This is a significant development, since the previous practice of the NCERT preparing the National Curriculum Framework (NCF) was purely advisory in nature. Under the Act, its role has become mandatory and will also involve state governments.

Under the Act, state governments will also specify academic authorities that will lay down curriculum and evaluation procedures at the state level. However, state curriculums must be prepared according to certain common principles described in Section 29(2) of the RTE Act. In fact, the Act legalizes the principles shared in the NCF 2005.

2. Prohibition of Holding Back and Expulsion or Physical Punishment and Mental Harassment

The RTE Act states that no child admitted to a school will be held back in any class or be expelled till the completion of his elementary education. It also states that no child will be subjected to physical punishment or mental harassment.

3. Duties of Teachers (Sections 24)

With a view of enhancing the professionalism of teachers, Section 24 of the RTE Act describes the key duties of teachers, including maintenance of regularity and punctuality, completion of the entire curriculum within a specified time, assessing the learning ability of each child and providing suitable instruction, including supplementary instruction, if necessary. Teachers are also required to hold regular meetings with parents and guardians to apprise them of key details relating to their wards' progress.

D. Adaptability

1. Admission of students belonging to socially disadvantaged groups.
2. Right of transfer to a school [Section 5(1)]: Section 5(1) provides right of transfer to another school to any child pursuing elementary education in a government or government-aided school.

Conclusion

Education is the responsibility of the Government. RTE needs to apply first to the Government schools. The ACT clearly states that the State Government is responsible for ensuring adequate number of schools and the infrastructure. The RTE is an effective tool that the Government has to use to improve enrolment and quality of education in fully aided schools first. We have seen in this paper that the Right to Education is now a Fundamental Right for all children in the age group of six to fourteen years. In simple word, it means that the Government will be responsible for providing education to every child up to the eight standards, free of cost, irrespective of class and gender. Part III of the Constitution of India gives all force to every child to get free and compulsory education through Article 21, and insertion of Article 21-A by the 86th Amendment is also a landmark in this respect.

The 4As are to be respected, protected and fulfilled by the government, as the prime duty-bearer, but there are also duties on other actors in the education process: the child as the privileged subject of the right to education and the bearer of the duty to comply with compulsory-education requirements; the child's parents, who are the 'first educators'; and professional educators, namely teachers. By using a participatory process, this framework of the 4As can become a tool to enable people to think through what the right to education means to them and compare their current reality to this ideal context.

References

1. A. Sen (1993). Capability and Well-Being in M. Nussbaum and A. Sen (eds.), *The Quality of Life*, Oxford: Clarendon Press, 30-53.

2. Committee on the Rights of the Child, *General Comment No 1*, CRC/GC/2001/, 17 April 2001, §§ 2, 15: http://www2.ohchr.org/english/bodies/crc/docs/GC1_en.doc.
3. Committee on Economic, Social and Cultural Rights, *General Comment No 13*, § 6, c: http://www.unhchr.ch/tbs/doc.nsf/(Symbol)/ae1a0b126d068e868025683c003c8b3b?Opendocument.
4. Committee on Economic, Social and Cultural Rights, *General Comment No 13*, § 6, d: http://www.unhchr.ch/tbs/doc.nsf/(Symbol)/ae1a0b126d068e868025683c003c8b3b?Opendocument.
5. ILO *Convention N° 182*, adopted 17 June 1999, entered into force 19 November 2000.
6. ILO *Convention N° 138*, adopted 26 June 1973, entered into force 19 June 1976.
7. Indigenous and Tribal Peoples Convention, adopted 27 June 1989, entered into force. 5 September 1991: http://www.ilo.org/ilolex/cgi-lex/convde.pl?C169.
8. K. Watkins (2000). *The Oxfam Education Report*, Oxford: Oxfam.
9. Special Rapporteur on the Right to Education, Annual Report, 55th Commission on Human Rights, E/CN.4/1999/47, 13 January 1999, §13: http://www2.ohchr.org/english/issues/education/rapporteur/annual.htm.
10. Special Rapporteur on the Right to Education, Annual Reports, 57th Commission on Human Rights E/CN.4/2001/52, 11 January 2001; 58th Commission on Human Rights, E/CN.4/2002/60, 7 January 2002: http://www2.ohchr.org/english/issues/education/rapporteur/annual.htm.
11. Special Rapporteur on the Right to Education, Annual report, 61st Commission on Human Rights, E/CN/4/2005/50, 17 December 2004, §§ 107-108: http://www.iidh.ed.cr/Documentos/Informes/Informe-relator-dic04-ingles.pdf.
12. Tomasevski, K. (2003). *Education Denied: Costs and Remedies.* London: Zed Books, 2003.
13. Tomasevski, K. (1999). Children's Rights, Adult's Duties. International Consultative Forum on Education for All. *Education – A Right or a Privilege? Student journalists report on the right to education worldwide.* 1999, p. 3.
14. Tomaševski K. (1999). *Preliminary Report of the Special Rapporteur on the right to education*, paragraphs 42-74; UN Committee on Economic, Social and Cultural Rights, *General Comment No. 13: The right to education*, UN document E/C.12/1999/10, 1999, paragraph 6.

16

The Inclusion of Diverse Learners
Issues and Challenges

D. Venkateshwarlu

The RTE Act ensures that the inclusion of children with diverse needs within the meaning of children belonging to disadvantaged group. Inclusion of children with diverse needs is significant in achieving the dream of Education for All. To enable the implementation of this Act, teacher education institutions will need to reframe their programme courses to include the perspective, concept and strategies of inclusive education.

Curriculum Framework for Teacher Education, 2009, recommended making the curriculum flexible and appropriate to accommodate the diversity of school children including children with special needs.

Indian Society is naturally more inclusive than segregationist in nature. Starting from the Gurukul System, efforts have been made to bring people in, rather than to keep them out. Inclusion, like learning is a dynamic process, not a static condition – a journey, not a destination (Topping and Maloney, 2005).

The phrase "inclusive education" has attracted much attention in recent years. However, an examination of literature and practice shows that the term has come to mean different things to different people.

'Inclusive education' means a system of education wherein all students – i.e. those with and without disability – learn together, most or all of the time, and the system of teaching-learning is suitably adapted to meet the learning needs of different types of students such that the learning outcomes of comparable/satisfactory quality are achieved for all students (*The Rights of Persons with Disabilities Bill, 2012*).

Inclusion means full inclusion of children with diverse abilities in all aspects of schooling that other children are able to access and enjoy. It involves regular schools and classrooms genuinely adapting and changing to meet the needs of children as well as celebrating and valuing differences. This definition of inclusion does not imply that children with diverse abilities will not receive specialized assistance or teaching outside of the classroom when required. For the severely disabled, there are provisions for home schooling. Most activists are, however, against home based education.

Inclusion is both a process for and outcome of understanding, acceptance and valuing of differences among today's school children and youth. It is both a process and an outcome for achieving social justice and equity in the society.

Meaningful inclusion in schools requires administrators, teachers and parents not only to value diversity, but also question the traditional practice of segregating students, who are different. Schools need to be provided with full range of resources necessary to deliver a full curriculum to all children, through a combination of class teacher, specialist, semi specialist, resource teacher, consultancy and ancillary staff, as necessary. That needs more staff. It is rather a question of improved and more differentiated quality than greater quantity.

The fundamental principle of inclusive school is that all children should learn together wherever possible, regardless of any difficulty or differences that they may have. Inclusive schools may recognize and respond to the diverse needs of their students, accommodating both different styles and rates of learning and ensuring quality education to all through appropriate curricula, organizational arrangements, teaching strategies, resources and partnership with their community.

We find two kinds of exclusion prevalent in schools largely because of an inadequate preparation of teachers to address diversity in the classroom. The first is the exclusion of the children with special needs. Neither does the teacher understand their needs nor what s/he can do to make learning possible for them. The RTE Act provides for free and compulsory education to all children including children with special needs. To enable the implementation of this Act, teacher education institutions will need to reframe their programme courses to include the perspective, concept and strategies of inclusive education.

More than a billion people around the world experience one or other form of disability according to the World Health Organization and World Bank 2011 report. On other estimates, about ten per cent of the population of developing countries are disabled. In India, an estimated 2.1 crore population are disabled.

UNESCO studies have suggested that only one-two per cent of children with disabilities in developing countries receive any education. It is estimated that only two per cent of people with disabilities in developing countries have access to rehabilitation and appropriate basic services. Women and girls with disabilities are particularly vulnerable to abuse.

About 1.40 million (NIEPA, 2005) children with special needs are in regular schools. Census and NSSO surveys estimated that 2.1-1.8 per cent of children with special needs are in regular schools.

The Government of India has to accelerate the new scheme of inclusive education to achieve the target of Education for All (EFA). According to IAMR (Institute of Applied Manpower Research) report, there is a shortage of 1,58,595 professionals to cater to the needs of children with special needs.

The second and more insidious pattern of exclusion is the social exclusion of children, who come from socially and economically deprived backgrounds, like the Scheduled Castes (SCs), Scheduled Tribes (STs), minority and other communities, girls and children with diverse learning needs. There is a dire need to equip teachers to overcome their biases in this regard and to develop professional capacities to address these challenges. The education of socially and economically disadvantaged groups, especially the SCs/STs and minorities has remained a primary national concern of education for several years. Though the literacy percentage among the SCs and STs has increased manifold, it is still much lower than the general category students.

Teachers will have to be equipped if social deprivation has to be overcome through education and Constitutional goals of social justice are to be achieved. Inclusive education refers to a philosophical position as well as an arrangement of institutional facilities and processes. This is to ensure access to and conditions of success in education for everybody, including those on the margins, because of physical or mental disabilities or because of their social position. The aim is to create an integrated school setting, providing equal opportunities to children with special abilities, varied social backgrounds and diverse learning needs.

Teachers need to be equipped to sensitively bring and include girls in the classroom transaction. It is necessary that teachers, who teach and manage the classrooms, are sensitized and made aware of the philosophy of inclusive education and oriented to the different kinds of adjustments that schools have to make in terms of infrastructure, curriculum, teaching methods and other school practices to relate teaching to the needs of all learners.

For effective implementation of inclusive education, teachers need an understanding of the educational needs of these children. Use appropriate strategies to help accomplish the lesson with maximum achievement for the students, e.g., use of cooperative learning, inquiry and graphic organizers. Give extra time as needed for children with special needs; provide feedback on completed work at the earliest. Make use of learning aids, like computers, calculators, projectors, etc. The attitude of teachers towards inclusive education should be positive.

A country's ability to develop support services at the school level may go a long way to ensuring that inclusion succeeds. Developing inclusive schools that cater to a wide range of pupils requires a clear policy on inclusion with adequate financial provisions, an effective public information effort to combat prejudice and create informed and positive attitudes, an extensive programme of orientation and staff training, and the provision of necessary support services. To make inclusion possible, the present education system, educational structure and educational practices need to be more flexible, more inclusive and more collaborative. The concern is to make teacher education *liberal*, *humanistic* and responsive to the demands of *inclusive education*.

References

1. Curriculum Framework for Teacher Education (2009). Towards Preparing Professional and Humane Teacher, National Council for Teacher Education (NCTE), New Delhi.
2. Right of Children to Free and Compulsory Education Act, 2009. The Gazette of India, August 27, 2009, New Delhi.
3. Topping, K. and Maloney's (Eds) (2005). *Inclusive Education*, London: Routledge Falmer.
4. UNESCO (1993). *Special Needs in the Classroom: Teacher Resource Pack.* Paris: UNESCO.

17

The Right to Education and Children with Disability

From Social Exclusion to Social Inclusion through Inclusive Education

Indrajeet Dutta

> *Education is not a static commodity to be considered in isolation from its greater context; it is an ongoing process and holds its own inherent value as a human right. Not only do people have the right to receive quality education now, they also have the right to be equipped with the skills and knowledge that will ensure long-term recognition of and respect for all human rights. A rights-based approach to education is imperative. Schooling that is respectful of human rights —both in words and in action, in schoolbooks and the schoolyard— is integral to the realization of quality education for all.*
>
> —UNESCO document on Education for All, 2007

Education is increasingly seen as a key to the inclusive and sustained development of a society. Experiences in many countries demonstrate that persistent social and economic inequalities and exclusion can lead to disaffection, social fragmentation and even conflicts. Furthermore, exclusion from quality educational opportunities is often related to inequalities in society. In this context, there is growing attention to disparities and inequalities in education, and to systematically addressing exclusion in education. The principle of equal educational opportunities is at the core of the right to education. Indeed, it inspired the movement for Education for All (EFA). What represents a more recent ambition is that education should not only be available to all, but that it has a crucial role in progress towards creating more inclusive and just societies. With this ambition, international consensus is converging towards a view that if there is a phenomenon of exclusion in an education system, then, it is not considered to be a quality education system. The re-orientation of education systems towards more inclusive and just societies, therefore, requires addressing exclusion in its diverse manifestations, while simultaneously taking a departure from deeply held assumptions about education and society. The first step of this challenging process, thus, necessarily entails a close and detailed look at the current education system in relation to the current situation of exclusion, together with reflection on how differently, rather than how much more, systems of education can be developed.

Inclusive, Integrated and Segregated Education

Globally, Children with Disabilities (CWD) count for one-third of all children out-of-school. In developing countries, the numbers are even more staggering, with 90 per cent of all children with disabilities being out-of-school. Although it is imperative that children with disabilities receive an education, it is also being recognized by bodies around the world that the type of education that children with disabilities receive is just as important. There are three basic types of Special Education, although many different models of classroom organization and teaching are available within each type.

Segregated education occurs when students with disabilities learn completely separate from their peers. Often, especially in "developing" countries, segregated education takes place in the form of special schools created specifically for the education of students with disabilities, or in completely separate classrooms for students with disabilities. Segregated education pinpoints the child as the problem in the system, the impediment to learning, and as a result, these students will often receive a completely different curriculum and different methods of testing, rather than being taught the same curriculum as their peers. This separation in school often creates separation within other areas of life as well. Integrated education is similar to inclusive education, but without any ideological commitment to equity. Integration places students in a mainstream classroom with "some adaptations and resources." However, students are expected to "fit in with pre-existing structures, attitudes and an unaltered environment. Integration is often mistaken for inclusion because students are placed in a mainstream classroom, which is a step towards inclusion. However, if there has not been a paradigm shift within the school and these students are not perceived as equals, if curriculum is not taught for the understanding of all instead of some, then, the students are integrated, but not included in the school.

Inclusive education "is a process of strengthening the capacity of the education system to reach out to all learners". "It involves restructuring the culture, policies and practices in schools, so that they can respond to the diversity of students in their locality." For a school to be inclusive, the attitudes of everyone in the school, including administrators, teachers, and other students, are positive towards students with disabilities. Inclusive education means that all children, regardless of their ability level, are included in a mainstream classroom, or in the most appropriate or least restrictive environment (LRE), that students of all ability levels are taught as equals, and that teachers must adjust their curriculum and teaching methodologies, so that all students benefit. This also avoids wasting resources, and "shattered hopes", which often occurs in classrooms that are "one size fits all", Studies have shown that systems that are truly inclusive reduce drop-out rates and repetition of grades, and have higher average levels of achievement; compared to systems that are not inclusive. People, who believe in inclusive education, believe that the education system is the impediment to learning for a child, and that every child is capable of learning!

Who Experiences Exclusion?

The right to education is high on the agenda of the international community. It is affirmed in numerous human rights treaties and recognized by governments as pivotal in the pursuit of development and social transformation. This recognition is exemplified in the international goals, strategies and targets that have been set during the past 20 years. The Education for All goals were established at Jomtien (Thailand) in 1990 and reaffirmed at the 2000 World Education Forum in Dakar (Senegal). In the Millennium Development Goals, established in 2000, the world's governments committed to achieving universal access to free, quality and compulsory primary education by 2015. In 'A World Fit for Children', the outcome document from the United Nations General Assembly Special Session on Children in 2002, governments reaffirmed these commitments and agreed to a range of strategies and actions to achieve them. However, the progress made to date is far from adequate. UNESCO statistics on enrolment indicate that 77 million children in 2004 were still not enrolled in school. According to UNICEF sources, this figure may be as high as 90 million children for 2005-2006 in terms of school attendance figures from household surveys. In India, according to the recent independent study by the Ministry of Human Resource Development (2008), an estimated 3.7 per cent of children in the age-group 6-10 and 5.2 per cent in the age-group 11-13 were out of school in 2008. In terms of numbers, about eight million children in the age-group 6-13 are out of school, about 6.7 million in rural and 1.3 million in urban areas. If attendance rate, instead of enrolment ratio, is used as the indicator to measure progress against MDG 2, the progress in achievement of universal education will not be as swift. With this attendance rate, the estimated number of children out of school or facing exclusion from primary education in the age group 6-13 would be higher.

International human rights treaties prohibit any exclusion from or limitation to educational opportunities on the bases of socially ascribed or perceived differences. They include differences in "sex," "race," "ethnic origin," "language," "religion," "political or other opinion," "national origin," "birth," "descent," "economic condition, "property," "social origin," "disability," and "the status, activities, expressed opinions, or beliefs of the child's parents, legal guardians, or family members." This means that a country needs to ensure that educational opportunities are not limited for anyone due to such differences listed above. Still, today, millions of children, youth and adults continue to experience exclusion in education in its various forms and expressions around the world. The statistics on global illiteracy and children out of school are a stark reminder that Education for All (EFA) is clearly *not for all.* Those, who are out of school, are in most societies the most marginalized and disadvantaged, the hard and hardest to reach. Out of them, children with disability are the ones, who are the most deprived and the hardest to reach. If Education for All is to be achieved by 2015, then the education rights and needs of these excluded groups must become paramount.

Disability and Social Exclusion

Our educations system is always concerned with literacy rate, dropout rate, attendance rate, enrolment rate of general, marginalized, deprived sections of the society and that's why various governmental, non-governmental and international bodies carried out all kind of surveys to estimate their numbers and possible solutions to achieve the MDG. When it is the case of disabled people, we even fail to find out their approximate numbers, leave alone their literacy and other rates. In our Census surveys, we hardly bothered to include them. Very few countries have in their Census a column for information about them. UNESCO GMR Report on MDG—Reaching the Marginalised (2010) states that "Disability is one of the least visible, but the most potent factors in educational marginalization." It is an accepted fact that it is the social, institutional and attitudinal barriers that limit the full inclusion of people with disabilities. Though time and again, society has reiterated about integration and inclusion based education, yet current statistics shows us that around 150 million children worldwide live with disabilities (Unicef and WHO, 2008). Around four in five children with disabilities live in developing countries. In addition, many millions of children live in households with parents or relatives, who have disabilities. At all ages, levels of both moderate and severe disability are higher in low and middle income countries than rich countries. The scale of disability and its concentration in the world's poorest countries contributes significantly to the marginalization in education. This is particularly so in rural areas or urban slums in developing countries. Systematic under reporting of disability is a serious problem. The probable reason cited in many of the documents is the stigmatization, which often makes parents and children reluctant to report disability.

India is the signatory of all these treaties and, therefore, has the compulsion of providing free and compulsory education to all children irrespective of the background. During these 20 years, India has made every possible effort either in terms of making policies or provision to provide education to CWD either in the form of integrated or inclusive education. These treaties or policies establish an entitlement to free, compulsory primary education for all children; an obligation to develop secondary education, supported by measures to render it accessible to all children, as well as equitable access to higher education; and a responsibility to provide basic education to individuals, who have not completed primary education. Furthermore, they affirm that the aim of education is to promote personal development, strengthen respect for human rights and freedoms, enable individuals to participate effectively in a free society, and promote understanding, friendship and tolerance. The right to education has long been recognized as encompassing not only access to educational provision, but also the obligation to eliminate discrimination at all levels of the educational system, to set minimum standards and to improve quality. In addition, education is necessary for the fulfilment of any other civil, political, economic or social right.

International Cooperation: Education for Persons with Disability

India is a signatory to the 1990 United Nations World Declaration on Education for All (EFA), which reaffirmed the rights of all children including children with disabilities to access education in regular school settings and to the Biwako Millennium Framework for Action towards an inclusive, barrier free and rights based society for persons with disability, the Declaration on the Full Participation and Equality of People with Disabilities in the Asia Pacific Region. India also subscribes to the philosophy of the 1993, UN Standard Rules on the Equalization of Opportunities for Persons with Disabilities and the Salamanca Statement and Frame work for Action (1994). This, perhaps, sets out in concise terms for the first time the concept of inclusive education and as one needing global consensus and urged all "governments to adopt as a matter of law and policy the principle of inclusive education and emphasized that "children with special needs must have access to regular schools." The Normalization Principle of Wolfensberger had much earlier placed focus on the person with disability and the slogan "change the environment to suit the child, not the child to suit the environment" became a well known quote.

The various international conventions related to right to education and inclusive education where there is an emphasis for social inclusion of these groups rather than social exclusion, are mentioned below:

Geneva Declaration of the Rights of the Child Adopted on 26 September 1924

The very first convention on the rights of the child was held in Geneva in 1924 named as "Declaration of Geneva", wherein it was mentioned that men and women of all nations, recognizing that mankind owes to the Child the best that it has to give, declare and accept it as their duty beyond and above all considerations of race, nationality or creed. Moreover it was resolved that the child, who is backward, must be helped.

Universal Declaration on Human Rights (1948)

The Universal Declaration of Human Rights, which was adopted by the UN General Assembly on 10 December 1948, was the result of the experience of the Second World War. With the end of that war, and the creation of the United Nations, the international community vowed never again to allow atrocities like those conflicts happen again. World leaders decided to complement the UN Charter with a road map to guarantee the rights of every individual everywhere. The document that they çonsidered, and which later became the Universal Declaration of Human Rights, was taken up at the first session of the General Assembly in 1946. The Assembly reviewed this draft Declaration on Fundamental Human Rights and Freedoms and transmitted it to the Economic and Social Council "for reference to the Commission on Human Rights for consideration. in its preparation of an international bill of rights." The first draft of the Declaration was proposed in September 1948 with over 50 Member States participating in the final drafting. By its resolution 217A (III) of 10 December 1948, the General Assembly, meeting in Paris, adopted the Universal Declaration of Human Rights. The General Assembly proclaims this Universal Declaration of Human Rights as a common standard of achievement for all peoples and all nations, to the end that every individual and every organ of society, keeping this Declaration constantly in mind, shall strive by teaching and education to promote respect for these rights and freedoms and by progressive measures, national and international, to secure their universal and effective recognition and observance, both among the peoples of Member States themselves and among the peoples of territories under their jurisdiction. In that declaration, almost 30 articles related to various aspects of human rights were charted out and one of them was on education. The article 26 relates to education whereas, especially Article 26(1) relates to elementary education wherein it was stated that "Everyone has the right to education. Education shall be free, at least in the elementary and fundamental stages. Elementary education shall be compulsory." This means elementary education is a fundamental right of every child irrespective of its background.

Declaration of the Rights of the Child adopted by the General Assembly on 20 November 1959

The principles related to this declaration are as follows:

Principle 5

The child, who is physically, mentally or socially handicapped, shall be given special treatment, education and care required by his particular condition.

Principle 7

The child is entitled to receive education, which shall be free and compulsory, at least in the elementary stages. He shall be given an education, which will promote his general culture and enable him, on the basis of equal opportunity, to develop his abilities, his individual judgement, and his sense of moral and social responsibility, and to become a useful member of society.

Convention against Discrimination in Education Adopted by the General Conference at its Eleventh Session, Paris, 14 December 1960

The General Conference of the United Nation's Educational, Scientific and Organization, meeting in Paris from 14 November to 15 December 1960. In its eleventh session, recalling that the Universal Declaration of Human Rights asserts the principle of non-discrimination and proclaims that every person has the right to education. Considering that discrimination in education is a violation of rights enunciated in that Declaration. The United Nation's Educational, Scientific and Cultural Organization has the purpose of instituting collaboration among the nations with a view to furthering for all universal respect for human rights and equality of educational opportunity.

International Covenant on Economic, Social and Cultural Rights (1966)

The States Parties to the present Covenant recognize the right of everyone to education. They agree that education shall be directed to the full development of the human personality and the sense of its dignity, and shall strengthen the respect for human rights and fundamental freedoms. They further agree that education shall enable all persons to participate effectively in a free society, promote understanding, tolerance and friendship among all nations and all racial, ethnic or religious groups, and further the activities of the United Nations for the maintenance of peace.

Convention on the Rights of the Child (1989)

The UN Convention on the Rights of the Child (1989) adopted and opened for signature, ratification and accession by General Assembly resolution 44/25 of 20 November 1989 was another important statement at the international level, which focus on the rights of disabled pupils to mainstream education and throughout the world 177 countries have ratified this statement. The major articles related to the right to education of disabled children are as follows:

World Declaration on Education for All: Meeting Basic Learning Needs

This World Conference on Education for All held at Jomtein, Thailand, March 1990 wherein almost 183 countries participated and reaffirmed the commitment that has been committed more than 40 years ago, in the Universal Declaration of Human Rights, and asserted that "everyone has a right to education". Despite notable efforts by countries around the globe to ensure the right to education for all, the following realities persist. The article III shows the concern about the gloomy status of primary education prevailing in different countries.

Article III - Universalizing Access and Promoting Equity

Basic education should be provided to all children, youth and adults. To this end, basic education services of quality should be expanded, and consistent measures must be taken to reduce disparities.

For basic education to be equitable, all children, youth and adults must be given the opportunity to achieve and maintain an acceptable level of learning.

The most urgent priority is to ensure access to, and improve the quality of, education for girls and women, and to remove every obstacle that hampers their active participation. All gender stereotyping in education should be eliminated.

An active commitment must be made to remove educational disparities. Underserved groups—the poor; street and working children; rural and remote populations; nomads and migrant workers; indigenous peoples; ethnic, racial, and linguistic minorities; refugees; those displaced by war; and people under occupation – should not suffer any discrimination in access to learning opportunities.

The learning needs of the disabled demand special attention. Steps need to be taken to provide equal access to education to every category of disabled persons as an integral part of the education system.

It was reiterated in the conference that there will be Universal access to and completion of primary education (or whatever higher level of education is considered as "basic") by the year 2000.

Dakar Framework for Action (2000)

The Dakar Framework for Action is a re-affirmation of the vision set out in the World Declaration on Education for All in Jomtien a decade ago. It expresses the international community's collective commitment to pursue a broad-based strategy for ensuring that the basic learning needs of every child, youth and adult are met within a generation and sustained thereafter. The World Education Forum (26-28 April 2000, Dakar) adopted the Dakar Framework for Action, Education for All: Meeting our Collective Commitments. In doing so, its participants reaffirmed the vision of the World Declaration on Education for All adopted ten years earlier (Jomtien, Thailand, 1990). The Dakar Framework is a collective commitment to action. Governments have an obligation to ensure that EFA goals and targets are reached and sustained.

> *We re-affirm the vision of the World Declaration on Education for All (Jomtien 1990), supported by the Universal Declaration of Human Rights and the Convention on the Rights of the Child, that all children, young people and adults have the human right to benefit from an education that will meet their basic learning needs in the best and fullest sense of the term, an education that includes learning to know, to do, to live together and to be. It is an education geared to tapping each individual's talents and potential, and developing learners' personalities, so that they can improve their lives and transform their societies.*

The Dakar Framework for Action is based on the most extensive evaluation of education ever undertaken, the Education for All (EFA) 2000 Assessment. Called for by the World Conference of Education for All, the Assessment produced a detailed analysis of the state of basic education around the world.

The Assessment shows that progress has been achieved, proving that Education for All is a realistic and achievable goal. But it needs to be frankly acknowledged that progress has been uneven and far too slow. At the start of a new millennium, the EFA 2000 Assessment shows the following:

- Of more than 800 million children under six years of age, less than a third benefit from any form of early childhood education.
- Some 113 million children, 60 per cent of whom are girls, have no access to primary schooling.
- At least 880 million adults are illiterate, of whom the majority are women.

We welcome the commitments made by the international community to basic education throughout the 1990s, notably at the World Summit for Children (1990), the United Nations Conference on Environment and Development (1992), the World Conference on Human Rights (1993), the

World Conference on Special Needs Education: Access and Quality (1994), the International Conference on Population and Development (1994), the World Summit for Social Development (1995), the Fourth World Conference on Women (1995), the Mid-Term Meeting of the International Consultative Forum on Education for All (1996), the Fifth International Conference on Adult Education (1997), and the International Conference on Child Labour (1997). The challenge now is to deliver these commitments.

Education is a fundamental human right. It is the key to sustainable development and peace and stability within and among countries, and thus an indispensable means for effective participation in the societies and economies of the twenty-first century, which are affected by rapid globalization. Achieving EFA goals should be postponed no longer. The basic learning needs of all can and must be met as a matter of urgency.

Equalization of Opportunities for Persons with Disabilities (1993)

Another international standard, which gives powerful support for the development of inclusive education for Children with Special Needs is the UN Standard Rules on the Equalisation of Opportunities for Persons with Disabilities (1993). According to the UN Standard rules on the Equalization of Opportunities for Persons with disabilities, (1993), countries should recognize the principle of equal primary, secondary and tertiary educational opportunities for children, youth and adults with disabilities in integrated settings. They should ensure that the education of people with disabilities is an integral part of the educational system. Marching towards the inclusion Vaughan cited in Hegarty and Alur, (2002) points out Rule 6 of UN Standard, which covers education and says that states should ensure that the education of disabled people is an integral part of the education system. The basic objective of this rule is to make school system in such a way that could meet the basic requirements of children with special needs, such as buildings must be accessible (this means that a wheel-chair user student should not find difficulty in mobility because of the structure of the building; there must be a ramp). Secondly, interpreter and support services, a flexible curriculum plus addition and adaptation. Further, every those aspects that are connected to the education of children with disabilities must be fulfilled, like parents and organisations of the disabled people to be involved in the education.

The Salamanca World Conference on Special Needs Education: Access and Quality

On international platform, there have been a number of encouraging pronouncements in recent years, affirming the principle of inclusive education and the importance of 'working towards schools for all—institutions, which include everybody, celebrate differences, support learning and respond to individual needs (Salamanca Statement, 1994).

Globally, the Salamanca Framework for Education for All is one of the important international events in the direction of declaring equal rights of person with disabilities. The Salamanca conference held in 1994, set the stage for inclusive education, wherein 92 countries became the signatories of the Salamanca statement including India and United Kingdom (UK) (UNESCO 1994). To give the highest policy and budgetary priority to improve the education system of the signatory nations, the Salamanca statement called upon the governments of respected nations to enable them to include all children regardless of individual differences or difficulties' (UNESCO,1994). The Salamanca statement can be considered as an important event because the nations committed to the UNESCO's vision of educating all children including children with special educational needs (SEN) and disabilities are then motivated to create an inclusive education system and an inclusive society at large. The basic objectives of Salamanca EFA are as follows:

- Every child has a fundamental right to education, and must be given the opportunity to achieve and maintain an acceptable level of learning,
- Every child has unique characteristics, interests, abilities and learning needs,
- Education systems should be designed and educational programmes implemented to take into account the wide diversity of these characteristics and needs,
- Those with special educational needs must have access to regular schools, which should accommodate them within child centred pedagogy capable of meeting these needs,
- Regular schools with this inclusive orientation are the most effective means of combating discriminatory attitudes, creating welcoming communities, building an inclusive society and achieving education for all; moreover, they provide an effective education to the majority of children and improve the efficiency and, ultimately, the cost-effectiveness of the entire education system.

Monitoring the Convention on the Rights of Persons with Disabilities: Guidance for Human Rights Monitors (2010)

Understanding Disability as a Human Rights Issue

It is estimated that over 650 million people, ten per cent of the world's population, have a disability. Eighty per cent live in developing countries. Some women, men and children with disabilities are fully integrated in society, and are participating in and actively contributing to all areas of life. However, the great majority face discrimination, exclusion, isolation and even abuse.

Many persons with disabilities live in extreme poverty, in institutions without education or employment opportunities and face a range of other marginalizing factors. In some countries, they are denied the right to own property and it is common for persons with disabilities to be denied the right to make decisions for themselves. The discrimination they face is widespread, cutting across geographical boundaries and affecting people in all spheres of life and all sectors of society. The entry into force of the Convention on the Rights of Persons with Disabilities and its Optional Protocol in May 2008 marked the beginning of a new era in the efforts "to promote, protect and ensure the full and equal enjoyment of all human rights and fundamental freedoms by all persons with disabilities, and to promote respect for their inherent dignity" (Article 1). Although persons with disabilities have always been entitled to the same rights as everyone else, it is the first time that their rights are set out comprehensively in a binding international instrument. The development of the Convention reflects the shift that has taken place in the way disability and persons with disabilities are seen. Historically, disability has been considered to be a personal condition residing in the individual. As an individual deficit, the status of "being disabled" has been viewed as the natural cause for some people being unable to attend a regular school, get a job or participate in social life. When disability is perceived in this way, society's responses are restricted to only one of two paths: individuals can be "fixed" through medicine or rehabilitation (medical approach); or they can be cared for through charity or welfare programmes (charity approach). According to this old model, the lives of persons with disabilities are handed over to professionals, who control such fundamental decisions as to where they will go to school, what support they will receive and where they will live.

Over the past few decades, there has been an important change in the way disability is understood. The focus is no longer on what is wrong with the person. Instead, disability is recognized as the consequence of the interaction of the individual with an environment that does not accommodate that individual's differences and limits or impedes the individual's participation in society. This approach is referred to as the social model of disability. The Convention on the Rights of Persons with Disabilities endorses this model and takes it forward by explicitly recognizing disability as a human rights issue.

From this perspective, the social, legal, economic, political and environmental conditions that act as barriers to the full exercise of rights by persons with disabilities need to be identified and overcome. For example, their marginalization and their exclusion from education are not the result of their inability to learn, but of insufficient teacher training or inaccessible classrooms; their exclusion from the labour market might be due to a lack of transport to the workplace or negative attitudes among employers and colleagues that a person with disabilities is unable to work; and their inability to participate in public affairs might result from the lack of electoral material in accessible formats, such as Braille or voting booths that are physically inaccessible to persons with disabilities.

Viewing disability from a human rights perspective involves an evolution in thinking and acting by States and all sectors of society, so that persons with disabilities are no longer considered to be recipients of charity or objects of others' decisions, but holders of rights. A rights-based approach seeks ways to respect, support and celebrate human diversity by creating the conditions that allow meaningful participation by a wide range of persons, including persons with disabilities. Protecting and promoting their rights is not only about providing disability-related services. It is about adopting measures to change attitudes and behaviours that stigmatize and marginalize persons with disabilities. It is also about putting in place the policies, laws and programmes that remove barriers and guarantee the exercise of civil, cultural, economic, political and social rights by persons with disabilities. To achieve a genuine exercise of rights, the policies, laws and programmes that limit rights need to be replaced, such as: immigration laws that prohibit entry to a country based on disability; laws that prohibit persons with disabilities to marry; laws that allow the administration of medical treatment to persons with disabilities without their free and informed consent; laws that allow detention on the basis of mental or intellectual disability; and policies that deny medical care to a person because he or she has a disability. Moreover, programmes, awareness-raising and social support are necessary to change the way society operates and to dismantle the barriers that prevent persons with disabilities from participating fully in society. Furthermore, persons with disabilities need to be provided with the opportunities to participate fully in society and with the adequate means to claim their rights.

The Convention on the Rights of Persons with Disabilities—The Need for a Convention

The core international human rights instruments that precede the Convention on the Rights of Persons with Disabilities recognize the rights of all, including persons with disabilities. While these instruments offer significant potential to promote and protect the human rights of persons with disabilities, this potential has not yet been fully realized. The Convention on the Rights of Persons with Disabilities marks the end of a long struggle by persons with disabilities and their representative organizations to have disability fully recognized as a human rights issue, which began back in 1981, with the International Year of Disabled Persons and the World Programme of Action concerning Disabled Persons, adopted as the outcome of that Year. The adoption, in 1993, by the United Nations General Assembly of the Standard

Rules on the Equalization of Opportunities for Persons with Disabilities, the reports of the Special Rapporteurs on Disability and of the Sub-Commission on Prevention of Discrimination and Protection of Minorities, and a series of resolutions by the Commission on Human Rights in 1998, 2000 and 2002, contributed significantly to pave the way for a human rights approach.

Defining Disability

The Convention does not include a definition of disability or persons with disabilities in the strict sense, but rather provides some guidance on the concept of "disability" and its relevance to the Convention. The preamble clearly endorses a social approach to disability—referred to as the social model of disability—by recognizing that "disability is an evolving concept and that disability results from interaction between persons with impairments and attitudinal and environmental barriers that hinders their full and effective participation in the society on an equal basis with others." The explicit reference to the barriers that are external to the subject as constituting factors of disability represents an important step away from notions that equated disability to the existence of functional limitations. Accordingly, Article 1 states: "Persons with disabilities include those, who have long-term physical, mental, intellectual or sensory impairments, which in interaction with various barriers may hinder their full and effective participation in society on an equal basis with others" (emphasis added). From this perspective, persons with disabilities' participation in society—be it having a job, going to school, visiting a doctor or running for elections—is limited or excluded not because of their having an impairment, but because of various barriers, which might include physical barriers, but also legislation and policies in some cases. For persons with physical disabilities, these barriers might include uneven terrains, steps to connect different levels, heavy doors or narrow passages. For example, a person using a wheelchair might be excluded from attending a meeting if the door to the meeting room is too narrow for the wheelchair to pass, or if there is no ramp or lift. The inexistence or inadequacy of accessibility standards in building codes could also amount to a barrier. The Convention does not preclude the use of definitions in national legislation and, in fact, definitions might be particularly necessary in some sectors, such as employment or social security. It is important, however, for such definitions to reflect the social model of disability enshrined in the Convention and for definitions based on a list or a description of impairments or on functional limitations to be revised. Monitors should observe whether national legislation: (a) recognizes that discrimination can occur in relation to mental, intellectual, sensory or physical impairments; (b) incorporates the social model by referring to disability as the result of the interaction between the person with an impairment and external barriers; (c) focuses on the prohibition of discrimination and the promotion of equality rather than on the categorization of various disabilities.

The Convention's Principles

Article 3 of the Convention identifies a set of overarching and foundational principles. These guide the interpretation and implementation of the entire Convention, cutting across all issues. They are the starting point for understanding and interpreting the rights of persons with disabilities, providing benchmarks against which each right is measured.

What do these Principles Mean?

Respect for inherent dignity, refers to the worth of every person. When the dignity of persons with disabilities is respected, their experiences and opinions are valued and are formed without fear of physical, psychological or emotional harm. Respect for dignity is denied when, for example, workers, who are blind, are forced by their employer to wear a shirt with the word "blind" printed on the back.

Individual autonomy means to be in charge of one's own life and to have the freedom to make one's own choices. Respect for the individual autonomy of persons with disabilities means that persons with disabilities have, on an equal basis with others, reasonable life choices, are subject to minimum interference in their private life and can make their own decisions, with adequate support where required. The principle pervades the Convention and underpins many of the freedoms that it explicitly recognizes, such as the freedom from non-consensual medical intervention and the requirement that health care should be provided on the basis of free and informed consent. From this perspective, for example, a person with mental disabilities should be offered a range of options for mental health care, such as psycho-therapy, counselling, peer support and psychiatric medication, and should have the freedom to make a meaningful choice based on personal preferences. Likewise, a landmine survivor with a physical impairment should be provided with devices that facilitate his or her personal mobility, so that he or she can enjoy as much independence as possible.

The principle of non-discrimination means that all rights are guaranteed to everyone without distinction, exclusion or restriction based on disability or on race, colour, sex, language, religion, political or other opinion, national or social origin, property, birth, age, or any other status. Discrimination on the basis of disability means any distinction, exclusion or restriction, which has the purpose or effect of impairing or nullifying the recognition, enjoyment or exercise by persons with disabilities, on an equal basis with others, of all human rights and fundamental freedoms, and includes the denial of reasonable accommodation. Discrimination occurs, for example, when a woman is not allowed to open a bank account on the grounds that her disability would not allow her to manage her money. Discrimination also occurs when a man, who was offered a job after an interview, is later told to go home and wait for written confirmation from the administration after the employer realizes that the man has a visual impairment and needs to hold books very close to his eyes. The correspondence never arrives and the man never takes up the job. Persons with disabilities might also experience multiple forms of discrimination; for example, a woman with disabilities might experience discrimination on the basis of sex as well as disability. The recognition of the principle of non-discrimination in Article 3 underlines the importance of considering discrimination in all its forms.

Equality means creating societal conditions that respect difference, address disadvantages and ensure that all women, men, girls and boys participate fully on equal terms. Equality is denied when a girl with a disability is taken out of school by her parents. Despite her good grades, her parents decide that it is useless to spend money on her education because of her disability. Achieving equality sometimes requires additional measures, such as the provision of assistance to persons with psycho-social or intellectual disabilities in order to support them in making decisions and in exercising their legal capacity on an equal basis with others.

The concept of full and effective participation and inclusion and accessibility means that society, both in its public and in its private dimensions, is organized to enable all people to take part fully. Being fully included in society means that persons with disabilities are recognized and valued as equal participants. Their needs are understood as integral to the social and economic order and not identified as "special". To achieve full inclusion, an accessible, barrier free physical and social environment is necessary. For instance, full and effective participation and inclusion mean that political election processes do not exclude persons with disabilities, ensuring, for example, that voting locations are accessible and election procedures and materials are available in multiple formats and easy to understand and use. Linked to the concept of participation and inclusion is that of universal design, which is defined in the Convention as the "design of products, environments, programmes and services that should be usable by all people, to the greatest extent possible, without the need for adaptation or specialized design" (Article 2). In other words, the design phase should consider the needs of all members of society, to ensure that special adaptations are not required later on.

The Rights of Persons with Disabilities

The Convention on the Rights of Persons with Disabilities is a wide-ranging human rights treaty covering the full spectrum of civil, cultural, economic, political and social rights. The Convention does not establish new rights for persons with disabilities; instead, it elaborates on what existing human rights mean for persons with disabilities and clarifies the obligations of State parties to protect and promote these rights. In order to ensure an environment conducive to the fulfilment of the rights of persons with disabilities, the Convention also includes Articles on awareness-raising, accessibility, situations of risk and humanitarian emergencies, access to justice, personal mobility and rehabilitation, as well as statistics and data collection.

Article 24—Education

The right to education requires, inter alia, examining whether pupils and students with disabilities are not excluded from the general education system on the basis of their disability, that reasonable accommodation of the pupil's requirements is provided in the general education system and that effective individualized support measures are provided to maximize academic and social development consistent with the goal of inclusion.

The United Nations Conventions on the Rights of the Child (1989), the UN Standard Rules on the Equalisation of Opportunities for Persons with Disabilities (1993) and the above mentioned UNESCO's Salamanca Statement and Framework for Action and the latest of them, the Convention on the Rights of Persons with Disabilities (2010) visualise and support 'Inclusion' as a powerful tool to bring every child under the roof of equality of education and further support it as a right of children with Special Education Needs (SEN) to become active members of mainstream schools. Altogether these documents make a strong case for inclusion and provide a unique opportunity to place inclusion firmly on the agenda of the national Governments (Bhatt, M).

The Convention on the Rights of Persons with Disabilities (2007)

The Convention on the Rights of Persons with Disabilities (UNCRPD) and its Optional Protocol was adopted at the UN headquarters in New York. The following March, the UNCRPD and Optional Protocol were open for signatures and ratifications, and this particular convention had "the highest number of signatories in history to a UN Convention on its opening day." Article 24 of the UNCRPD addresses education. Article 24, titled simply "Education", is split up into five sections. Section one addresses why it is a right for people with disabilities to access the same mainstream education that people without disabilities receive. Inclusive education is imperative for people with and without disabilities because it allows people of all ability levels to develop skills and become effective members in a "free society". Section one points out that education of people with disabilities isn't just a human right, but is imperative for the development of humans to their fullest potential.

Education gives people of all ability levels dignity. Section two specifically discusses inclusion. This section mandates that people with disabilities "are not excluded from the general education system on the basis of disability". Specifically, people with disabilities should be able to access "free and compulsory" primary and secondary education in the community within which they live. According to Section two of Article 24, inclusion means including "reasonable accommodation" for children with disabilities, and providing "effective individualized supports" in "environments that maximize academic and social development". Section three delves deeper into communication and mobility tools that will ensure "full and equal participation" in both school and the community. It mandates that students with disabilities learn and have access to materials in Braille, sign language, and alternative script, as well as the proper mobility aids. Most importantly, section three specifies that education is delivered "in the most appropriate languages and modes and means of communication for the individual."

The last two Sections touch on teacher training and tertiary education or vocational training. Section four discusses employing teachers, "including teachers with disabilities," who know Braille, sign language, and other alternative forms of communication, and letting these teachers spread their knowledge to mainstream teachers, including information regarding disability awareness. The last Section, five, discusses the importance of making tertiary education or vocational training available to all people with disabilities and emphasizes the importance of ensuring that people with disabilities are not discriminated against in the entry process and throughout these programmes.

Policy, Laws or Acts Related to PWD in India

India has a long experience of policy and practice with respect to disability, including collection of Census information on disability from as early as 1872, and special schools and institutions operating since the 19th century. Like many countries, it also had specific provision for people with mental illness and retardation under the Indian Lunacy Act of 1912. After independence, when the Constitution of India was framed in 1950, 'right to education and work' was mentioned in Article 41 and 'free compulsory education for all children up to the age of 14 years was quoted in Article 15. However, there were little efforts geared in this direction.

The Constitution of India also acknowledged general state obligations towards PWDs in Article 41, and the State List under "Relief of the disabled and unemployable". Subsequently, specific measures, such as employment concessions were introduced from the 1960s. However, *it was not until the 1980s that policy commitment to full participation of PWD in Indian society evolved.* The outcomes of this policy shift were realized in several key pieces of legislation: (i) the Mental Health Act, 1987; (ii) the Persons with Disabilities

(Equal Opportunities, Protection of Rights and Full Participation) Act, 1995 (PWD Act); (iii) the Rehabilitation Council of India Act, 1992 and amended in 2000 (RCI Act); and (iv) the National Trust for Welfare of Persons with Autism, Cerebral Palsy, Mental Retardation and Multiple Disabilities Act, 1999 (National Trust Act). Each legislation has its strong points that benefit children with disabilities and weaknesses too. Thus, the author will critically examine each legislation suggesting its good points and the point that made it weak (Kundu, 2000).

India Lunacy Act (ILA) (1912)

The mental health legislation is essential to protect the rights and dignity of persons with mental disorders, and they could develop accessible and effective mental health services (Trivedi). Mental illness and mental retardation are two distinct conditions. However, in ILA, persons suffering from mental illness and mental retardation are grouped together and similar laws are applicable to the mentally ill and retarded persons. This was the biggest drawback in this legislation (*ibid*).

Mental Health Act (MHA) (1987)

As per the Mental Health Act (1987), the Government of India, Ministry of Law and Justice, (Trivedi), "mentally ill Person" means person, who is in need of treatment by reason of any mental disorder other than mental retardation. The another important point that needs to be noted is that the Mental Health Act clearly excludes the persons with mental retardation from the definition of persons with mental illness. With this exclusion, for the first time, the legal interests of the persons, who are mentally ill and those, who are retarded, are not being jointly considered (*Ibid*).

He further points out that MHA, 1987 primarily deals with treatment and institutionalization of the mentally ill, protection and management of their property. The right to legal aid and representation has also been granted to the mentally ill by this Act. With the enforcement of the MHA, the Indian Lunacy Act of 1912, which was the operative law on these areas for the persons with mental retardation, became nonexistent. This Act does differentiate the two – mental illness and mental retardation – but is not applicable for mentally retarded, a legal vacuum that prevailed in with regard to the rights of protection of the persons with mental retardation till the introduction of the Disability Act 1995. Therefore, these are some important points about this Act. Looking forward to further Acts, the important thing that need to be considered is that these Acts are not only beneficial to person with disabilities, but also give importance to the professionals dealing with the mentally sick or retarded and their parents in direct or indirect way. This will be discussed thoroughly in further parts of the paper (Kundu, 2000).

Rehabilitation Council of India Act (RCI) (1992)

The Rehabilitation Council of India (RCI) is a statutory body under the Ministry of Social Justice and Empowerment to regulate and introduce uniformity in the human resource development in country. Under this Act, every rehabilitation practitioner including special educators are expected to register with RCI after qualifying from Training Institutes recognised by RCI to ensure maintenance of standards. The RCI Act is a major move by the Government of India for quality assurance in the education, training and management of persons with disabilities. Furthermore, a list of recognised rehabilitation qualifications granted by universities or institutions in India is also approved by the Rehabilitation Council of India Act (Vijayan and Naomi, 2006). As previously mentioned, the educational policies and legislation not only benefit pupils, but also the concerned people. This legislation was basically for regulation, standardization and recognition of training programme in the field of rehabilitation of person with disabilities.

Persons with Disabilities (Equal Opportunities, Full Participation and Protection of Rights) Act 1995

This Act came into enforcement on February 7, 1996 as an important and significant step in the direction to ensure full participation of persons with disabilities in the nation building (Kundu, 2000). The Act provides preventive and promotional aspects of rehabilitation, like education, employment, and vocational training, reservation, research and manpower development, creation of barrier free environment, unemployment allowance, special insurance scheme for the disabled employees and establishment of homes for person with severe disabilities (Vijayan and Naomi, 2006).

Basically, this Act consists of 14 major chapters focusing on specific demands made by the disabled people in order to ensure that the promise made in this Act are honoured by the government. The Chapter 4 tells about Education, which is as follows:

A. The appropriate Governments and the local authorities shall:

- Ensure that every child with a disability has access to free education in an appropriate environment till he attains the age of eighteen years;
- Endeavour to promote the integration of students with disabilities in the normal schools;
- Promote setting up of special schools in Government and private sector for those in need of special education, in such a manner that children with disabilities living in any part of the country have access to such schools;
- Endeavour to equip the special schools for children with disabilities with vocational training facilities.

B. The appropriate Governments and the local authorities shall by notification make schemes for:

- Conducting part-time classes in respect of children with disabilities, who having completed education up to class fifth and could not continue their studies on a whole-time basis;
- Conducting special part-time classes for providing functional literacy for children in the age group of sixteen and above;
- Imparting non-formal education by utilizing the available manpower in rural areas after giving them appropriate orientation;
- Imparting education through open schools or open universities;
- Conducting class and discussions through interactive electronic or other media;
- Providing every child with disability special books and equipments needed for his education free of cost.

C. The appropriate Government shall initiate or cause to be initiated research by official and non-governmental agencies for the purpose of designing and developing new assistive devices, teaching aids, special teaching materials or such other items as are necessary to give a child with disability equal opportunities in education.

D. The appropriate Governments shall set up adequate number of teachers' training institutions and assist the national institutes and other voluntary organizations to develop teachers' training programmes specializing in disabilities, so that requisite number of trained manpower is available for special schools and integrated schools for children with disabilities.

E. Without prejudice to the foregoing provisions, (be appropriate Governments shall by notification prepare a comprehensive education scheme, which shall make Provision for:

- Transport facilities to the children with disabilities or any other alternative financial incentives to parents or guardians to enable their children with disabilities to attend schools;
- The removal of architectural barriers from schools, colleges or other institutions imparting vocational and professional training;
- The supply of books, uniforms and other materials to children with disabilities attending school;
- The grant of scholarship to students with disabilities;
- Setting up of appropriate fora for the redressal of grievances of parent, regarding the placement of their children with disabilities;
- Suitable modification in the examination system to eliminate purely mathematical questions for the benefit of blind students and students with low vision;

- Restructuring of curriculum for the benefit of children with disabilities;
- Restructuring the curriculum for benefit of students with hearing impairment to facilitate them to take only one language as part of their curriculum.

National Trust for Welfare of Persons with Autism, Cerebral Palsy, Mental Retardation and Multiple Disabilities Act (1999)

It is well known that some of the disabilities need lifelong care of varying degrees, despite best of training and rehabilitation efforts. Parents always have the big question in their mind, "What will happen to our child after us?" The National Trust Act is an answer to this question. India is a country with close-knit families and the children are always with the families. Thus, keeping in mind all these basic things, the Act has made provisions for appointment of guardians for those, who have applied and residential facilities by organisations, which will have to maintain minimum standards prescribed by the Act in terms of space, staff, furniture, rehabilitation and medical facilities. This is an Act to provide for the constitution of a body at the National Level for the welfare of persons with autism, cerebral palsy, mental retardation and multiple disabilities and for matters connected therewith or incidental thereto (Kundu, 2000).

Government Interventions for Inclusive Education

Though in policy documents, the government has shown its commitment towards inclusive education and it is reflected through the programmes it has launched, but none of the programmes has its impact on the system. The first time government made an attempt of inclusive Education through its policy document, National Education Commission (1964-66) and thereafter in National Policy of Education (1968). But later on, it is the National Policy of Education (1986), which had changed the scenario of inclusive education wherein government commitment was seen much more aggressively. Later on, schemes like UEE, DPEP, Lok Jumbish, Mahila Samakhya, Bihar and Andhra Education Project, SSA etc. programmes were launched and one of the objectives of these schemes was to integrate the special children in mainstream schools. Some of the schemes launched by the government are as follows:

Integrated Education for Disabled Children (IEDC)

The Ministry of Welfare, now Social Justice and Empowerment, implemented the Integrated Education for Disabled Children (IEDC) scheme from 1974 to 1982, when it was transferred to the Department of Education (Dasgupta, 2002). The scheme was apparently intended to encourage co-operation between mainstream and special schools in order to support integration, although Julka (2005) believes that this co-operation did not happen. Singal (2005b) too, argues that the programme is seen as an overall failure by those outside the government. Unfortunately, the researcher was not able to access literature exploring these failures further, reflecting the need for valid and reliable data to enable improved project planning in the future. IEDC has been replaced by the Integrated Education for the Disabled (IED) component of the national District Primary Education Project (DPEP), and supports community mobilization and early detection, in-service teacher training, architectural design in schools (Mukhopadhyay, nd), the establishment of resource centres, teacher training, identification and assessment of children with disabilities, and the supply of specialist aids and appliances (Mukhopadhyay, 2003).

Project on Integrated Education for Disabled (PIED)

In 1987, UNICEF and the government-funded National Council of Educational Research and Training (NCERT) launched the Project on Integrated Education for Disabled (PIED) in ten blocks (the administrative level between district and village (Thomas, 2005b)) that focused on teacher training in order to encourage integration. PIED was later amalgamated with the DPEP and SSA (see below) and by 2002, it was extended to 27 States (Julka, 2005). While enrolment of children with disabilities in the mainstream increased and the retention was high (Julka, 2005; Jangira and Ahuja, 1994), the coverage has been "miniscule" with only two-three per cent of children with disabilities getting integrated in mainstream institutions (Julka, 2005: 9). Criticisms made in the project evaluation pointed to implementation issues, such as children getting financial assistance, who were not classified as disabled, or teacher training courses being un-regulated (Julka, 2005). However, the design of the project, which encouraged continued labelling of children and withdrawal of those with disabilities from particular activities in school, was not highlighted (Ainscow *et al.*, 1995 cited in Singal, 2005b; Jangira and Ahuja, 1994). Further, despite aiming to deliver learner-centred teacher training courses, much of the course instruction was found to be traditionally formal (Jangira and Ahuja, 1994), hence, failing in one of its key objectives of instigating change in pedagogy through teacher training.

District Primary Education Programme (DPEP)

The 1995 District Primary Education Programme (DPEP), funded 85 per cent by the Central Government via a World Bank loan and support from the European Community, UNICEF and the UK and Netherlands Governments, and fifteen per cent by the State governments, focused on the universalization of primary education, particularly for the girls. The intention was for district-specific planning to make the programme contextual, and for participatory processes to empower and build capacity at all levels (GOI, 2002). However, Kobayashi (2006) found that the programme focused on quantitative targets and educational administration capacity-building more than participation, hence, failing to empower local communities, unlike Lok Jumbish. Children with disabilities were included with the aim of achieving EFA.

Extensive construction led to the creation of 200,000 new schools, and a teacher-training component led to the in-service training of all teachers. Alur (2002) argues that there were failures not so willingly reported, such as corruption in the form of budgets for non-existent non-formal education centres, tribal dropout, the difficulty of multi-grade teaching in one-teacher schools, low learning achievement, and no integration of children with disabilities due to continued reliance on special school systems. However, it is arguable that the existence of special school systems does not necessarily obstruct locational integration in the mainstream. Due to a lack of data, it is not possible to confirm how many children with disabilities were, or were not, integrated under the auspices of DPEP.

Janshala

This community school programme started in 1998 and is now replaced by the SSA (see below), was a collaboration between the Government of India and the UNDP, UNICEF, UNESCO, the ILO, and UNFPA, and supported the government drive towards universal primary education. It covered 120, mainly rural, blocks in nine States where there is evidence of low female literacy, child labour, and SC/ST children not catered for under DPEP (Mukhopadhyay, 2005). Unfortunately, due to limited availability of data, it is not possible to elaborate on any issues arising on the *Janshala* programme, which has a component designed to improve the attendance of difficult to reach groups of children, including children with disabilities.

Sarva Shiksha Abhiyan (SSA)

Sarva Shiksha Abhiyan (SSA) is the government's millennial Education for All umbrella programme for all education schemes, which aims to universalise elementary education. The goals are that all children aged 6-14: i) will receive some form of education by 2003; ii) will complete five years' primary education by 2007; and iii) will complete eight years' education by 2010 (GoI, 2002). Disability indicators are included in the government agreement for SSA (Thomas, 2005a), although what exactly these are and whether they are taken on at local level is unclear. In fact, although one of the official SSA objectives is the enrolment of children with disabilities, the World Bank (2004) SSA project appraisal does not list disability as a key indicator, unlike gender, SC and ST. The fact that there are still many children out-of-school in 2006 demonstrates not only how behind this programme already is, but also how over-ambitious the infrastructure-led SSA goals were in the first place. For example, of the one million new classrooms that should have been built by 2007, there are only 300,000; 100,000 of which are not fully functional (Lal, 2005). Part of the "compelling" rationale for World Bank assistance to SSA was the continuous monitoring and evaluation and the "built-in accountability mechanism at the school and community levels" (World Bank, 2004: 2). With donor support of the government feedback system, it was hoped that, "the development of mechanisms to assure cross-state and cross district observation, dialogue and learning for programme refinement could be among SSA's most enduring features" (World Bank, 2004).

However, despite an awareness of SSA lagging so far behind in the achievement of its intended targets, there is apparently no sign of accelerated political momentum to lend a sense of urgency to the task (Lal, 2005). This is perhaps a reflection of there being "...no condition of effectiveness..." in the World Bank interest-free loan contributing towards the funding of SSA (World Bank, 2004: 8). With a planned central: state government budget ratio of 85:15 changing to 50:50 in 2007, there is a high risk of some states not being able to afford to finance the programme (Govinda and Biswal, 2006; Lal, 2005), and perhaps an accompanying weakening of political will and programme implementation. The lack of political voice of the poorest people, whom this programme is intended to assist, further pushes education to the lower strata of politicians' agendas (Lal, 2005). While criticism from the Indian media may be justified and necessary to raise awareness, it remains to be seen whether SSA will be able to adapt and become more effective over the next four years.

National Policy for Persons with Disabilities (2006)

The most broad and comprehensive policy related to CWD was brought in by the Government of India in the year 2005 wherein all kinds of disabilities and its severity is encompassed along with the mention of role and responsibilities of various agencies. The opening statement of the policy reiterated, "The Constitution of India ensures equality, freedom, justice and dignity of all individuals and implicitly mandates an inclusive society for all including persons with disabilities. In the recent years, there have been vast and positive changes in the perception of the society towards persons with disabilities. It has been realized that a majority of persons with disabilities can lead a better quality of life if they have equal opportunities and effective access to rehabilitation measures." The main provisions related to elementary education in this policy are as follows:

- Education is the most effective vehicle of social and economic empowerment. In keeping with the spirit of Article 21A of the

Constitution guaranteeing education as a fundamental right and Section 26 of the Persons with Disabilities Act, 1995, free and compulsory education has to be provided to all children with disabilities up to the minimum age of 18 years. According to the Census, 2001, fifty-one per cent persons with disabilities are illiterate. This is a very large percentage. There is a need for mainstreaming of persons with disabilities in the general education system through Inclusive education.

- Sarva Shiksha Abhiyan (SSA) launched by the Government has the goal of eight years of elementary schooling for all children including children with disabilities in the age group of 6-14 years by 2010. Children with disabilities in the age group of 15-18 years are provided free education under Integrated Education for Disabled Children (IEDC) Scheme.
- Under SSA, a continuum of educational options, learning aids and tools, mobility assistance, support services, etc. are being made available to students with disabilities. This includes education through an open learning system and open schools, alternative schooling, distance education, special schools, wherever necessary home based education, itinerant teacher model, remedial teaching, part time classes, Community Based Rehabilitation (CBR) and vocational education.
- IEDC Scheme implemented through the State Governments, Autonomous Bodies and Voluntary Organizations provides hundred per cent financial assistance for various facilities, like special teachers, books and stationery, uniform, transport, readers allowance for the visually handicapped, hostel allowance, equipment cost, removal/ modification of architectural barriers, financial assistance for the purchase/production of instructional material, training of general teachers and equipment for resource rooms.
- There will be concerted effort on the part of the Government to improve identification of children with disabilities through regular surveys, their enrolment in appropriate schools and their continuation till they successfully complete their education. The Government will endeavour to provide right kind of learning material and books to the children with disabilities, suitably trained and sensitized teachers and schools, which are accessible and disabled friendly.

PWD Act and RTE Act: Two Contradictory Policies

If we look closely at both the RTE and PWD Acts, one would find dichotomy in their versions. The PWD Act was passed by the government to provide every child with a disability access to free education in an appropriate environment till he attains the age of eighteen years; whereas if we look at the RTE Act, it talks about the age group of 6-14 years. Was the difference of four years overlooked while framing the policy of RTE? Since the RTE Act has the restriction of providing free education up to 14 years, where will the disabled children study?

Next point of contradiction is that in the PWD Act, provision is that "the state shall endeavour to promote the integration of students with disabilities in the normal schools. Moreover, promoting setting up of special schools in Government and private sector for those in need of special education, in such a manner that children with disabilities living in any part of the country have access to such schools; whereas we are talking about inclusive education in the RTE Act. It is indeed difficult to gauge how the two Acts with different provisions will make our schools inclusive.

Marginalized Groups and People with Disabilities

There are several areas across which people with disabilities receive unequal services in India. One of those is the difference between urban and rural areas and the services available in both. Seventy-five per cent of people with disabilities live in rural areas in India. This is an overwhelming majority. The number becomes worrisome in comparison to where the majority of services are offered; which is in urban areas. Less than fifteen per cent of national services for people with disabilities are located in rural areas, and of those, most are expensive and/or private. The discrepancy in services is directly reflected in educational achievement and enrolment in schools. Kalyanpur, drawing data from the National Census, states that in terms of educational levels, only eleven per cent of children with disabilities between the ages of 5-18 years living in urban areas (less than 1% in rural areas) were enrolled in special schools, while 55 per cent of adults with disabilities were illiterate (59% in rural and 40% in urban areas), with only seven per cent in rural and 18 per cent in urban areas having completed secondary education. Most of the data available follows this trend, suggesting that services are significantly more available in urban areas and people and students with disabilities are more marginalized in rural areas.

However, interestingly, in the National Census, the data is the opposite in regards to inclusive schooling, or at least attending a mainstream school. Per 1000 students with a disability between the ages of 5-18, enrolment years in mainstream schools were actually higher in rural areas versus urban areas; 475 out of 1000 students with disabilities attended a mainstream school in rural areas, versus 444 out of 1000 students with disabilities in urban areas. This may be because there is a higher prevalence of special schools in urban areas, which would make sense considering that urban areas have significantly more resources. Another area of inequity between persons with disabilities is gender. The Government of India National Census pointed out extreme inequities between girls and boys with a disability. In numbers, there are fewer girls than boys with a disability.

The hierarchy of Indian society results in selective abortion, female infanticide and female foeticide of female children with a disability. Females with a disability are not considered an educational investment, because they marry and go to the husband's family, whereas boys stay with and provide for their extended families all of their life. As a result 68 per cent of girls with a disability are not in school. Girls with disabilities have a lower enrolment rate in the school than boys with disabilities across many sectors; urban vs. rural, by type of schooling, by level of schooling, and in primary versus secondary schooling. According to the World Bank, the educational divide specially begins after grade school, although in general, school attendance is never more than 70 per cent for boys and 66 per cent for girls. Families also worry about their girls with a disability being vulnerable in the community, if they don't go to school the family will be able to supervise them closely. Although these gender trends are also true for girls without disabilities. Both socio-cultural and political-economic factors have led to women and girls with disabilities becoming "one of the most marginalized groups in the society." People with disabilities in India are also discriminated against based on their type of disability.

The National Census did not break down types of disability according to the Diagnostic and Statistical Manual of Mental Disorders IV (DSM IV) or a similar text, but rather by the categories, such as "locomotor, multiple, mental retardation (intellectual disability), mental illness, blindness, low vision, hearing and speech. "Out of the 70-110 million people, who are disabled in India, their disabilities break down as follows: 53 per cent have a locomotor disability, thirteen per cent have a visual disability, ten per cent have an auditory disability, and four per cent have an intellectual disability. Generally, people with an intellectual disability are discriminated against and marginalized more than people with physical disabilities. In terms of disability, people with Intellectual Disabilities (Mental Retardation) had the lowest enrolment rates in schools—they are four times less likely to go to school than children with physical disabilities; and are the least likely to be employed, and the least likely to get married. There are several reasons why children with intellectual disabilities are so marginalized. There are fewer services available for children with intellectual disabilities, partly because educators have to make changes to the curriculum to accommodate these students, whereas students with physical or locomotor disabilities are often able to learn with the same material as students without disabilities.

In addition, due to social stigma, parents and families are more likely to keep their children with intellectual disabilities at home, hiding these family members. As a result, almost three fourths of people with "severe" disabilities are illiterate, whereas one-half of people with "moderate" or "mild" disabilities are illiterate. The World Bank does not define what "severe" versus "moderate" and "mild" mean in this instance, but their data comes from the National Census. Gender, urban versus rural living, and type of disability are just three of the many categories that further marginalize children with disabilities. Statistics do vary; however, all of them point to the gaps in the education system that are preventing children with a disability from being in school.

Barriers to Inclusive Education

The education system in India has compromised on many levels. We no longer see the child as priority. We have become very conscious of the need to educate our children but it is hardly academic motivation, which generates this interest, but rather an economic motivation. Education is largely seen as the route to white collar jobs and this is due to our present education system, which has moulded generations to the thinking that all worth is measured in terms of money. Very often, the knowledge of the English language becomes the measure of this worth. So, inclusive education in India needs must contend with the present system of education, which is provided under the Integrated Education Programme for children with mild disabilities in a regular school and in special school for the more severely disabled child under the Ministry of Social Justice and Empowerment implemented through state governments and NGO's.

Some questions will inevitably have to be confronted. Perhaps, the most important is not whether inclusive education is relevant for us in India, but the problems associated with its implementation. A major deterrent has been the lack of statistics on the prevalence of intellectual disability. Surveys conducted by the NSSO (National Sample Survey) in 2002 and the Census in 2001 show varying figures with the NSSO quoting 1.8 per cent (1.85 crore of the country's population) and the census quoting 2.19 per cent of the population (2.19 crore). The large number of children in most schools is another reason since most of our schools except the elitist ones have classes where the student-teacher ratio is anywhere between 40 to 60. What passes for education in most free educational institutions offering services to the poor and even in some middle class communities catering to a major chunk of educable children can hardly earn the title of quality. The disparity between elite educational institutions and their poorer counterparts are too glaring even to be mentioned.

Challenges of Social Inclusion

There are many challenges of social inclusion at different stages, which are as follows:

At Policy Level

- Inclusive education alone cannot build an inclusive society.
- Inclusive education refers to a goal as much as a gradual process, it serves as a gateway to the fulfilment and enjoyment of other rights.
- Inclusive education viewed as a moral issue or a learning strategy?
- Policies must take a rights-based approach, supported by appropriate legislation.
- There is no strong consensus on how to implement inclusion at the classroom level (differentiated teaching within a regular school or separation between regular and special schools).
- Policies should provide a basis for the development of citizenship skills in students and for assuring quality.
- The need for extensive collaboration and support from all sectors of society to achieve a consensus through participatory, multi-sectoral dialogue between the multiple groups involved (stakeholders).
- The financing of inclusive education (issues relating to competition, privatization and decentralization) and the impact of market-based forces.
- Debate about the contribution of private institutions to inclusive education.
- Provide resources to prepare and support teachers and professional educators, who play a fundamental role in achieving quality education.
- The key role of the state in promoting inclusive education as a public good, which contrasts with the trend towards the privatization of educational services.
- Multi-sectoral public policies on inclusive education must be accompanied by and in accordance with other social, cultural and language policies, etc.
- The wide dissemination and sharing of public policies on inclusive education as a way to strengthen a global partnership committed to inclusion

At the Learners' and Teachers' Levels

- There is a need to strengthen teachers' competencies/skills in inclusive education, and to reform teacher training in its form and content.
- Teacher training alone is not sufficient as inclusive education begins with the attitude of a teacher.
- The status of students with special educational needs: from a clinical approach to a rights-teacher based approach.
- The challenge of inequality and discrimination among students based on socio-economic, ethnic and cultural profiles (e.g. the competencies and learning outcomes achieved).

- What is expected of students: the relevance of having high expectations about their performance
- The need to build networks and communities of practice for teachers and strengthen partnerships between the parents and the school.
- The use of ICTs to support the development of a culture of achievement and to promote the principles of equity and inclusion.
- Increased opportunities to learn and share best practices, research and pilot projects.
- The dialogue between learners and teachers and the importance of listening to students.
- Recognizing that teachers are strengthened and empowered through practical support in schools and classrooms and through the engagement of families and communities.
- Disagreements over how to deal with specific issues, such as religious instruction in the classroom.
- Schools as the places to protect and take care of children in conflict situations.

At Systems, Links and Transitions Level

- Need for a holistic approach based on inclusive education that can be adapted to the complexities and specificities of national situations.
- Interfaces between the formal and non-formal education and methods to assess competencies in both types of education.
- Partnerships with families, who play an active role in shaping positive attitudes towards inclusion.
- Importance of access to early childhood education.
- Partnerships between various actors and institutions (stakeholders, collaboration of civil society and international organizations with national governments).
- Transitions within the school system and between the education system and work.
- The challenges of designing curriculum to include all students and ensure equal access to all levels of education and all types of schools (including access, processes and results).

Challenges to Implement Inclusive Education

The main challenges to implement inclusive education are as follows:

The Challenge of Poverty Associated with Disability

With an estimated 1,027 million people, India is the world's second most populated country. It has 17 per cent of the global population and 20 per cent of the world's out-of-school children. Despite impressive gains in the last few decades (11th largest industrial power, 4th largest economy in terms of purchasing power parity), India still has more than 260 million people living in poverty (Canadian International Development Agency [CIDA], 2003). A large number of children with disabilities live in families with income significantly below the poverty level. According to Rao (1990), while disability causes poverty, it is also possible that in a country like India, poverty causes disability. The combination of poverty and disability results in a condition of "simultaneous deprivation". According to Harris-White (1996), this is a syndrome that sets up barriers to the participation of persons with disabilities in the normal routines and activities of the community, including regular schooling. Recently, the Ministry of Rural Development, Government of India, has allocated three per cent funds in poverty alleviation programmes targeting families of children with disabilities (B.L. Sharma, 2001). However, motivating poor families, with all the associated costs to send their child to school, is proving to be a big challenge.

The Challenge of Modifying Deeply Held Attitudes

Attitudes of the non-disabled are proving to be a major barrier in the social integration of persons with disabilities. "The more severe and visible the deformity is, the greater is the fear of contagion, hence the attitudes of aversion and segregation towards the crippled" (Desai, 1990, p. 19). Such attitudes reinforced by religious institutions may militate against any attempts to include students with disabilities into regular schools. For example, Hindus (who constitute 85 per cent of the total population in India) believe that disability is a consequence of misdeeds performed in the previous life (often referred to as the doctrine of Karma). Many Hindu religious institutions and temple trusts, therefore, do not think that a part of their duty is to help persons with disabilities, because they consider the disability to be the result of a person's misdeeds in his previous life (Rao, 1990). Any attempts to improve the life of a person with a disability may be considered a "defiance of the wills of Allah or as interference with a person's karma" (Harris-White, 1996, p.7 [also see Miles, 1995]). Alur (2001), in her study found that disability in India is not seen as something "normal" or "natural," rather it is seen as an "evil eye". Guilt, stigma and different kinds of fears tend to be paramount in such families. She further concludes that "the contradiction here was that Indian society, although integrated in accepting and valuing diversity in so many ways, has a social role construct of disability, which is negative, discriminatory and exclusionary" (n.p.). Kannan (2000) states that in order to harness the great potential of more than 30 million people with disabilities, it is essential that "prejudice, mental and irrational myths concerning disability are eradicated."

Dissemination and Public Education

People, including parents and school personnel, are largely unaware of the full intent of the recent legislation passed by the Indian Parliament. A large number of school personnel are also not aware of funding available to include students with disabilities in regular schools. There is some evidence that those educators, who are knowledgeable about government policies and laws concerning integrated education tend to have positive attitudes toward implementing such programmes (U. Sharma, 2001). There is also evidence that when parents are knowledgeable and supportive of integrated education, they tend to have a positive effect on the school personnel (U. Sharma, 2001). Thus, unless people, especially parents of children with disabilities and school personnel, are made knowledgeable about various provisions enshrined in the Act, the Central and State governments' commitment to providing integrated education will be in vain. Although some attempts are being made to disseminate information about the Persons with Disabilities Act to parents, to government officials and non-government organizations (B.L. Sharma, 2001), they have been extremely limited in coverage (Chatterjee, 2003).

There is also a greater need to have a National Resource Centre for Disabilities. Such a centre would work to collect and disseminate information on various aspects of disability (B.L. Sharma, 2001). The centre would provide information through various TV and radio programmes as well as through the Internet (B.L. Sharma, 2001). The centre would also fulfil the role of scrutinizing all mass communication programmes (TV, radio and even entertainment programmes) to ensure that disability is not portrayed in a negative manner.

The centre could also start documentary projects (e.g. video programmes) that feature inclusion being implemented in different parts of India. Such programmes are likely to make a positive impact on school educators, who often believe that inclusion can work only in Western or developed countries.

The Challenge of Providing Adequate Levels of Training to Key Stakeholders

The majority of school personnel in India are not trained to design and implement educational programmes for students with disabilities in regular schools. Most teacher training programmes in India do not have a unit on Disability Studies (Myreddi and Narayan, 2000). The universities, which do cover some aspects of special education in their teacher training programmes, fail to train teachers adequately to work in integrated settings. For example, there is limited coverage of information about practical strategies (Myreddi and Narayan, 2000). Also, placement of pre-service teachers in special or integrated schools is rarely given consideration (Jangira, Singh and Yadav, 1995).

Great variations are noted in the content, process, and examination of existing special education programmes as well in the country (Myreddi and

Narayan, 2000). However, the situation may improve in the coming years as the Rehabilitation Council of India (RCI) will periodically evaluate special education programmes to ensure that each programme meets minimum standards (Rehabilitation Council of India, 1996). The number of trained special educators is also limited. The most recent report of the Rehabilitation Council of India (1996) states that the number of trained special education teachers is extremely small, considering the number of children with disabilities that require their services. At the time of the publication of this report there were only 9,492 specially trained teachers. Of these, 4,295 were trained to teach students with mental retardation, 1,079 were trained to teach students with visual disabilities, 4,011 were trained to teach students with hearing impairments, and 107 were trained to teach students with locomotor disabilities in India. To address this severe shortage of trained teachers, the Rehabilitation Council of India recommended that an additional 44,000 teachers needed to be trained by the end of the Ninth Five-Year Plan (1997-2002). However, it should be noted that even if these targets were to be achieved, *only* ten per cent of the population of children with disabilities would be served (Rehabilitation Council of India, 1996). RCI must consider reformulating existing teacher training programmes for special educators, with greater emphasis on integrated education. Special educators could be a key resource as they can be used to train regular school educators in implementing integrated education. They can also act as itinerant teachers working in partnership with a number of regular school educators to advise them on practical issues related to the education of students with disabilities.

Inadequate Resources

The majority of schools in India are poorly designed and few are equipped to meet the unique needs of students with disabilities. The lack of disability friendly transportation services and accessible buildings are considered by some to be far greater problems than social prejudice and negative attitudes (for example, Chatterjee, 2003). Both the Central and State governments will have to provide increased resources to cater to this aspect of education to ensure successful implementation of integrated practices in schools.

Over and above, some of these challenges that India shares with other developing countries are some distinctive features that will make the implementation of educational reform particularly difficult. India is a multilingual, multicultural, multi-religious country, and its people are stratified along sharp socio-economic and caste lines. Therefore, unless the challenges are carefully identified and systematically addressed, inclusion will remain a policy on paper. The forthcoming section presents some strategies that policy makers in India may find useful to implement integrated education successfully.

Strategies to Address the Challenges

The main strategies to address the challenges regarding the inclusive education of children with disabilities are as follows:

Training of Teachers

If integrated education is to become a reality in India, then the training of teachers has to become a top priority. The educational authorities in India may adopt a policy of training one teacher from each school or a cluster of schools. The teacher would need to be provided with intensive training to work with various disabilities and could then act as an integration specialist or an inclusion facilitator for one or a number of schools located in close proximity. A similar strategy has already worked well in certain parts of India when several school teachers were specifically trained to work in integrated settings under the PIED programme and is recommended by several researchers in India (Jangira, 1995; Jha, 2002; Myreddi and Narayan, 2000). Also in-service teachers would need continued training to update their skills and knowledge of integrated education strategies.

It is clear that regular school educators need training in issues related to the implementation of integrated education. A question that arises with regard to such training is the identification of specific content that should be included in these training programmes. Given the enormous diversity in India (cultural, linguistic, socio-economic, etc.), further research is clearly warranted. Sharma (1992) suggests that the curriculum for pre-service training programmes should be carefully developed, incorporating feedback from special and regular educators. Some research has been conducted in India that points out that educators need basic skills, professional knowledge, communication and interaction skills (K. Sharma, 1992; U. Sharma and Pillay, 1997), knowledge about assessment techniques, and resource management (Das and Pillay, 1999), knowledge of multi-grade teaching, instructional techniques, and peer-tutoring and cooperative learning techniques to include students with disabilities into regular classes.

Need to Design Innovative System of Training

Several authors have cautioned that India will not be able to successfully implement integrated educational services unless regular school educators are trained at mass scale. Comments on this situation are as follows: "The number of persons, who need training, is very large and the conventional training methods cannot simply meet the requirements." Therefore, there is a need to design some innovative models to train educators at mass level. One possibility to educate such a large number of teachers is by using Distance Open Learning or DOL (Ramanujam, 2001). Indira Gandhi National Open University (IGNOU) has a history of successfully running courses for a larger number of students using DOL mode. IGNOU, in association with Rehabilitation Council of India, is considering offering various courses to the trainers of children with disabilities, including teachers. It is expected that such training, accompanied with ongoing in-service training, would prove very useful for school educators. It would, however, be important that practical aspects of implementing integrated education form a key part of any such course.

Need for Collaboration between Different Ministries

Different ministries in India administer various services for persons with disabilities (Alur, 2001). For example, while "integrated education" is the responsibility of the Ministry of Human Resource Development, education in special schools is the responsibility of Ministry of Social Justice and Empowerment. This is just one example of the waste of already limited resources. India cannot afford to have such administrative arrangements. There is a need for streamlining administrative arrangements so that funds provided to different ministries for persons with disabilities can be used effectively.

Involve NGO's in Implementing Integrated Education Programmes

There are more than one million NGOs workings in India (Canadian International Development Agency, 2003). Although not all of them are working in the education sector, a large number still provide educational services to children with disabilities. These organizations can play a significant role in implementing integrated education because they are widely located in India and can serve both urban and rural school communities. Unfortunately, a large majority of NGOs still believe that segregated education is the best way to educate students with disabilities (Alur, 2001). It would, therefore, be necessary to train the key stakeholders in these NGO's about the benefits of integrated education as well as practical aspects of implementing integrated education in regular schools.

Establish an Alternate System of Examination

Most school educators in India are concerned that integration of students with disabilities would result in lowering school standards because these students won't be able to pass exams (U. Sharma and Desai, 2002). This seems to be a genuine concern of teachers because it can influence their promotion. Thus, it is necessary to establish an alternative system of examination for students with disabilities. Such an examination system is already in practice in the USA. Students in this system are asked to do activities that demonstrate their abilities rather than disabilities. It is expected that teachers in India would feel more comfortable including students with disabilities in their classrooms if such a system existed.

School-University Partnership

The multilingual, multi-cultural and multi-religious nature of India is often cited as a challenge in implementing any educational reforms. Local universities in each of the States and Union Territories may play a significant role in overcoming this challenge. Pilot projects involving local schools could be initiated by universities to explore strategies that may be appropriate for each region. Also, texts on practical strategies can be produced in the common language spoken by educators in each of the States.

Evidence from a number of Western countries indicates that such collaborative projects can produce positive results for students with disabilities as well as for school educators. An example of one such project is the Learning Improves in Networking Communities (LINC) programme that was conducted in partnership between the Catholic Education Commission, Victoria (CECV) and Monash University in Melbourne, Australia. The project was geared to identify the factors within the school environment that most effectively contribute to successful integrated practices, building learning communities and to positive student learning outcomes and learning opportunities. A collaborative inquiry approach was employed with approximately 45 teachers undertaking a Postgraduate Diploma in Education (Special Education) in eight primary and secondary schools over the three-year study (2001-2003). The school-based professional development was focused on priorities identified by the schools themselves, linking teacher evidence-based practice to student outcomes. Results highlighted a shift away from a "special needs" delivery approach to disabilities, towards one that emphasizes collaboration, critical reflection and evidence-gathering for the purpose of informing instructional or organizational practices. Improvements in student outcomes were reported in all schools, but value-added analysis indicates that conditions in the school context contributed to the better-than-expected improvement in two of the schools (Deppeler and Harvey, 2004).

Conclusion

Inclusive education is concerned with removing all barriers to learning, and with the participation of all learners vulnerable to exclusion and marginalization. It is a strategic approach designed to facilitate learning success for all children. It addresses the common goals of decreasing and overcoming all exclusion from the human right to education, and enhancing access, participation and learning success in quality basic education for all *(2000 Bulletin, UNESCO No. 32, 1998).*

The history of education of children with special educational needs (SEN) is a progression from segregation to integration and now to inclusion. Inclusion refers to the opportunity for persons with disability to participate fully in all of the educational employment, consumer, recreational, community and domestic activities that typify every society (ILSMH 1994).

Inclusion is a philosophy built on the belief that all people are equal and should be respected and valued, as an issue of basic human rights. An "unending set of process" in which children and adult with disabilities have the opportunity to participate fully in ALL community activities offered to people, who do not have disabilities. *(UNESCO—at the committee on rights of the child, October 6, 1997—Centre for Human Rights, Geneva).*

Inclusive education happens when children with and without special educational needs participate and learn together in the same classes. Research shows that when a child with special educational needs attends classes alongside peers, who do not have disabilities, good things happen. For a long time, children with special educational needs were educated in separate classes or in separate schools. People got used to the idea that special education meant separate education. But we now know that when children are educated together, positive academic and social outcomes occur for all the children involved. We also know that simply placing children with and without disabilities together does not produce positive outcomes. Inclusive education occurs when there is on-going advocacy, planning, support and commitment.

References

1. Aggarwal, R. (1994). In K. Mazurck and M.A. Winzer (Eds.), *Comparative Studies in Special Education*, pp. 179-203. Washington D.C.: Gallaudet University Press.
2. Alur, M. (2001). Inclusion in the Indian Context. *Humanscape, 8*(6), 1-8.
3. Azad, Y.A. (1996). *Integration of Disabled in Common Schools: A survey-study of IEDC in the country.* New Delhi: National Council of Educational Research and Training.
4. Baquer, A. and Sharma, A. (1997). *Disability: Challenges vs. Responses.* New Delhi: Concerned Action Now.
5. Das, A.K. and Pillay, A.N. (1999, December). *Inclusive Education for Disabled Students: Challenges for Teacher Education.* Paper presented at the 5th UNESCO-ACEID Conference, Bangkok, Thailand.
6. Jangira, N.K. (1995). Rethinking Teacher Education. *Prospects, 25*(2), 261-272.
7. Jangira, N.K. and Ahuja, A. (1993). Special Education in India. *Asia Appraiser* (October-December), 6-11.
8. Jangira, N.K., Singh, A. and Yadav, S.K. (1995). Teacher Policy, Training Needs and Perceived Status of Teachers. *Indian Educational Review, 30*(1), 113-122.
9. Jha, M.M. (2002). *Barriers to Access and Success: Is Inclusive Education An Answer?* Paper presented at the Commonwealth of Learning (2002) Pan-

Commonwealth forum on open learning: Open learning: transforming education for development, 29 July - 2 August 2002, p. 16, Durban, South Africa.

10. Kannan, K. (2000). *Wherefore Change?* Website: http://www.webcottage.net/dij/nov2000/article3.htm
11. Karna, G.N. (1999). *United Nations and Rights of Disabled Persons: A Study in Indian Perspective*. New Delhi: A.P.H. Publishing Corporation.
12. Mani, R. (1988). *Physically Handicapped in India*. Delhi: Ashish Publishing House.
13. Mastropieri, M.A. and Scruggs, T.E. (2004). *The Inclusive Classroom: Strategies for Effective Instruction*. NY: Pearson.
14. Miles, M. (1995). Disability in an Eastern Religious Context: Historical Perspectives. *Disability and Society,* 10(1), 49-69.
15. Miles, M. (1997). Disabled Learners in South Asia: Lessons from the Past for Educational Exporters. *International Journal of Disability, Development and Education, 44*(2), 97-104.
16. Miles, M. (2000). Disability in South Asia-Millennium to Millennium. *Asia Pacific Disability Rehabilitation Journal,* 11(1), 1-10.
17. Ministry of Information and Broadcasting. (2000). *India 2000: A Reference Annual*. New Delhi: Publication Division.
18. Ministry of Law Justice and Company Affairs. (1996). The Persons with Disabilities (Equal Opportunities, Protection of Rights and Full Participation) Act, 1995, Government of India. India.
19. Ministry of Welfare. (1997). *Mid-term review meeting on the progress of implementation of the agenda for action for the Asia and Pacific Decade of Disabled Persons*. New Delhi: Govt. of India.
20. Myreddi, V. and Narayan, J. (2000). Preparation of Special Education Teachers: Present Status and Future Trends. *Asia Pacific Disability Rehabilitation Journal,* 10(1), 1-8.
21. NCERT. (1987). *Project Integrated Education for the Disabled (PIED)*. New Delhi: National Council of Educational Research and Training.
22. Pandey, R.S. and Advani, L. (1997). *Perspectives in Disability and Rehabilitation*. New Delhi: Vikas Publishing House Pvt. Ltd.
23. Rane, A. (1983). *An Evaluation of the Scheme of Integrated Education for Handicapped Children Based on a Study of the Working of Scheme in Maharashtra.* Bombay: Unit for Child and Youth Research, Tata Institute of Social Sciences.
24. Rehabilitation Council of India. (1996). *Report on Manpower Development*. New Delhi: Ministry of Welfare, Govt. of India.
25. Sharma, B.L. (2001). *United Nations expert group meeting on disability-sensitive policy and programme monitoring and evaluation: Country paper-India*. New York: UNHQ.
26. Sharma, K. (1992). *Integrating Children with Special Needs*. Agra: National Psychological Corporation.
27. Sharma, U. (2001). *The Attitudes and Concerns of School Principals and Teachers Regarding the Integration of Students with Disabilities into Regular Schools in India.* Unpublished Ph.D. Thesis, University of Melbourne, Melbourne.

28. Sharma, U. and Desai, I. (2002). Measuring Concerns about Integrated Education in India. *Asia and Pacific Journal on Disability, 5*(1), 2-14.
29. Sharma, U. and Pillay, A.N. (1997). *Collaborative Consultation Skills Needed by Teachers to Develop Effective Teaching Programs.* Paper presented at the 33rd Annual Conference of Australian Association for the Study of Intellectual Disability (ASSID), Brisbane, Australia.
30. Singh, R. (2001, February). *Need of the Hour – A Paradigm Shift in Education.* Paper presented at the North South Dialogue on Inclusive Education, Mumbai, India.
31. UNICEF (2011) The Situation of Children in India: A profile UNCIEF, New Delhi.

Webliography

1. Ramanujam, P.R. (2001). *DOL and Disability Studies.* Retrieved July 10, 2003, from www.fernuni-hagen.de/ZIFF/rampoten.doc
2. Canadian International Development Agency (CIDA). (2003). *India Country Program Framework (2002-2007).* Retrieved 10th June, 2003, from www.acdi-cida.gc.ca
3. Chatterjee, G. (2003, April). *The global movement for inclusive education.* Retrieved 10 July 2003, from http://www.indiatogether.org/2003/apr/edu-inclusive.htm
4. Convention on the Rights of Persons with Disabilities. *UN Enable.* The United Nations. Web. 18 January 2012. <http://www.un.org/disabilities/default.asp?id=150>.
5. Disabled Persons in India: NSS 58th Round. *National Sample Survey Organization.* Ministry of Statistics and Programme Implementation, Government of India. December 2003. Web. 31 November 2011. <http://mospi.nic.in/rept%20_%20pubn/485_final.pdf>.
6. Fact Sheet on Persons with Disabilities. *UN Enable.* The United Nations. Web. 15 March 2012. http://www.un.org/disabilities/documents/toolaction/pwdfs.pdf.
7. Government of India. *The Constitution of India.* 1 December 2007. Web. 18 March 2012. http://lawmin.nic.in/coi/coiason29july08.pdf
8. Government of India announces plan to make education disabled-friendly by 2020. *UNICEF India.* The United Nations. Web. 14 April 201. http://www.unicef.org/india/media_610.htm
9. Inclusive Education of the Disabled at the Secondary Stage (IEDSS): Ministry of Human Resource Development." Government of India, 2009. Web. 2 April 2012 http://www.india.gov.in/govt/viewscheme.php?schemeid=2061.
10. Infoexchange India. "India to notify right to education act." One World South Asia. 17 February 2010. Web. 29 March, 2012. http://southasia.oneworld.net/todaysheadlines/india-tonotify right-to-education-act.
11. Integration is not Inclusion. *The Alliance for Inclusive Education.* The Alliance for Inclusive Education. Web. 3 January, 2012 http://www.allfie.org.uk/pages/useful%20info/integration.html.
12. International Day of Persons with Disabilities. *EduInfo.* UNESCO. 2009. Web. 19 April 2012 http://portal.unesco.org/education/en/ev.php.

13. Mahatma Gandhi on Education. Infed. 1 December 2011. Web. 25 February 2012. infed.org/thinkers/et-gand.htm.
14. Making Schools Inclusive: How Change can Happen. *Save the Children UK*, Save the Children UK. 2008. http://www.eenet.org.uk/resources/docs/Making%20schools%20inclusive%20SCUK.pdf.
15. The Medical Model. *The Alliance for Inclusive Education*. The Alliance for Inclusive Education. Web. 3 January 2012 http://www.allfie.org.uk/pages/useful%20info/medical.html>.
16. National University of Educational Planning and Administration. "Status of Education in India National Report. *Department of Higher Education,* Ministry of Human Resource Development, Government of India. 2012. Web. 16 April 2012 http://www.nse2012.com/images/images/State%20of%20Edcuation%20in%20India National%20Report.pdf.
17. Nearly 80 pct of India lives on half a dollar a day, *Reuters,* Reuters, 10 August, 2007, Web. 17 April 2012, http://www.reuters.com/article/2007/08/10/idUSDEL218894.
18. The Persons with Disabilities (Equal Opportunities, Protection of Rights and Full Participation) Act, 1995. *Ministry of Social Justice and Empowerment,* Government of India. 2009. Web. 9 October 2011. http://socialjustice.nic.in/pwdact1995.php?pageid=14.
19. People with Disabilities in India: from Commitments to Outcomes. The World Bank Human Development Unit, South Asia Region. July 2009. Web. 25 September 2011, 59, http://wwwwds. worldbank.org/external/default/WDSContentServer/WDSP/IB/2009/09/02/0003349 5_20090902041543/Rendered/PDF/502090WP0Peopl1Box0342042B01PUBLIC1.pdf>.
20. Policy guidelines on Inclusion in Education. *UNESCO*. The United Nations. 2009. Web. 15 April 2012. http://unesdoc.unesco.org/images/0017/001778/177849e.pdf.
21. The Rehabilitation Council of India Act, 1992. Government of India. 1 September 1992. Web. 28 October 2011. http://rehabcouncil.nic.in/engweb/rciact.pdf.
22. Right to Education Act. Government of India. 2005. Web. 27 December 2011. http://www.india.gov.in/spotlight/spotlight_archive.php?id=74.
23. The Salamanca Statement and Framework for Action on Special Needs Education. *UNESCO*, The United Nations. 10 June 2012. Web. 2 November 2011. http://www.unesco.org/education/pdf/SALAMA_E.PDF.
24. Sarva Shiksha Abhiyan. *Sarva Shiksha Abhiyan: a programme for the universalization of inclusive education.* Ministry of Human Resource Development, Department of School
25. Education and Literacy. Government of India. 2007. Web. 16 March 2012 http://ssa.nic.in/. 2005. Web. 12 March 2012
26. Translated: Sarva Shiksha Abhiyan. Education for All. Central Plan. 2005. Web. 12 March 2012. http://www.bharat.gov.in/spotlight/spotlight_archive.php?id=32.
27. Translation: Right to Education, *Primary Education*, Government of India: Ministry of Human Resource Development, 20 January 2012, Web, 15 March 2012, <http://mhrd.gov.in/hi/retH>.
28. Sharma, Umesh and Deppeler, Joanne. Integrated Education in India: Challenges and Prospects. *Disability Studies Quarterly,* 25.1 (2005). Society for Disability Studies. Web. 13 February 2012. http://dsq- sds.org/article/view/524/701.

29. The Social Model of Disability. *Office for Disability Issues*. Department for Work and Pensions. 4 November 2010. Web. 29 March 2012. http://odi.dwp.gov.uk/about-theodi/the-social-model.php.
30. Teach India: Don't kill the Right to Education Bill. *The Times of India*. 8 July, 2008. Web. 22 December 2011. <http://articles.timesofindia.indiatimes.com/2008-07-8/india/27916558_1_education-bill-seats-for-poor-children-private-schools>.
31. UN at a Glance. *The United Nations*. The United Nations. Web. 20 April 2012. <http://www.un.org/en/aboutun/index.shtml>.
32. United Nations Decade of Disabled Persons 1983-1992. *United Nations Enable*. The United Nations. Web. 13 March 2012. <http://www.un.org/esa/socdev/enable/disunddp.htm>.
33. UNESCO. *Salamanca Statement, 1994*. Retrieved November 17 2004, from United Nations Educational, Scientific, Cultural Organization. Website: http://portal.unesco.org/education/en/ev.php-URL_ID=10379&URL_DO= DO_TOPIC&URL_SECTION=201.html for link to PDF: http://unesdoc.unesco.org/images/0009/000984/098427eo.pdf
34. Verma, Gajendra K., Christopher Bagley, and Madan M. Jha. *International Perspectives on Educational Diversity and Inclusion: Studies from America, Europe and India*. London: Routledge, 2007.
35. World Declaration on Education for All and Framework for Action to Meet Basic Learning Needs. World Conference Education for All: *Meeting Basic Learning Needs*. 9 March 1990. Web. 8 October 2011. <http://www.unesco.org/education/pdf/JOMTIE_E.PDF>.

18

Attitude of Society towards HIV/AIDS Impacting Child Education

G.K. Tripathi

Acquired Immuno Deficiency Syndrome (AIDS) is one of the most dreaded entities that modern medicine has ever had to tackle. The interaction between HIV/AIDS and human rights is most often illustrated through the impact on the lives of individuals due to neglect, denial, and violation of their rights in the context of the HIV/AIDS epidemic. This applies, albeit in different ways, to women, men, and children infected with, affected by, and vulnerable to HIV. As a major actor in the development of human resources—through the teaching of literacy and numeracy, the transmission of basic knowledge and skills for survival, and the delivery of vocational, tertiary and professional training – the education system bears both a special burden in terms of being affected by AIDS and special responsibilities for responding to its impact (Shaeffer 1994, p. 8). The present discussion seeks to underline the way the perception of HIV/AIDS afflicted people contravenes human rights and children's right to be educated along with making suggestions to overcome the dreaded entity through education.

Acquired Immuno Deficiency Syndrome as a Social Stigma

The HIV continues to be marked by discrimination against population groups: those who live on the fringes of society or who are assumed to be at risk of infection because of behaviours, race, ethnicity, sexual orientation, gender or social characteristics that are stigmatized in a particular society.

Studies by UNAIDS (2007) found out that people living with HIV/AIDS have been judged and found guilty, by means of their disease and seen as having promiscuous behaviour. Kengeles, Coates, Christopher and Lazarus (1989) further stipulated that stigma is applied in varying degrees depending on moral judgement on the basis of the mode of acquisition. In addition, Busza

(2001) stated that children born of parents infected by HIV/AIDS become ultimate defence victims, same to family members of people living with HIV/AIDS of stigma and discrimination.

Community level stigma and discrimination can manifest as ostracism, rejection, verbal and physical abuse. In addition, stigma and discrimination can result in murder in extreme cases. According to Avert (2010), murder cases have been reported in Brazil, South Africa and India among other countries. In South Africa, studies done by Avert (2010) indicate that in 1998 Gugu Dhlamini was stoned and beaten to death after speaking openly on World AIDS Day. In India, studies by Avert (2010) indicated that people living with HIV/AIDS face violent attacks and killed on the basis of their HIV status. In addition, children living with HIV/AIDS face rejection by family members and the community. The study further showed that children living with HIV/AIDS were denied access to medical treatment on the basis of HIV positive condition.

From the studies carried out in Indonesia, Busza (2001) has taken notice of the families that have been found to separate household items, clothing and personal belongings of people, including children, living with HIV/AIDS. Sarjana and Wiyadnyana (1999) asserted that in extreme cases, the family experiences rejection by the wider community. Children rejected and thrown out of the community miss attending school, thus, infringing the right to education. Brown (1994) found that HIV positive women were pressured to undergo surgical contraception or if already pregnant to have abortion.

Holzemer and Uys (2004) described various phrases used to refer to people living with HIV/AIDS, which have negative implication. In Tanzania, as Nyblade, Pande, Mathur, MacQuarrie (2003) have noted, people living with HIV/AIDS are called "Maiti inayotembea" (walking corpse) and "Marehemu mtarajiwa" (expected to die). In Africa, people living with HIV/AIDS suffer name calling and being referred to as Satan's people by church members. Stigmatizing phrases in school make children drop out of school, thus, denying the child access to education and association.

Children with HIV/AIDS or associated with HIV through infected family members have been stigmatized and discriminated against in educational settings in many countries. Stigma has led to teasing by classmates of HIV-positive school children or children associated with HIV (Gilborn *et al.* 2001). Discrimination against HIV-positive children in the USA and Brazil, including exclusion from collective activities or expulsion from school, has led to non-discrimination legislation (Public Media Centre 1995; Galvão 2000). However, less concern has been shown for young people, who are perceived to be responsible for their HIV infection and who are already stigmatized and discriminated against, because they are sexually active, homosexual, or drug users. In the USA, for example, HIV-positive young gay men have been expelled from school and, in some cases, subjected to violence (Kirp *et al.* 1989).

The HIV/AIDS Threatening Human Rights in the Education Sector

The HIV continues to spread throughout the world, shadowed by increasing challenges to human rights, at both national and global levels. People infected with HIV may suffer from violations of their rights when, for example, they face government-condoned marginalization and discrimination in relation to access to health, education, and social services (Cohen1990). In this context, the realization of rights by people living with HIV would require non-discriminatory access within a supportive social environment.

The strong focus in the 1980s on the human rights of people living with HIV/AIDS helped lead to increased understanding in the 1990s of the importance of human rights as a factor in determining people's vulnerability to HIV infection and their consequent risk of acquiring HIV infection as well as the probability of their accessing appropriate care and support (Gruskin, Tarantola, 2000).

Department of AIDS Control 2010 asserted that India has the third largest population living with HIV/AIDS and amongst them, children have emerged as a significant group. While there are no current official estimates of children living with HIV in India, we have to accept that approximately 100,000 children in India are HIV-positive (UNICEF, 2007). However, these figures do not reveal that the number of children affected by HIV/AIDS is far larger than those infected. For every child, who is infected, there are apparently another fifty who are affected – have an HIV positive parent or have been orphaned by AIDS. Some of the HIV high prevalence states in India, such as Karnataka, Tamil Nadu, Andhra Pradesh, Maharashtra, Manipur and Nagaland are grappling with increased numbers of children infected and affected by HIV and AIDS.

Prakash Kumar (2012) reported that over 60 children were denied admissions in the schools in various states in the last four years because they were infected with HIV. Such children continued to face discrimination despite a law guaranteeing the right to free and compulsory education to children came into effect on April 1, 2010. The instances of the violation of the fundamental rights of these children from 2008-09 to 2011-12 have been recorded by the National AIDS Control Organisation (NACO).

The Human Resource Development Ministry claims that the Central Board of Secondary Education (CBSE) conducts advocacy programme to sensitise principals and teachers to ensure that students infected with HIV/AIDS are treated with dignity and respect. But CBSE claims that there is 'no clear policy' to deal with such cases. The RTE Act prohibited such kind of discrimination, but Andhra Pradesh, which accounts for five lakh cases of HIV/AIDS as per a latest government report, topped the list with the NACO recording as many as 27 cases in the state, where children infected with HIV were denied admissions in schools. West Bengal came second where at least 13 such cases were reported. In Haryana, at least nine such children were denied admissions, four in Kerala, three in Uttar Pradesh and one in Maharashtra. The number of such cases would be much higher than the data collected by the NACO, asserted a non-government organisations and activists working to protect the rights of the HIV infected persons.

From Ukraine, CRIN (2010) reported that preschools and primary schools refused to admit children living with HIV/AIDS. Children living with HIV/AIDS have been turned away and excluded from primary schools, which are against the country's anti-discrimination laws. According to UK, National IDS Trust in CRIN (2010), a child, who discovered her status from the teacher, was bullied by other children until she was forced by stigma to drop out of the school. The right to education of the child was infringed.

Education and Human Rights in the Context of HIV/AIDS

It is difficult to overstate the role that the education sector can play in fulfilling human rights—not only of those participating in the education system as learners or as teachers, but of whole groups in society. This section examines how the education sector can strengthen the fulfilment of human rights, and then continues from the HIV/AIDS perspective.

The UNGASS Declaration of Commitment on HIV/AIDS states that:

> *The full realization of human rights for all is an essential element in a global response to HIV/AIDS, including in the areas of prevention, care, support and treatment. It reduces vulnerability to HIV/AIDS and prevents stigma and discrimination against people living with HIV/AIDS, or at risk of it (UNGASS Declaration, para.16, 2001).*

The relationship between education and AIDS is complex: As a major factor in the development of human resources, the education system, as pointed above, bears both a special burden in terms of being affected by AIDS and special responsibilities for responding to its impact. Shaeffer identifies three issues for discussion: first, changes needed in the education system in order to effectively deliver messages (including those related to human rights) about the epidemic; second, the question of how to deal with the immediate impact of AIDS on the education system itself (including human rights violations or gaps in policies and laws protecting people living with HIV/AIDS); and third, the longer-term response of the education.

The role of education in the community changes as more and different demands are put on it (Shaeffer, 1994; Kelly, 2000; Coombe, 2001). The school must become an important entry point into the community for awareness-raising and teaching activities aimed at decreasing stigma and discrimination of people living with HIV/AIDS in the community, as was shown convincingly in a community-based multi-sectoral response project implemented in Sampatong District, Northern Thailand (Devine, 2001). Teachers and school administrators (as well as monks and other influential people in the community) can play a major role in convincing community members that living side-by-side with people, who have HIV or AIDS, is safe; that these people deserve care and support; and that they have basic human rights (including the right to education) that need to be upheld (Devine, 2002).

Responsibilities of the Government

With the applicability of international law to HIV/AIDS, governments are publicly accountable for their actions toward people in the context of HIV/AIDS. Given the reality of violations that continue to occur, it is useful to consider the specific human rights responsibilities of governments. Governments are responsible for not violating rights directly, as well as for ensuring the conditions that enable people to realize their rights as fully as possible. It is understood that, for every human right, governments have responsibilities at three levels: the governments must (1) respect the right, (2) protect the right, and (3) fulfil the right (Eide, 1995).

As an illustration, consider governmental obligations in the context of HIV, using one right – the right to education:

- Respecting the right means that states cannot violate the right directly. This means that the right to education is violated if children are barred from attending school on the basis of their HIV status.
- Protecting the right means that a state has to prevent violations of rights by non-state actors and offer some sort of redress that people know about and have access to if a violation does occur. A state has to ensure, for example, that religious groups are not successful, when they try to stop adolescents from accessing reproductive health education.
- Fulfilling the right means that the states have to take all appropriate measures—legislative, administrative, budgetary, judicial, and otherwise—toward fulfilling the right. If a state fails to provide essential HIV/AIDS prevention education in enough languages and media to be accessible to everyone in the population, this in and of itself could be understood to be a violation of the right to education.

Dearth of Laws

India had enacted laws to protect the rights of various sections including those suffering from disability but, there is no law to protect the rights and interests of people suffering from HIV/AIDS. We need a strong legislation statute to address HIV/AIDS—its prevention, its treatment, and the manner in which we respond to the people affected by it.

The newly passed "prohibition of unfair practices in schools Bill 2012 makes refusal of admission or expulsion of students on grounds of having contracted HIV/AIDS a 'cognisable offence'." Schools denying admission would be liable to pay a monetary penalty and the school principal or any other officer, responsible for the functioning of the institution, would face imprisonment of up to three years or fine or both. The Bill has been prepared by a committee set up by CABE in 2011 and headed by the then Minister of State for Human Resource Development, D. Purandeswari. CABE is the highest advisory body to inform the Centre and state governments on education issues.

Although, the Right to Education (RTE) Act 2010 guarantees education to all children (irrespective of any disability or ailment) in the age group of six to fourteen years, this is the first time that a specific provision has been conceived to protect the rights of students with HIV/AIDS. Section 6 (4) of the law states: "No school shall deny admission or expel any student on the ground of having HIV/AIDS or any other serious ailment."

"Under the RTE Act, a school could be derecognised for violating a child's right to education." But de-recognition affects all the children of the school.

Developing a New Conceptual Framework

Why do we need a new way of thinking? It is a well-accepted fact that HIV/AIDS related S&D are linked to the actions and attitudes of families, communities, and societies (UNAIDS, 2000). However, current thinking largely focuses on stigma and discrimination as individual processes – or as what some individuals do to other individuals—rather than as social processes. The dominant definition describes stigma as a "discrediting attribute" and stigmatized individuals as those, who possess an "undesirable difference," and ignores aspects that describe stigma as something that is socially constructed (Goffman 1963; Marshall 1998). This has resulted in the notion that stigma is a static individual feature or characteristic, limiting the analysis of the underlying causes and possible responses to HIV/AIDS-related stigma and discrimination. We need to move beyond current thinking toward a conceptual framework that is based on an understanding that stigma and discrimination are social processes and that, consequently, stigma and discrimination can be resisted and challenged by social action.

Understanding Stigmatization and Discrimination as Social Processes

Stigma and discrimination are used to produce, legitimize, and perpetuate social inequality. Social and political theory can help us to understand that stigmatization and discrimination are not isolated phenomena or the expression of individual attitudes, but are social processes used to create and maintain social control and to produce and reproduce social inequality.

Stigma is something that is "produced" and used to help order in the society. For example, most societies achieve conformity by contrasting those, who are "normal" with those, who are "different" or deviant. Culture, therefore, produces difference in order to achieve control. In many non-Western societies, local knowledge systems may perform the same function at a more localized level (Geertz 1983). Similarly, concepts of symbolic violence and hegemony highlight the role of stigmatization in establishing social order and control, and identify stigmatization as part of the social struggle for power. Symbolic violence is a process where words, images and practices promote the interests of dominant groups (Bourdieu, 1977; Bourdieu, 1984; Bourdieu and Passeron, 1977), and hegemony is achieved through the use of political, social and cultural forces to promote dominant meanings and values that legitimize unequal social structures (Foucault, 1977 and 1978; Williams, 1977; Williams, 1982). So all cultural meanings and practices embody interests and are used to enhance social distinctions between individuals, groups, and institutions.

Sociological analyses of discrimination are also useful because they emphasize the structural aspects of discrimination and "concentrate on patterns of dominance and oppression, viewed as expressions of a struggle for power and privilege" (Marshall, 1998).

Following the notion that stigmatization is a process that involves identifying differences between groups of people, and using these differences to determine where groups fit into the structures of power, is the idea that stigma and discrimination are used to produce and reproduce social inequality. Stigmatization, therefore, not only helps to create difference, but also plays a key role in transforming difference based on class, gender, race, ethnicity, or sexuality into social inequality.

Stigmatization is also used by dominant groups to legitimize and perpetuate inequalities, and concepts of symbolic violence and hegemony can also help us understand how it is that those, who are stigmatized and discriminated against so often, accept and even internalize the stigma to which they are subjected. This is because the processes of symbolic violence and hegemony convince the dominated to accept existing hierarchies and allow social hierarchies to persist over generations, without generating conscious recognition from those, who are dominated. In addition, these processes limit the ability of oppressed and stigmatized groups and individuals to resist the forces that discriminate against them.

Responding to Stigmatization and Discrimination through Social Action

An understanding of stigmatization and discrimination as political and social processes can also help us to reconsider responses to HIV/AIDS-related S&D. For example, identity theory suggests that those, who are stigmatized, can take action to resist the forces that discriminate against them (Castells, 1997; Hall, 1990). Those, who are marginalized, generate "resistance identities" and use them to build a new identity that redefines their position in society and, thus, seeks the transformation of overall social structure. This would include resistance through mobilization of movements, at community, national and international levels, aimed at social change.

Implications of Re-conceptualizing Stigma and Discrimination

These ideas offer important insights for re-conceptualizing HIV/AIDS-related stigmatization and discrimination within a broader social, cultural, political, and economic framework rather than as individual processes. They offer a framework for understanding S&D as social processes that are used to create a social hierarchy by differentiating between the stigmatized and the non-stigmatized, as well as to produce and reproduce social inequalities and to make these inequalities seem reasonable.

Such a framework improves our ability to analyze the causes of S&D and the ways in which HIV/AIDS S&D interacts with and reinforces pre-existing S&D and social exclusion. More important, a better understanding of the processes that produce S&D, as well as of the processes that produce resistance to S&D, would enable us to develop more effective responses to HIV/AIDS-related S&D. Such a framework implies new approaches to research, including exploratory studies to identify and assess concepts that take account of the social, cultural, political, and economic determinants of S&D and contribute to our understanding of the processes of change; investigative studies to explore these processes in a range of contexts and evaluate the potential of interventions intended to reduce S&D; and strategic and policy-oriented studies to inform implementation of effective responses.

Such a framework also implies new approaches to programme development and intervention that engage societies, communities, and those, who experience stigma and discrimination. If S&D are understood to be the products of social rather than individual processes, it follows that challenging S&D requires social action to change the context within which individuals and communities respond to HIV/AIDS rather than just individual action. Creating a climate in which S&D are no longer tolerated, therefore, requires environmental interventions – in particular, social and community mobilization and empowerment of marginalized groups to resist S&D – and structural interventions, especially laws and policies that protect the rights of PLHA and those affected by the HIV/AIDS epidemic.

References

1. Avert (2010). *AIDS Orphans.* Brighton Road Horsham West Sussex RH135 BA UK
2. Bourdieu, P. (1984). *Distinction: A Social Critique of the Judgement of Taste.* Cambridge: Cambridge University Press.
3. Bourdieu, P. (1977). *Outline of a Theory of Practice.* Cambridge: Cambridge University Press.
4. Bourdieu, P. and J.C. Passeron. (1977). *Reproduction in Education, Society and Culture.* London: Sage.
5. Brown, T. (1994). *Social policy, human rights, and HIV/AIDS in Asia and the Pacific.* AIDS, 8, S207-S213.
6. Busza J.R. (2001). *AIDS care* Carfax: Bangkok
7. Castells, M. (1997). *The Power of Identity.* Oxford: Blackwell Publishers, Inc
8. Cohen, R.L. Wiseberg. (1990). *Double jeopardy-threat to life and human rights: discrimination against persons with AIDS.* Cambridge, MA: Human Rights Internet.
9. Coombe, C. (2001). "*Rethinking Some of Our Perceptions about HIV/AIDS and Education.*" Paper prepared for the Southern African Development Community meeting on HIV/AIDS and Education, University of Pretoria, Faculty of Education, 26-28 February
10. Coombe, C. (2001). *"Mitigating the Impact of HIV/AIDS on Education Supply, Demand and Quality: A Global Review."* A paper prepared for UNICEF Innocenti Research Centre, Florence, Italy,
11. CRIN (2010). *Discrimination: Briefing on discrimination and HIV/AIDS.* East Studio London: Ponty pool place
12. Devine, S. (2001). *A Multi-sectoral Approach to Planning Services for AIDS Orphans, Sanpatong District, Chiang Mai* [Thailand]. Bangkok: UNICEF,
13. Eide, A. (1995). Economic, Social and Cultural Rights as Human Rights. In: A. Eide, C. Krause, A. Rosas, (eds). *Economic, Social and Cultural Rights: A Textbook.* Dordrecht: Martinus. Nijhoff, 21-40.
14. Galvao J. (2000). *AIDS.* Brasil, Sao Paulo and Rio de Janeiro: Editorial 34, ABIA.
15. Geertz, C. (1983). *Local Knowledge.* New York: Basic Books.
16. Gilborn *et al.* (2001). *Making a Difference for Children Affected by AIDS*: Baseline Findings from Operations research in Uganda. Washington, DC: Population Council.
17. Goffman I. (1963) *Stigma: Notes on the Management of Spoiled Identity.* Prentice-Hall,
18. Gruskin, S.; Tarantola, D. (2000). HIV/AIDS, Health and Human Rights. In: P. Lamptey, H. Gayle, P. Mane, (eds). *HIV/AIDS Prevention and Care Programs in Resource-Constrained Settings: A Handbook for the Design and Management of Programs.* Arlington, Virginia: Family Health International, HIV/AIDS 1(3), 165-174.
19. Hall, S. (1990). Cultural Identity and Diaspora, in *Identity: Community, Culture, Difference*, ed. J. Rutherford. London: Lawrence and Wishart.
20. Holzemer W. and Uys L. (2004). Managing AIDS stigma. *Journal of Social Aspects of HIV/AIDS* 1(3), 165-174

21. Kelly, M. (2000). *Planning for Education in the Context of HIV/AIDS.* Fundamentals of Educational Planning Series #66.Paris: International Institute for Educational Planning/UNESCO.
22. Kelly, M. (2000). *The Encounter Between AIDS and Education.* Harare: UNESCO,
23. Kengeles, S. M.L., Coates, T.J., Christopher, A and Lazarus J.L. (1989). Perceptions of AIDS: The Continuing Saga of AIDS- related Stigma. *AIDS, 3,* S253-S258.
24. Kirp, D. *et al.* (1989). *Learning by Heart: AIDS and School Children in America's Communities.* New Brunswick, NJ: Rutgers University Press.
25. Marshall, G. (1998). *Oxford Dictionary of Sociology*, pp.163, 522, Oxford and New York: Oxford University Press.
26. Nyblade, L.; Pande, R.; Mathur, S.; MacQuarrie, K.; Kidd, R.; Banteyerga, H. (2003). *Disentangling HIV and AIDS: Stigma in Ethiopia, Tanzania and Zambia.* Washington, DC: International Centre for Research on Women. Retrieved from http://www.icrw.org/docs/stigmareport093003.pdf
27. Prakash Kumar (2012). Schools across country spurn HIV-hit children. DHNS New Delhi, October 21, 2012
28. Public Media Centre. (1995). The Impact of Homophobia and Other Social Biases on AIDS. *A Special Report by the Public Media Centre,* San Francisco, California.
29. Sarjana, I.G., and Wiyadnyana, I.B. (1999). *Reception of People with HIV/ AIDS by* health care providers and by the community. A qualitative study on social discrimination experienced by people with HIV/AIDS (ODHA) in Bali. Unpublished.
30. Shaeffer, S. (1994). *The Impact of AIDS on Education: a Review of Literature and Experience.* Paris: UNESCO, Section for Preventive Education.
31. UN. *UNGASS* (2001). *Declaration of Commitment on HIV/AIDS.* New York: UN.
32. UNAIDS. (2007). *HIV and AIDS-related stigmatization discrimination and denial: Forms, contexts and determinants, research studies from Uganda and India* (prepared for UN AIDS by Peter Aggleton). Geneva, UNAIDS.
33. UNAIDS. (2000). *HIV and AIDS-related stigmatisation, discrimination and denial: forms, contexts and determinants, research studies from Uganda and India* (prepared for UNAIDS by Peter Aggleton). Geneva, UNAIDS.
34. UNICEF, (2007). *Barriers to Services for Children with HIV Positive Parents,* July 2007.
35. Williams, R. (1977). *Marxism and Literature.* Oxford: Oxford University Press.
36. Williams, R. (1982). *The Sociology of Culture.* New York: Schoken Book.

19

The Right to Education

Some Critical Issues

Neeti Dutta

Education is the most potent mechanism for the advancement of human beings. It enlarges, enriches and improves the individual's image of the future. A man without education is no more than an animal. Education emancipates the human beings and leads to liberation from ignorance. According to Pestalozzi, education is a constant process of development of innate powers of man, which are natural, harmonious and progressive. It is said that in the twenty-first century, "a nation's ability to convert knowledge into wealth and social good through the process of innovation is going to determine its future." Accordingly, the twenty-first century is termed as the century of knowledge. In this situation, it is an obligation on the part of the state to provide education of comparable quality to all of its citizens free of cost.

Historical Perspective

It may be stated that education in India has been notorious for not being socially inclusive. Till the 19th Century, it was largely considered a privilege restricted to persons at the higher end of the caste or class hierarchy. History is replete with examples of caste, class and gender-based discrimination in imparting education in India. The system of education was clearly not accessible to all persons. The neglect of education by the British was also acknowledged by the Wood's Despatch.

In this context, the demand for Free and Compulsory Education (FCE) in India can be traced back to the early stages of the freedom struggle in British India. It subsequently became an integral part of the freedom struggle. The Indian National Congress fought valiantly for the expansion of elementary education and literacy, in general, and in rural India, in particular. In the evidence placed before the Education Commission (Hunter Commission) appointed in 1882, Dadabhai Naoroji and Jyothiba Phule from Bombay demanded state-sponsored free education for at least four years. This demand was indirectly acknowledged in the Commission's recommendations on primary education. The commission also recommended that schools should be open to all castes and classes. But it became a futile exercise. The first law on compulsory education was introduced by the State of Baroda in 1906. This law provided for compulsory education for boys and girls in the age groups of seven to twelve years in seven to ten years, respectively. In 1911, Gopal Krishna Gokhale moved a Bill for compulsory education in the Imperial Legislative Council, albeit unsuccessfully. The Legislative Council of Bombay was the first amongst the Provinces to adopt a law on compulsory education, which was transferred to Indian Ministers under the Government of India Act, 1919. However, even though Provincial Legislatures had greater control and autonomy in enacting laws, progress in universalizing education was poor due to lack of control over resources. The next landmark development in the history of FCE in India was the Post War Plan of Education Development of 1944, also called the Sargent Plan, which recommended FCE for eight years (6-14 year age group).

The period spanning between 1950 to the judgement in Unnikrishnan's case in 1993 to the passage of the Right of the Children to Free and Compulsory Education Bill by the Lok Sabha on 4 August 2009 saw several legal developments. After independence, the Constitution framers gave a prominent place to educational endeavour when they included Article 45 and Article 46 in the Directive Principles of the State Policy. In Article 45, it is laid down that "The State shall endeavour to provide, within a period of ten years from the commencement of this Constitution, for free and compulsory education for all children until they complete the age of fourteen years." Further, Article 46 declares that "the state shall promote with special care the educational and economic interests of the weaker section of the people." But the Constitutional obligation was time and again deferred.

The Indian Education Commission (Kothari Commission) 1964-1966, reviewed the status of education in India and made a prominent recommendation of introducing a common school system with a view to eliminate inequality in access to education. The common school system means the national system of education that is founded on the principles of equality and social justice and provides education of a comparable quality to all children in an equitable manner, irrespective of their caste, creed, language, gender, economic or ethnic background, location or disability (physical or mental), and wherein all categories of schools —i.e., government, local body or private, both aided and unaided, or otherwise will be obliged to (a) fulfil certain minimum infrastructural (including those relating to teachers and other staff), financial, curricular, pedagogic, linguistic and socio-cultural norms, and (b) ensure free education to the children in a specified neighbourhood from an age group and/or up to a stage, as may be prescribed, while having adequate flexibility and academic freedom to explore, innovate and be creative and appropriately reflecting the geo-cultural and linguistic diversity of the country. However, it was not supported by legal tools that could enforce such policy mandates.

A great legal breakthrough was achieved in 1992 when the Supreme Court of India held in *Mohini Jain v/s State of Karnataka* case that the 'right to education' is concomitant to fundamental rights enshrined under part III of the Constitution and that 'every citizen has a right to education under the Constitution'. The Supreme court subsequently reconsidered the above mentioned judgement in the case of *Unnikrishnan, J.P. v/s State of Andhra Pradesh*. The court (majority judgement) held that 'though right to education is not stated expressly as a fundamental right, it is implicit in and flows from the right to life guaranteed under Article 21 and must be construed in the light of the Directive Principles of the Constitution'. The Unnikrishnan Judgement empowered people with a legal claim to FCE. Several public interest litigation petitions were filed in different High Courts to enforce the Unnikrishnan Judgement and acquire admission into schools. This created tremendous pressure on the part of the state and thereafter a proposal for a Constitutional Amendment to include the right to education as a fundamental right was made in 1996. Accordingly, the Constitution (Eighty-third) Amendment Bill was introduced in the Rajya Sabha in July 1997. The 83rd Amendment proposed that Article 21-A be introduced (Fundamental Right to education for 6-14 years), former Article 45 be deleted (the then existing Directive Principle on FCE) and Article 51-A (k) fundamental duty on parents be introduced between 1997 and 2001. Due to change in Governments, the political will that was required to bring about the Amendment was absent. In November 2011, however, the bill was re-numbered as the 93rd Bill and the 83rd Bill was withdrawn. The 93rd Bill proposed that former Article 45 be amended to provide for early childhood care and education instead of being deleted altogether. This Bill was passed in 2002 as the 86th Constitutional Amendment Act. Currently under Article 21-A of the Constitution, every child between the ages of six to fourteen has a fundamental right to education, which the state shall provide in such manner as the state may by law determine. Early childhood care and education (for children in the age group of 0-6 years) is provided for as a Directive Principle of State Policy under Article 45 of the Constitution. Again, there has been a revolutionary change in the country's education sector with the passage of the Right of Children to free and Compulsory Education Bill by the Lok Sabha on 4 August 2009. Subsequently, on 26 August 2009, the Parliament received the assent of the President and the right of children to FCE 2009 was published in the Gazette of India on 27 August 2009.

Major Problems Related to RTE Act

There are lots of ambiguities in the interpretation of the Act and a lot of issues have been delineated. Some of them are discussed below:

Exclusion of ECCE from the Ambit of RTE

The present RTE Act gives right to free education to only the children in the age group of six to fourteen years, whereas it has been proven by ample research carried out by various organizations that 0-6 years is very critical as far as the developmental milestones are concerned. The exclusion of ECCE from the RTE where there is neither any norm nor standards for pre-school education in the country as well as any uniformity in the system, it gives the advantage to particular section of the society, who can afford ECE. Currently, a state may choose to provide ECCE under the RTE; thereby making ECCE optional. Many education activists have expressed concerns about the lack of a monitoring authority in this regard. The exclusion of pre-school education under the RTE has paved the way for an unregulated system of pre-school education in India. Also, ECCE has an immediate impact, like improvements in children's health, cognitive ability, maths learning, academic performance and school retention almost by 15-20 per cent gain. The long term impact is that it leads to higher incomes and incidence of home ownership, lower propensity to be on welfare and lower rates of crime and arrest. The evidence from neuro-science also indicates that brain almost develops 85 per cent during the first six years of life. If we provide the economic argument, it was found that the total cost of schooling including early learning up to grade two was eleven per cent lower for those, who participated in ECCE as compared to those who did not (Brazil PROAPE Project, 2002). Recent evidence indicated that the return on every dollar invested in ECCE was about $12.90 saved in subsequent years. Recent panel of nine Economists noted that benefits are substantially higher than costs. Thus, excluding ECCE from the ambit of RTE means depriving a large section of the society to reap the benefits of future life, and it is against the social welfare society.

Quality of Education

If one looks at Article 21A of RTE Act, it addresses the quality as "*satisfactory and equitable quality in a formal school, which satisfies certain essential norms and standards.*" It is hardly surprising that the large proportion of what is taught is completely alien and alienating to the average Indian child. The hapless middle class child doggedly goes through school anyway, because she or he has no choice. However, the poor child, the first-generation learner, often takes the easy way out and stays away. This is not to say that we need to have a different curriculum for the rich and for the poor-definitely not. The children of the poor cannot be short-changed in the name of local relevance, non-formal education, etc. In fact, a lot of confusion and well-intentioned bumbling is going on in this area right now. For example, 'non-formal education' is often posited against 'formal schooling', implying that the latter is stifling, irrelevant and undesirable by definition, and that the former is necessarily good. Obviously, this is not the case. If made truly relevant, interesting, child-centred and attractive to learners and parents, formal schooling can provide the poor child with a solid educational base that is in no way inferior to that available to her richer compatriot. On the other hand, non-formal programmes can, and often do, easily end up being extremely loose, without specific targets, and finally cheat the child of even basic literacy skills. To really provide equity in basic education, what is needed is a combination of the best of both approaches. On the solid framework of a core curriculum needs to be built a child-friendly, locally-relevant structure that is welcoming and appealing for the first-generation learner. The government has been making great efforts in the past few years to improve this situation by trying to develop a core curriculum, or minimum levels of learning, which will ensure basic equity in learning, and which can then be adapted locally and made more meaningful. Government-initiated teacher training programmes also emphasise 'child-centred, activity-based' learning. New and better textbooks have been developed by most states. However, these efforts have, by and large, been only theoretical. The vast majority of schools continue to burden the child with vast amounts of useless information, resulting in a crisis in confidence among rural and urban learners from poor families.

Common School System

The desire to have a common school system in India is as old as the Kothari Commission. No one, who is concerned with equity in education and the creation of a new citizenry, can disagree with this goal. Unfortunately, we are discussing about this goal at a point of time when private schools have mushroomed and become the institution of first choice for the children of the elite and even of the middle classes. India has provided highly stratified private schools in order to cater to different classes of people. These institutions are delivering "good results" for their respective clients, while the huge bulk of the less fortunate is consigned to government schools. Given the size of our population and the magnitude of illiteracy, no transformation is possible through the model of privatization. We have to make arrangement in such a manner that the government schools should come at par with these private schools and provide education of equal quality. Quality government schools, like KVS, NVS, KGBV and Model schools, which are at par with any private schools, should be opened almost at every kilometre, so that poor child along with the middle and upper middle class children receives education.

Public vs. Private Schools

In the last two decades, there is a mushrooming of private schools. Many of them are delivering the results as per the expectations of the parents. As a result, there is an increase in the percentage of population of children, who are going to these schools, whereas the trend is reversed in the case of government schools. The government school not only fails to attract the students, but also fails to deliver the goods as expected by the parents. As a result, the parents, who can afford, are sending their child to private school. Many a times, these private schools are even worse than government ones. The provision for reservation in private unaided schools is certainly admiring and plays a crucial role in bridging the gap between private and public schools. However, one should also acknowledge that in order to strengthen the campaign against inequitable schooling, the first step is to prioritize and strengthen government schools across the country. The problem of education today is largely attributable to a complete loss of faith in the quality of existing government schools. Therefore, purely with a view to achieving a strategic interim victory in people's struggle for the implementation of the right to education, the crisis of public schools and the problem of 'public versus private schools' may have to be solved out.

States Crying for Starvation of Funds

The Parliamentary Committee on HRD in its 21st report has said that the states will not be able to meet their share for Right to Education (RTE) Act. The Committee said that the implementation of RTE will require ₹ 1.71 lakh crore for a period of five years. The HRD ministry, later on, demanded ₹ 2.31 lakh crore for RTE's implementation over the next five years. The 13th Finance Commission sanctioned ₹ 24,000 crore for the states for the next five years. This has effectively brought down the total demand to ₹ 2.07 lakh crore. Moreover, the funding pattern has been revised to 65:35. In spite of such a large support from the centre, many of the states have their reservation, as they demanded for 90:10 or 75:25 funding pattern. It looks that majority of states are severely starved of funds. The enactment of RTE saw the approval of ₹ 2.31 lakh crore for the implementation of RTE-SSA. The total funds provided in the Eleventh Plan amounted to ₹ 78,000 crore, a figure that is not much higher than the original approved outlay of ₹ 71,000 crore, without the provision for RTE-related expenses. There is a significant shortfall of funds required for the implementation of the RTE-SSA programme, especially as the first two years called for the heaviest expenses, including hiring of additional teachers, enhancement of infrastructure and administrative changes required to move to the new rights-based regime. Due to staff shortages, the release of funds is delayed, ultimately leading to under-spending of allocated funds. This is a problem in itself. The government has spent just 70 per cent of the funds allocated for the SSA and RTE in 2010-11 compared to 78 per cent the previous year. On one hand, the states are crying for more funds to be allocated to meet RTE norms, whereas on other hand, the glaring fact is the non-utilization of funds available.

Problems of Qualified Teachers

The supply of qualified teachers in all schools has been even a bigger problem. While part of the problem could be due to managerial inefficiency at the systems level, there are also real problems of availability and quality. According to DISE data, during 2010-11, two schools in five failed to reach the primary grade norm of a pupil-teacher ratio of 1:30, and almost two out of three children are enrolled in schools that do not meet this requirement. Similarly, seven out of ten upper primary schools failed to attain the RTE teacher-pupil norm of 1:35; roughly one in two children are enrolled in schools that fail the norm. There are huge disparities, with nine out of ten primary schools in Bihar having a pupil-teacher ratio of over 1:30. Only the Andaman and Nicobar Islands met the PTR norm for primary and upper primary education, with Sikkim meeting the latter. In 2011-12, 8.86 per cent of schools had a single teacher—an almost insignificant improvement over 9.33 per cent in 2009-10. These numbers obviously mean that in the first year of implementation of the RTE Act, recruitments had not taken place. Since the Act was notified, and based on proposals received from the state governments, 6.31 lakh teacher posts have been sanctioned under the SSA to enable the states to meet RTE requirements.

However, according to government data, 689,268 sanctioned teacher posts remain vacant. This amounts to 36 per cent of the sanctioned total teacher force. Apart from it, a huge force of para-teachers is working in the schools, who are invariably employed on contract basis and most often do not have professional training and qualification. This is an issue that has attracted considerable criticism and needs careful consideration as the proportion of such para-teachers is continuously increasing in various states as such recruitments are supported by Central Government's funds through SSA. Many of the states have asked for extension of dates from the central government not only for recruitment of teachers, but also bring down the PTR to 1:30, which the central government has accepted in the proposal. Needless to say, the requirements of providing quality education at the upper primary level becomes quite complex, as specialized teachers are required to teach a diversified curriculum. As a result, the teacher student ratio may not be the right criteria for assessing teacher requirement. Equally true is the non-applicability of classroom teacher ratio at the upper primary level. The teacher requirement is to be based on the requirement of subject specialists in different schools. The teacher-student ratio and teacher-classroom ratio can form complementary criteria for determining the requirement of teachers. This can only bring up the complex issue of building a good quality teaching force to meet the expanding requirement of the school system.

Quality of In-Service Training

Continuous professional development holds key for the capacity building of teachers and, thus, ensuring quality of education. Since SSA programme has been merged with RTE, therefore, in-service training programme for teachers are usually being followed in the same pattern as provided in SSA. The capacity building of teachers essentially pertain to: (a) ensuring basic provisioning to enable improvement in the quality of classroom transactions, (b) focus on assessment of learning outcomes and their improvement, as key indicators of the quality of learning. It requires an annual in-service training for up to 20 days per teacher. The emphasis is on practical classroom related teacher training by providing for a maximum of ten days institutional training at BRCs level, and another ten days specifically at cluster/school level in order to ensure follow-up, peer learning and experience practical classroom transactions. SSA also provides for 30 day induction training for newly recruited trained teachers to orient them to their roles and responsibilities; the expectation of the SSA programme; and specific state/district priorities in quality education. Sixty day training is also provided for teachers that have not received pre service training in order to provide customized distance mode programmes for such teachers to acquire progressive qualifications in service mode. All trainings cover several pedagogical issues, including content and methodology, thereby improving teaching learning transactions at classroom level. Many States have started exploring several innovative means of imparting these trainings, including the use of distance, self-learning mode and use of educational technology. Teacher training under the SSA emphasizes child-centred pedagogy and activity based teaching learning. In one of the study conducted on the effectiveness of in-service education of teachers by Eshwaran and Ajit (2008) in the state of Tamil Nadu and Bihar, the following observations were made:

- In the state of Tamil Nadu, nearly 72 per cent teachers reported that the training content of the training programmes they underwent was relevant to their professional learning needs. The remaining teachers (28%) expressed that it was not relevant at all to their professional learning needs. Of the teachers, who perceived the training content relevant to their needs, nearly 94 per cent expressed that it was relevant to some extent. Only six per cent expressed that it was relevant to a great extent. Further, only 61 per cent of the teachers expressed that training content can be implemented in the classroom. Of these, nearly 93 per cent further expressed that it can be implemented to some extent only.

- Teachers from Tamil Nadu by and large further reported that no substitute teacher was posted against their position in the school during the period of their in-service training. As a consequence, learning of their students was affected adversely. They further reported that their image among parents/guardians of their students also declined because of their absence from the school due to their in-service training.
- Only 2.9 per cent teachers from Tamil Nadu reported that their teaching process improved to a large extent as a result of their in-service training under SSA. Nearly 73 per cent reported that it improved to some extent only. The remaining teachers (23.7%) reported that they do not perceive any improvement in their teaching process as a result of their in-service training.
- Nearly 74 per cent teachers reported that transactional approaches followed by facilitators/resource persons were appropriate to some extent only. About ten per cent reported that the approaches were appropriate to a great/large extent.
- Seventy five per cent teachers from Bihar reported that the training content was relevant to their professional learning needs. Further 23.7 per cent teachers reported that the training content can be implemented in the classroom to a great extent. Nearly 49 teachers reported that it can be implemented to some extent only.
- Nearly 24 per cent teachers from Bihar reported that training received by them was useful to them to a large extent. About 58 per cent teachers reported that it was useful to some extent only. The rest (18.4%) reported that it was not useful at all.
- Only 28 per cent teachers reported that the transactional approaches followed by resource persons/facilitators were appropriate to a great/large extent. More than 60 per cent reported that they were appropriate to some extent only.

Though majority of the in-service programmes are conducted by BRC, CRC or DIET level organizations, yet they are routine type and general rather locale specific and many times, it is not applicable to classroom transactions. This further becomes acute in the case of upper primary teachers.

Right Based Approach

The centre should undertake a detailed evaluation of all existing educational policies and schemes using the rights based approach. There is an urgent need to consolidate the experiences of providing elementary education in the last six decades and evolve a realistic pro-child rights based policy on education, which may then be translated into legislation. The institutional framework required to implement such a policy can also be determined only after the policy itself is evaluated and updated. Some of the non-negotiable minimum matrix of rights, which may be used to analyze the existing policies and developing institutional framework for implementation, are:

a) Identifying minimum quantitative indicators
b) Identifying minimum qualitative indicators
c) Respecting non-negotiable principles to implement the entitlements, like non-discrimination, equality and child participation.
d) Provision for capacity building of the right-holders as well as the duty-bearers.
e) Creating an enabling framework where solutions to barriers against FCE are provided.
f) Ensuring that relationship between child -state, parent-child, parent-state and community-child/parent-state is clearly defined.
g) Fixing social accountability on different actors and creating a grievance redressal mechanism. This would entail clear identification of duty-bearers at different levels – centre, state, district, local level bodies and school.
h) Ensuring sufficient budget as prescribed by various committees and individuals to ensure FCE.

Multiculturalism and Pedagogy

Presently what an Indian classroom looks like is very similar to a miniature Indian society wherein children from diverse backgrounds are studying together. The curriculum, which is operated in the schools, is heavily biased in favour of middle class professional households. Textbooks represent middle class lifestyle and preferences, and often portray them as models to emulate. The absence of any positive representation of the labour of the working poor alienates children from their own communities and families and negatively affects their self-esteem. The curricula do not teach about their struggles for equity and dignity or the oppressive nature of the caste system, and it is barely dealt with at the secondary level either. Further, school curricula are restricted to bookish and abstract learning, and do not utilize local examples, materials and modes of learning to teach these concepts.

A curriculum that includes the histories, living environments and livelihoods of poor and downtrodden communities in a positive manner is needed in order to promote a sense of self-worth and facilitate meaningful learning. However, current mainstream curricula do not give attention to the socio-cultural and economic realities and ideals of many of the communities. Using the native language as the medium of instruction has also long been recognized as an important factor for successful learning. This is especially important for children, who often speak dialects that are different from the regional or state language. The 1986 National Policy on Education and the more recent revised National Curriculum Framework (NCERT, 2005) recommend the use of local languages in the early stages of education. Except in some rare instances (due to the efforts of local NGOs), however, there has been no real attempt to develop primers using words and phrases from the local language or dialect. As a result, an increasing number of researchers strongly advocate the use of the mother tongue or home language as the medium of instruction in early stages of education. This assumes greater significance in the context of education of tribal children because their mother tongue is often quite distinct from the prominent languages in the state or regional languages. ST children face problems wherever teachers do not speak their dialect at all. From the perspective of language, it is desirable to have a local teacher from the same tribal community (Jha and Jhingran, 2002).

Conclusion

RTE is a historic development in the post-Independence era, especially in the field of elementary education, but entire effort of government will be futile if these myriad of problems are not being sorted out quickly. This needs serious attention and efforts of government machinery to overhaul the system, so that benefits can reach to the grassroots level.

References

1. Balagopalan, S. and Subrahmanian, R. (2003). Dalit and Adivasi Children in Schools: Some Preliminary Research Themes and Findings. *IDS Bulletin*, 34(1): pp. 4354. Brighton: Institute of Development Studies.
2. Banerjee, Upala Devi (2001). Primary Education: The Sankalp and Madhya Pradesh Educational Guarantee Scheme Models Case Studies of Rights-Based Approaches to Designing an Educational System for Marginalized and Vulnerable Children in India www.equalinrights.org/./OHCHR_2005_Accessing_Primary_Educat.Retrieved on 12th February 2013.
3. C.J. Sonowal (2008). Indian Tribes and Issue of Social Inclusion and Exclusion Study Tribes Tribals, 6(2): 123-134.
4. Census of India (2002). Primary Census Abstract: Census of India 2001. New Delhi: Government of India.
5. Drèze, J. and Gazdar, H. (1997). *Uttar Pradesh: The Burden of Inertia*. In Drèze, J. and Sen, A.K. (eds.), *Indian Development: Selected Regional Perspectives*. Delhi: Oxford University Press.

6. Drèze, J. and Sen, A.K. (2002). *India: Development and Participation*. New Delhi: Oxford University Press.
7. Duraisamy, P. (2001). Effectiveness of Incentives on School Enrolment and Attainment. *Journal of Educational Planning and Administration*. XV (2): pp. 155-177.
8. Eduwatch (2008). Report on Rhetoric vs. Reality: The State of Elementary Education in India.
9. Gautam, V. (2003). "Education of Tribal Children in India and the Issue of Medium of Instruction: A Janshala Experience." UN/Government Janshala Programme. New Delhi.
10. GOI (2012). Annual Report of Ministry of Tribal Affairs 2011-12, GOI, New Delhi.
11. Government of India (2002). Tenth Five-Year Plan. New Delhi: Government of India.
12. Government of India (2008). Selected Educational Statistics, 2005-2006, Abstract. New Delhi: Ministry of Human Resource Development, Department of Education, Planning, Monitoring and Statistics Division.
13. Illiah, K. (2000). The State Oppressions and Weaker Sections in Rao, C.S. and Francis, D. (eds.), *Development of Weaker Sections*. Jaipur and New Delhi: Rawat Publications.
14. Jeffrey, C., Jeffery, R. and Jeffery, P. (2002). Degrees without Freedom: The Impact of Formal Education on Dalit Young Men in North India. *Development and Change*, 35(5): pp. 963-986.
15. Jha, J. and D. Jhingran (2002). "Review of Elementary Education for Poorest and Other Disadvantaged Groups: The Real Challenge of Universalisation." Centre for Policy Research. New Delhi.
16. Kaul, R. (2001). Accessing Primary Education: Going Beyond the Classroom. *Economic and Political Weekly,* 13-19 January, 36(2): pp. 155-162.
17. Lewis, M.A. and M.E. Lockheed. (2007). "Getting All Girls into School." Finance and Development. *International Monetary Fund*. Volume 44. Number 2. June.
18. Mona Sedwal and Sangeeta Kamat (2008). *Education and Social Equity: With a Special Focus on Scheduled Castes and Scheduled Tribes in Elementary Education*, NUEPA.
19. National Commission on Scheduled Castes and Scheduled Tribes (1998). Annual Report. New Delhi: Government of India.
20. National Tribal Commission (2008). Education of Tribal People in India.
21. Reddy, P.S. (2000). District Primary Education Programme in Andhra Pradesh: A Social Assessment Study among the Tribal Groups. Report funded by DPEP, Government of Andhra Pradesh. Tirupati: Department of Anthropology, Sri Venkateswara University.
22. Secada, W.G. (1989). Educational Equity versus Equality of Education: An Alternative Conception. In Secada, W.G. (ed.), *Equity in Education*. New York: Falmer Press.
23. Subrahmanian, R. (2005). Education Exclusion and the Development State. In Chopra, R., and Jeffery, P. (eds.), *Educational Regimes in Contemporary India*. New Delhi: Sage Publications.

24. Sujatha, K. (2002). Education among Scheduled Tribes. In Govinda, R. (ed.), *India Education Report: A Profile of Basic Education*. New Delhi: Oxford University Press.
25. Sujatha, K. (2002). Education among Scheduled Tribes. In Govinda, R. (ed.), *India Education Report: A Profile of Basic Education*. New Delhi: Oxford University Press.
26. Sundaram, K. and Tendulkar, S.D. (2003). Poverty among Social and Economic Groups in India in the Nineteen Nineties. Centre for Development Economics Working Paper 118. Delhi: Delhi School of Economics.
27. Surajit, S. (2002). Tribal Solidarity Movements in India: A Review. In Shah, G. (ed.) *Social Movements and the State: Readings in Indian Government and Politics*. New Delhi: Sage Publications.
28. Thorat, S. (2002). Oppression and Denial: Dalit Discrimination in the 1990s. *Economic and Political Weekly*, 9 February, 37(6): 572-578.
29. Tilak, J.B.G. (2002). Determinants of Household Expenditure on Education in Rural India. National Council of Applied Economic Research Working Paper Series No. 88. Delhi: NCAER.
30. World Bank Report (2004). Report on reaching out to the Child an Integrated Approach to Child Development.

20

The Role of ICTs in Achieving Universal Primary Education

Noushad Husain

The UN Millennium Summit, in 2000, defined a set of goals to be achieved for a more peaceful and prosperous world. The eight Millennium Development Goals (MDGs) were agreed upon by the United Nation's member states (MDGs 2008). These were: "(1) Eradication of poverty and hunger; (2) Achieve universal primary education; (3) Promote gender equality and empower women; (4) Reduce child mortality; (5) Improve maternal health; (6) Combat HIV/AIDS, malaria and other diseases; (7) Ensure environmental sustainability; and (8) Develop a global partnership for development" (GRN 2004). The purpose of these eight MDGs aimed to tackle the vestiges of poverty by addressing factors that impacted negatively on the lives of communities in all member states and the eradication of these by year 2015 (MDGs 2008). That Declaration contains a commitment to "*ensure that the benefits of new technologies, especially information and communication technologies...are available to all.*" While access to ICTs can educate, entertain and enrich our lives, ICTs, together with other tools, can also play a part in helping to achieve the much broader goals of the Millennium Declaration.

Millennium Development Goals (MDGs)

As illustrated in Table 20.1, the MDGs (and their corresponding targets) cover a broad range of concerns, namely: poverty and hunger; primary education; gender equality; child mortality; maternal health; HIV/AIDS, malaria and other diseases; environmental sustainability; and global partnerships.

Information and Communication Technologies (ICTs)

Information and Communications Technologies (ICTs) cut across a variety of technologies including: computer, micro-electronics and related technologies

Table 20.1: Millennium Development Goals and Targets

The MDGs	*The Targets*
Goal 1: Eradicate Extreme Poverty and Hunger	**Target 1:** Halve, between 1990 and 2015, the proportion of people whose income is less than one dollar a day. **Target 2:** Halve, between 1990 and 2015, the proportion of people who suffer from hunger.
Goal 2: Achieve Universal Primary Education	**Target 3:** Ensure that, by 2015, children everywhere, boys and girls alike, will be able to complete a full course of primary schooling.
Goal 3: Promote Gender Equality and Empower Women	**Target 4:** Eliminate gender disparity in primary and secondary education, preferably by 2005, and to all levels of education no later than 2015.
Goal 4: Reduce Child Mortality	**Target 5:** Reduce by two-thirds, between 1990 and 2015, the under-five mortality rate.
Goal 5: Improve Maternal Health	**Target 6:** Reduce by two-thirds, between 1990 and 2015, the under-five mortality rate.
Goal 6: Combat HIV/AIDS, Malaria and other Diseases	**Target 7:** Have halted by 2015 and begun to reverse the spread of HIV/AIDS. **Target 8:** Have halted by 2015 and begun to reverse the incidence of malaria and other major diseases.
Goal 7: Ensure Environmental Sustainability	**Target 9:** Integrate the principles of sustainable development into country policies and programmes and reverse the loss of environmental resources. **Target 10:** Halve, by 2015, the proportion of people without sustainable access to safe drinking water. **Target 11:** By 2020, to have achieved a significant improvement in the lives of at least 100 million slum dwellers.
Goal 8: Develop a Global Partnership for Development	**Target 12:** Develop further an open, rule-based, predictable, non-discriminatory trading and financial System. **Target 13:** Address the Special Needs of the Least Developed Countries. **Target 14:** Address the Special Needs of land-locked countries and small island developing States. **Target 15:** Deal comprehensively with the debt problems of developing countries through national and international measures in order to make debt sustainable in the long term. **Target 16:** In co-operation with developing countries, develop and implement strategies for decent and productive work for youth. **Target 17:** In co-operation with pharmaceutical companies, provide access to affordable, essential drugs in developing countries. **Target 18:** In co-operation with the private sector, make available the benefits of new technologies, especially information and communications.

including microchip and microprocessor-based technologies; multimedia and other information processing technologies and systems; telecommunications technologies and infrastructure (fixed line, wireless, satellite based and mobile infrastructure); and communication network technologies and infrastructure (including local and wide area communications and computer networks for voice, data and video).

Other technologies that form part of ICTs include: broadcasting networks and technologies including radio and TV networks; production-based technologies including those used in computer-integrated manufacturing and production systems and operations, robotics technologies, biotechnology-related equipments and systems; and the Internet as a globally-based delivery platform—incorporating elements of computers, telecommunications, communication technologies and networks and other multimedia development and delivery technologies to form an integrated multimedia transmission and communication delivery infrastructure and platform with a global reach.

ICTs and MDGs

There are a number of important ways in which ICT is differentiated from other development sectors and technologies and this is not simply because of its status as a lucrative source of revenue and taxation for business and government. As an accelerator, driver, multiplier and innovator, the unique character of ICTs, both established (radio, television, video, compact disc) and emerging (wireless, Internet, broadband), make them a powerful if not indispensable tool in the massive scaling up and inter-linkage of development interventions and outcomes inherent in the MDGs.

ICTs are a powerful enabler of development goals, because it dramatically improves communication and the exchange of knowledge and information to strengthen and create new social and economic networks. Its uses and applications are pervasive and cross-cutting and can be applied to the full range of human activity from personal use to business and government. It propitiates an acceleration factor through the power of the network that becomes ever more powerful and useful, the more people are connected to it, thus creating network externalities or exponentially increasing returns as network usage increases. And it fosters the dissemination of information and exchange of knowledge by separating content from physical location and overcoming distance.

ICTs as an Enabler of Developmental Goals

There is now mounting evidence that ICTs can be used to facilitate various aspects of the socio-economic development process in both developing and developed countries. For example, research work based on a number of case studies, reported by Dzidonu (2001) suggests that ICTs can serve as a key resource essential for achieving broad-based development goals. The principal lesson being that although use of the technology is not a goal in itself, it can be used as an enabler of developmental goals and that for ICTs to have impact on development; its introduction should be fully integrated into the process of organizational and societal change and driven by real needs for economic, social and institutional development.

How ICTs Can Help Achieve the Millennium Development Goals

Table 20.2 clearly shows how we can use ICTs to achieve the millennium declaration goals:

Table 20.2: How ICTs Can Help Achieve the Millennium Development Goals

Goal/Target	*Role of ICTs*
1. Eradicate extreme poverty and hunger Halve, between 1990 and 2015, the proportion of people whose income is less than one dollar a day. Halve, between 1990 and 2015, the proportion of people who suffer from hunger.	Increase access to market information and reduce transaction costs for poor farmers and traders. Increase efficiency, competitiveness and market access of developing country firms. Enhance ability of developing countries to participate in global economy and to exploit comparative advantage in factor costs (particularly skilled labour).
2. Achieve universal primary education Ensure that, by 2015, children everywhere, boys and girls alike, will be able to complete a full course of primary schooling.	Increase supply of trained teachers through ICT-enhanced and distance training of teachers and networks that link teachers to their colleagues. Improve the efficiency and effectiveness of education ministries and related bodies through strategic application of technologies and ICT-enabled skill development. Broaden availability of quality educational materials/resources through ICTs.
3. Promote gender equality and empower women	Deliver educational and literacy programmes specifically targeted to poor girls and women using appropriate technologies. Influence public opinion on gender equality through information or communication programmes using a range of ICTs.
4. Reduce child mortality 5. Improve maternal health 6. Combat HIV/AIDS, malaria and other diseases Reduce infant and child mortality rates by two thirds between 1990 and 2015 Reduce maternal mortality rates by three-quarters between 1990 and 2015 Provide access to all, who need reproductive health services by 2015	Enhance delivery of basic and in-service training for health workers. Increase monitoring and information-sharing on disease and famine. Increase access of rural care-givers to specialist support and remote diagnosis. Increase access to reproductive health information, including information on AIDS prevention, through locally appropriate content in local languages.
7. Ensure environmental sustainability Implement national strategies for sustainable development by 2005 so as to reverse the loss of environmental resources by 2015. Halve, by 2015, the proportion of people without sustainable access to safe drinking water. Have achieved, by 2020, a significant improvement in the lives of at least 100 million slum dwellers.	Remote sensing technologies and communication networks permit more effective monitoring, resource management, mitigation of environmental risks. Increase access to/awareness of sustainable development strategies, in areas such as agriculture, sanitation and water management, mining, etc. Greater transparency and monitoring of environmental abuses/enforcement of environmental regulations. Facilitate knowledge exchange and networking among policymakers, practitioners and advocacy groups.

Source: ITU adapted from Department for International Development (United Kingdom).

From Table 20.2, it is clear that we can use ICTs to achieve the millennium development goals successfully within the time limit. The advantages of ICT in achieving millennium development goals can best understood with the help of Figure 20.1.

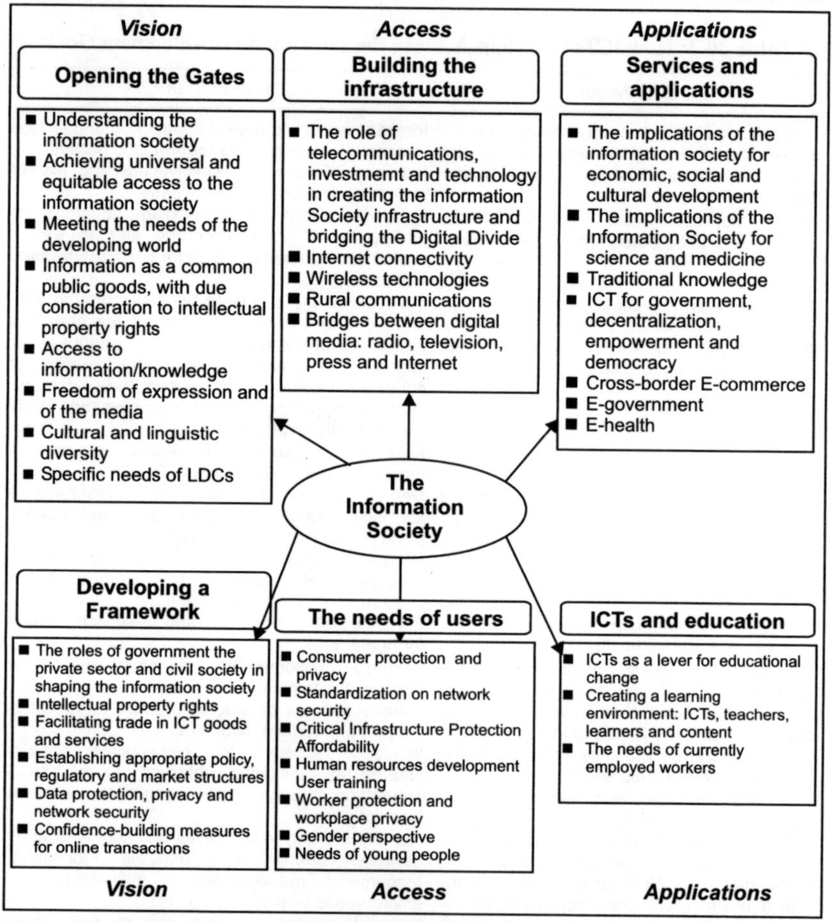

Figure 20.1: How Information and Communication Technologies (ICTs) can Help Achieve Broader Development Objectives, such as the Millennium Development Goals (MDGs).

ICTs and Primary Education (Goal 2)

There are many hurdles in achieving the MDG target of all children receiving primary school education. Of the 680 million children of primary school age in developing countries, 115 million do not attend school, with 60 per cent of these children being girls and 74 per cent living in South Asia and sub-Saharan Africa. ICTs can help countries facing budgetary constraints. UNESCO estimates that an additional 15-35 million educated and trained teachers will be needed over the next decade if all countries are to achieve the MDG of universal primary education by 2015. ICT-based distance training can overcome the shortage of primary school teachers by accelerating instruction. ICT can also supplement primary school teaching, thereby helping to overcome shortages. And via the traditional ICTs of radio and television, ICT could also be used to emphasize the importance of primary school attendance, particularly in areas with strong social or cultural barriers.

Based on extensive interviews in Bolivia, Ghana, India, Namibia and South Africa, the Global eSchools and Communities Initiative (GeSCI), backed by the United Nations and the Governments of Canada, Ireland, Sweden and Switzerland has recently identified five education building blocks with respect to key educational challenges and ICT solutions desired by schools:

- ***teachers***, with inadequate training and ICT-based (TV or computer) teacher training;
- ***infrastructure***, with long distance to schools in some areas and remote distance learning via ICTs;
- ***curriculum and content***, with outdated curricula and inclusion of ICT skills in curriculum, and ineffective distribution of content for teachers and ICT-based delivery of traditional and rich content;
- **teaching and learning tools**, with under-equipped laboratories and insufficient tools and materials for project work and ICT-based education tools for classroom teaching and for project work by learning;
- **administration**, with high volume of manual administration and for teachers and principals with basic ICT applications for administration.

ICTs for Achieving Universal Primary Education

There are a number of barriers to achieve the MDG target of all children receiving primary school education. One of the most pervasive one is a shortage of facilities and teachers, often due to financial constraints (UNDP, 2003). ICTs can help overcome these shortages in an efficient and economical way for countries facing budgetary limitations (Perraton, 2000).

ICT-based distance training can help overcome a lack of primary school teachers by accelerating instruction (Rowe, 2003). This is particularly relevant for countries with large rural areas where potential teachers have difficulty travelling to formal learning centres. There are a number of examples of primary teacher distance education programmes in developing nations (Shrestha, 1997). ICTs can enhance distance education through more rapid and interactive dissemination of learning materials compared to traditional correspondence-based formulas. Several nations have integrated old and new ICTs into primary teacher education programmes. Widespread adoption of ICT based training could help alleviate the teacher shortage and increase the capacity of countries to enrol more primary school students. One indicator to measure this would be the number of primary school teachers trained through ICT-based education.

ICTs can also supplement primary school teaching, thereby helping to overcome shortages. For example, a number of countries use radio programmes to broadcast subjects to primary schools while others have gone further by integrating ICTs, such as CD-ROMs and web-based software into the daily instruction time. An indicator that could measure the impact of new technologies for teaching students, might be the number of primary school pupils using ICTs for learning.

ICTs could also be used to emphasize the importance of primary school attendance, particularly where there are strong social or cultural barriers to doing so. Radio and television broadcasts could be used to emphasize this with a possible indicator of the number of students enrolled in primary school as a result of radio/television broadcasts.

Finally, many countries suffer from a shortage of primary school textbooks that affects learning and causes students to drop out. ICTs can help overcome this limitation through electronic learning materials. The growing trend towards the production of electronic textbooks could alleviate shortages in developing countries through innovative distribution techniques. The indicator number of primary school learning materials provided through ICTs and Internet could measure this.

ICTs as a Facilitator for Achieving Universal Primary Education (Goal 2)

The use of ICTs to facilitate educational delivery at all level of the educational system has been one of the popular applications of ICTs in a number of countries. Achieving universal primary education has for some years been a priority educational policy area and goal in a number of these countries and some of them have explored ways, so that ICTs can be used to enable them to make progress towards this goal. We examine below two broad areas of initiatives, which a number of countries are engaged in as a way of facilitating, among other things, the achievement of this MDG.

Access to Education and Training Resources

A number of countries are implementing various forms of e-education programmes and initiatives using ICTs to improve and widen access to educational resources in a number of ways including: improved access to learning materials and resources, widening of access to education through e-learning etc. A number of these initiatives are contributing to promote universal primary education in many of these countries. Also, a number of these countries are deploying ICTs to improve the effectiveness and efficiency of delivery of education at all level of the educational system, especially at the primary and secondary education levels. These efforts being undertaken by countries may in the long-run improve and widen access to primary and secondary education, which could translate into enabling these countries making progress towards achieving the targets set for the MDG 2—*Achieve Universal Primary Education.*

Widening Access to Education and Reducing Physical and Social Barriers to Education

Some countries are using ICTs to create new avenues of access to schooling for the underserved communities and vulnerable groups. A number of these countries are also deploying ICTs to provide innovative educational delivery mechanisms and systems to support the provision of education, especially distance education and non-formal education. The deployment and use of ICT-based educational delivery and support technologies and resources to complement the traditional mode of education as a step towards reducing physical, geographical and social barriers to education can also be identified as one area in which these countries are using these technologies to support education delivery at various levels of the educational system.

On the whole, these efforts directed at the use of ICTs to promote and support education in countries have the potential to have a positive impact on the achievement MDG goal of universal primary education in these countries.

Conclusion

Information and communication technologies hold great potential to help those seeking to achieve universal primary education and universal literacy in the near future. Even if these targets prove overly optimistic, ICT innovations in the educational sector should help improve access, efficiency and quality.

There is an almost magical quality in the Information Revolution, as complex, distributed social and economic processes have resulted in far faster dissemination and more profound application of the technology than anyone expected. The process has been compared to a viral process, teleonomic rather than teleologic. It seems likely that such teleonomic progress will continue to be made in the application of ICT in improving primary education and reducing illiteracy during the remainder period of the implementation of the MDG.

It also seems likely that development of appropriate policies and strengthening appropriate institutions can foster such progress, and can help avoid some of the negative consequences to which education in developing countries is vulnerable. Action is needed at all levels. For example, while radio offers great potential for improving primary education, that potential will not be realized unless radio curricula are designed, radio broadcasts prepared and made, and appropriate formative and summative evaluation processes put in place. Policies will have to be made or modified to permit schools and teachers to adopt radio education, and training will have to be offered as to how to incorporate the technology into the classroom and school. Thus, there are needs for planning and management even to support the "viral approach" to educational technology innovation.

Unfortunately, by most measures, the Digital Divide seems sure to expand. Rich countries, with per capita GDP orders of magnitude higher than the poorest countries, also tend to spend a larger portion of GDP on ICT. Many benefits from ICT will fall disproportionately to the already affluent.

There are perhaps more important measures. Life expectancy in developing nations has increased, without doubt as the result of better health and nutrition, and improved abilities of people to care for themselves and their children. If ICT can be brought to bear to help reduce and eradicate the worst poverty, and the worst aspects of poverty, then it will clearly help breach the development divide separating the rich from the poor. Bringing ICT to bear to extend basic education and literacy to all is a part of the effort to fight poverty.

References

1. Dzidonu C.K. (2001). The Socio-Economic Development Implications of the Digital Divide within the Context of African Countries, Presented at the, Joint African Finance and Economic Planning Ministers Meeting of the ECA, Algiers, Algeria, 8-10.
2. MDGs (2008). Millennium Development Goals (MDGs) Report. http://www.undp.org/mdg/.
3. GRN (2004). *Namibia 2004 Millennium Development Goals.* National Planning Commission Document.
4. Perraton, H. (2000). Teaching the Teachers. *Imfundo Project Background Paper #5*, UK Department for International Development (DFID). http://www.id21.org.
5. Rowe, M. (2003). E for Education. *The International Development Magazine.* Issue 22. http://www.developments.org.uk/data/Issue22/e-for-education.htm.
6. Shrestha, G. (1997). *A Review of Case Studies Related to Distance Education in Developing Countries.* http://www.undp.org/info21/public/review/pb-revke.html.
7. UNDP (2003). *Human Development Report.* http://www.undp.org/hdr2003.

21

A Rights Based Approach to Education

Noushad Husain and *Afaque Nadeem Khan*

Education has been formally recognized as a human right since the adoption of the Universal Declaration of Human Rights in 1948. This has since been affirmed in numerous global human rights treaties, including the United Nations Educational, Scientific and Cultural Organization (UNESCO) Convention against Discrimination in Education (1960), the International Covenant on Economic, Social and Cultural Rights (1966) and the Convention on the Elimination of All Forms of Discrimination against Women (1981). These treaties establish an entitlement to free, compulsory primary education for all children; an obligation to develop secondary education, supported by measures to render it accessible to all children, as well as equitable access to higher education; and a responsibility to provide basic education for individuals, who have not completed primary education. Furthermore, they affirm that the aim of education is to promote personal development, strengthen respect for human rights and freedoms, enable individuals to participate effectively in a free society, and promote understanding, friendship and tolerance. The right to education has long been recognized as encompassing not only access to educational provision, but also the obligation to eliminate discrimination at all levels of the educational system, to set minimum standards and to improve quality. In addition, education is necessary for the fulfilment of any other civil, political, economic or social right. The United Nations Convention on the Rights of the Child (1989) further strengthens and broadens the concept of the right to education; in particular through the obligation to consider in its implementation the Convention's four core principles: non-discrimination; the best interests of the child; the right to life, survival and development of the child to the maximum extent.

Principles Underpinning a Rights-based Approach to Education

A rights-based approach to education is informed by seven basic principles of human rights:

***Universality and Inalienability*:** Human rights are universal and inalienable, the entitlement of all people everywhere in the world. An individual cannot voluntarily give them up, nor can others take them away.

***Indivisibility*:** Human rights are indivisible. Whether civil, cultural, economic, political or social, human rights are all inherent to the dignity of every person.

***Interdependence and Inter-relatedness*:** The realization of one right often depends, wholly or in part, on the realization of others.

***Equality and Non-Discrimination*:** All individuals are equal as human beings, and by virtue of the inherent dignity of each person, are entitled to their rights without discrimination of any kind.

***Participation and Inclusion*:** Every person and all people are entitled to active, free and meaningful participation in, contribution to and enjoyment of civil, economic, social, cultural and political development.

***Empowerment*:** Empowerment is the process by which the capabilities of people to demand and use their human rights grow. The goal is to give people the power and capabilities to claim their rights in order to change their own lives and improve their communities.

***Accountability and Respect for the Rule of Law*:** A rights-based approach seeks to raise levels of accountability in the development process by identifying 'rights holders' and corresponding 'duty bearers', and to enhance the capacities of those duty bearers to meet their obligations.

Adopting Rights Based Approach to Education

Needs-based development approaches to education have, to date, failed to achieve the Education for All goals. Because it is inclusive and provides a common language for partnership, a rights-based approach—although certainly not without tensions and challenges—has the potential to contribute to the attainment of the goals of governments, parents and children. Girls' right to education, for example, can be achieved more effectively if measures are also implemented to address their rights to freedom from discrimination, protection from exploitative labour, physical violence and sexual abuse, and access to an adequate standard of living. Equally, the right to education is instrumental in the realization of other rights. A rights-based approach can contribute significant added value:

***It Promotes Social Cohesion, Integration and Stability*:** Human rights promote democracy and social progress. Even where children have access to school, a poor quality of education can contribute to disaffection. A rights based approach to education, which emphasizes quality, can encourage the development of school environments in which children know that their views are valued. It includes a focus on respect for families and the values of the society in which they are living. It can also promote understanding of other cultures and peoples, contributing to intercultural dialogue and respect for the richness of cultural and linguistic diversity, and the right to participate in cultural life. In this way, it can serve to strengthen social cohesion.

***It Builds Respect for Peace and Non-Violent Conflict Resolution*:** A rights-based approach to education is founded on the principles of peace and non-violent conflict resolution. In achieving this goal, schools and communities must create learning environments that eliminates all forms of physical, sexual or humiliating punishment by teachers and challenges all forms of bullying and aggression among students. In other words, they must promote and build a culture of non-violent conflict resolution. The lessons children learn from school-based experiences in this regard can have far reaching consequences for the wider society.

***It Contributes to Positive Social Transformation*:** A rights-based approach to education that embodies human rights education empowers children and other stakeholders and represents a major building block in efforts to achieve social transformation towards rights—respecting societies and social justice.

***It is More Cost Effective and Sustainable*:** Treating children with dignity and respect—and building inclusive, participatory and accountable education systems that respond directly to the expressed concerns of all stakeholders—will serve to improve educational outcomes. In too many schools, the failure to adapt to the needs of children, particularly working children, results in high levels of dropout and repeated grades. Children themselves cite violence and abuse, discriminatory attitudes, an irrelevant curriculum and poor teaching quality as major contributory factors in the inability to learn effectively and in subsequent dropouts. In addition, health issues can diminish the ability of a child to commence and continue schooling, and for all children, especially girls, an inclusive education can reduce the risk of HIV infection.

A rights-based approach is, therefore, not only cost-effective and economically beneficial, but also more sustainable.

***It Produces Better Outcomes for Economic Development*:** A rights-based approach to education can be entirely consistent with the broader agenda of governments to produce an economically viable workforce. Measures to promote universal access to education and overcome discrimination against girls, children with disabilities, working children, children in rural communities, and minority and indigenous children will serve to widen the economic base of society, thus strengthening a country's economic capability.

***It Builds Capacity*:** By focusing on capacity-building and empowerment, a rights-based approach to education harnesses and develops the capacities of governments to fulfil their obligations and of individuals to claim their rights and entitlements.

Obligations to Ensure the Right to Education for Children

When governments across the region ratified the Convention on the Rights of the Child, they undertook to take all necessary measures to ensure that children's rights are realized. This involves action to:

- **Fulfil the right to education** by ensuring that education is available for all children and that positive measures are taken to enable children to beneût from it, such as by tackling poverty, adapting the curricula to the needs of all children or engaging parents to enable them to provide effective support to their children's education.
- **Respect the right to education** by avoiding any action that would serve to prevent children from accessing education, such as legislation that categorizes certain groups of children with disabilities as uneducable.
- **Protect the right to education** by taking the necessary measures to remove the barriers to education posed by individuals or communities, such as cultural barriers to education or violence and abuse in the school environment.

A Conceptual Framework for Promoting the Right to Education

The development of a human rights-based approach to education requires a framework that addresses the right of access to education, the right to quality education and respect for human rights in education. These dimensions are interdependent and interlinked and a rights-based education necessitates the realization of all three.

The right to education requires a commitment to ensuring universal access, including taking all necessary measures to reach the most marginalized children. But getting children into schools is not enough; it is no guarantee of an education that enables individuals to achieve their economic and social objectives and to acquire the skills, knowledge, values and attitudes that bring about responsible and active citizenship. Achieving a quality education is also a challenge in industrialized nations. Recent studies show that large numbers of students in rich countries do not acquire the basic skills to be competent in today's world.

To ensure quality education in line with the Dakar Framework for Action (2002) and the aims of education elaborated by the Committee on the Rights of the Child, attention must be paid to the relevance of the curriculum, the role of teachers and the nature and ethos of the learning environment. A rights-based approach necessitates a commitment to recognizing and respecting the human rights of children while they are in school – including respect for their identity, agency and integrity. This will contribute to increased retention rates and also makes the process of education empowering, participatory, transparent and accountable. In addition, children will continue to be excluded from education unless measures are taken to address their rights to freedom from discrimination, to an adequate standard of living and to meaningful participation.

Quality education cannot be achieved without regard to children's right to health and well-being. Children cannot achieve their optimum development when they are subjected to humiliating punishment or physical abuse.

This conceptual framework highlights the need for a holistic approach to education, reflecting the universality and indivisibility of all human rights. The following paragraphs set out the central elements that, therefore, need to be addressed in each of the three dimensions mentioned above.

Right of Access to Education

The right of access to education comprises three elements: the provision of education throughout all stages of childhood and beyond, consistent with the Education for All goals; the provision of sufficient, accessible school places or learning opportunities; and equality of opportunity.

Obligations to Ensure the Right of Access to Education

Provide free and compulsory primary education.

- Develop forms of secondary education that are available and accessible to everyone, and introduce measures to provide free education and financial assistance in cases of need.
- Provide higher education that is accessible on the basis of capacity by every appropriate means.
- Provide accessible educational and vocational information and guidance.
- Introduce measures to encourage regular attendance and reduce drop-out rates.
- Provide education on the basis of equal opportunity.
- Ensure respect for the right to education without discrimination of any kind on any grounds.
- Ensure an inclusive education system at all levels.
- Provide reasonable accommodation and support measures to ensure that children with disabilities have effective access to and receive education in a manner conducive to achieving the fullest possible social integration.
- Ensure an adequate standard of living for physical, mental, spiritual, moral and social development.

- Provide protection and assistance to ensure respect for the rights of children, who are refugees or are seeking asylum.
- Provide protection from economic exploitation and work that interferes with education.

Sources: Article 26, Universal Declaration of Human Rights; Articles 2, 22, 23, 27, 28 and 32, Convention on the Rights of the Child; Article 13, International Covenant on Economic, Social and Cultural Rights; Article 10, Convention on the Elimination of All Forms of Discrimination against Women; Articles 4 and 5, UNESCO Convention against Discrimination in Education; Article 24, Convention on the Rights of Persons with Disabilities (opened for signature 30 March 2007).

Right to Quality Education

The Dakar Framework for Action commits nations to the provision of primary education of good quality and to improving all aspects of educational quality. Although there is no single definition of 'quality', most attempts to define it incorporate two fundamental perspectives. First, cognitive development is a primary objective of education, with the effectiveness of education measured against its success in achieving this objective. Second, education must promote creative and emotional development, supporting the objectives of peace, citizenship and security, fostering equality and passing global and local cultural values down to future generations.

These perspectives have been integrated into the aims of education set out in the Convention on the Rights of the Child, which formulates a philosophy of respect for children as individuals, recognizing each child as "unique—in characteristics, interests, abilities and needs". It sets out a framework of obligations to provide education that promotes children's optimum development. Article 29 implies "the need for education to be child-centred, child-friendly and empowering, and it highlights the need for educational processes to be based on the very principles it enunciates". Every child has a right to an education that empowers him or her by developing life skills, learning and other capacities, self-esteem and self-confidence. The provision of a quality education demands attention to the content of the curriculum, the nature of the teaching and the quality of the learning environment. It implies a need for the creation of flexible, effective and respectful learning environments that are responsive to the needs of all children.

Obligations to Ensure Right to Quality Education

- Develop children's personalities, talents, and mental and physical abilities to their fullest potential.
- Promote respect for human rights and fundamental freedoms, and prepare children for a responsible life in a spirit of peace, tolerance, equality and friendship.

- Promote respect for the child's, his or her parents' and others' cultural identity, language and values.
- Promote respect for the natural environment.
- Ensure the child's access to information from a diversity of sources.
- Ensure that the best interests of children are a primary consideration.
- Promote respect for the evolving capacities of children in the exercise of their rights.
- Respect the right of children to rest, leisure, play, recreation, and participation in arts and culture.

Sources: Article 26, Universal Declaration of Human Rights; Articles 3, 5, 6, 12, 17, 29, 31, Convention on the Rights of the Child; Article 13, International Covenant on Economic, Social and Cultural Rights; and Article 24, International Convention on the Rights of Persons with Disabilities (opened for signature 30 March 2007).

Right to Respect in the Learning Environment

Human rights are inalienable. In other words, they are inherent in each human being. Accordingly, they must be respected in all learning environments. The right to education must be understood as incorporating respect for children's identity, their right to express their views on all matters of concern to them, and their physical and personal integrity.

Obligations to Respect Children's Rights in the Learning Environment

- Respect every child equally without discrimination on any grounds.
- Teach respect for human rights and fundamental freedoms, for difference and for life in a society where there is understanding, peace, tolerance, equality and friendship.
- Give primary consideration to the best interests of the child.
- Respect the evolving capacities of the child.
- Respect the right of children to express their views on all matters of concern to them and have those views given due weight in accordance with children's age and maturity.
- Recognize the right to freedom of expression, religion, conscience, thought and assembly.
- Respect the privacy of children.
- Take all appropriate measures to ensure that school discipline is administered in a manner consistent with the child's dignity and all other rights in the Convention on the Rights of the Child.
- Protect children from all forms of physical violence, injury or abuse, neglect or negligence, maltreatment or exploitation, including sexual abuse.

Sources: Articles 2, 3, 5, 12, 13, 14, 15, 16, 19, 28, 29, Convention on the Rights of the Child; Articles 1, 2, Universal Declaration of Human Rights; Articles 18, 19, 27, International Covenant of Civil and Political Rights.

Conclusion

Education does not exist in a vacuum. Ensuring that every child has access to quality and respectful learning environments throughout his or her childhood necessitates action far beyond the ministries of education. The right to education can only be realized in a political and economic environment that acknowledges the importance of transparent, participatory and accountable processes, as well as broad-based collaboration both across government and in the wider society. It needs a long-term strategic commitment to the provision of adequate resources, development of cross-departmental structures, engagement with the energies and capacities of parents and local communities, and partnership with non-governmental organizations.

To ensure the realization of the right to education for all children, States have three levels of obligations:

- *To Fulfil the Right to Education* by ensuring that education is available for all children and that positive measures are taken to enable children to benefit from it, for example, by tackling poverty, adapting the curricula to the needs of all children or engaging parents to enable them to provide effective support to their children's education.
- *To respect the right to education* by avoiding any action that would serve to prevent children from accessing education, for example, legislation that categorizes certain groups of children with disabilities as uneducable.
- *To protect the right to education* by taking the necessary measures to remove the barriers to education posed by individuals or communities, for example, cultural barriers to education or violence and abuse in the school environment.

References

1. CARE Human Rights Initiative, 'Basic Introduction to Human Rights and Rights-Based Programming: Facilitators' guidebook', Care International, London, 2004, www.reliefweb.int/rw/rwt.nsf/db900SID/NVEA5ULK9G/$File/carehrguide.pdf?OpenElement.
2. Human Rights Watch, *Failing our Children: Barriers to Education,* HRW, New York, 2005.
3. Office of the United Nations High Commissioner for Human Rights, *Frequently Asked Questions on a Human Rights-Based Approach to Development Cooperation,* United Nations, New York and Geneva, 2006.
4. Santos Pais, Marta, 'The Convention on the Rights of the Child', in Office of the High Commissioner for Human Rights, United Nations Institute for Training and Research, and United Nations Staff College Project, *Manual on Human*

Rights Reporting Under Six Major International Human Rights Instruments, United Nations, Geneva, 1997.

5. Save the Children, *Child Rights Programming: How to apply rights-based approaches to programming*, 2nd ed., Save the Children Sweden, Stockholm, 2005.
6. Tomaševskí, Katarina, and United Nations Educational, Scientific and Cultural Organization Bangkok, *Manual on Rights-Based Education: Global human rights requirements made simple*, UNESCO Bangkok, Bangkok, 2004.
7. United Nations, 'The Human Rights-Based Approach to Development Cooperation: Towards a common understanding among UN agencies', Report of The Second Interagency Workshop on Implementing a Human Rights-based Approach in the Context of UN Reform, Stamford, May 2003.
8. United Nations Children's Fund, *The 'Rights' Start to Life: A statistical analysis of birth registration*, UNICEF, New York, 2005.
9. United Nations Committee on Economic, Social and Cultural Rights, *General Comment No. 16: The equal right of men and women to the enjoyment of all economic, social and cultural rights (article 3)*, 2005.
10. United Nations Committee on the Elimination of Discrimination against Women, *General Recommendation No. 3: Education and public information programmes*, 1987.
11. United Nations Committee on the Rights of the Child, *General Comment No. 7: Implementing child rights in early childhood*, 2005.
12. United Nations Educational, Scientific and Cultural Organization, *EFA Global Monitoring Report*, UNESCO Publishing, Paris, annually, 2002–ongoing.
13. ______, *Overcoming Exclusion through Inclusive Approaches to Education*, UNESCO, Paris, 2003.
14. ______, *Education in a Multilingual World*, Education Position Paper, UNESCO, Paris, 2003.
15. ______, *Education for All: Initiatives, issues and strategies*, Report of the Working Group on Education for All held at UNESCO Headquarters, 22-24 November 2000, UNESCO, Paris, 2001.
16. ______, *Country Guidelines on the Preparation of National EFA Plans of Action*, UNESCO, Paris, 2000.
17. ______, *World Education Report: The right to education*, UNESCO, Paris, 2000.

22

The Right to Education

Financial Implications

Shobhit Wadhwa and *Sucheta Arora Wadhwa*

The National Policy on Education (NPE) 1968 and the NPE 1986 has laid special emphasis on the fulfilment of the Constitutional Directive of universalization of elementary education (UEE). Five Year Plans have repeatedly promised to take the nation towards achieving this goal. Elementary education was also included in the 'National Programme of Minimum Needs' in the Five Year Plans, and this inclusion has significant implications for allocation of resources. This was expected to ensure favourable treatment in the allocation of resources, and to protect it from reallocation of approved outlays away from elementary education. Education was also made an important component of the 'national human development initiative' in the Union Budget of 1999-2000. Thus, much before the Jomtien Conference (1990) and the adoption of the World Declaration on education for all (EFA) at the same conference, the Government of India had repeated its resolve to universalize elementary education in the country as early as possible, and also to increase the public funding of education to at least six per cent of national income, so that education, elementary education in particular, does not suffer from paucity of financial resources.

RTE: A New Face of Education

On 1 April 2010, the State finally undertook the endeavour described in the Constitution, although with some modifications of the target age-group. This date marked the enforcement of the Right of Children to Free and Compulsory Education Act (RTE). The Right to Education was made a fundamental right in 2002, under Section 21A of the Constitution, by way of the Constitution Act (Eighty-sixth Amendment). Between then and now, the legislation to implement the RTE has been drafted and redrafted several times, specifically in 2003, 2004, 2005 and 2008. The 2008 Bill was taken forward, and approved, with minor changes, in 2009. India became one of 135 countries to make education a fundamental right of every child when the Act came into force on 1 April 2010.

The Constitution (Eighty-sixth Amendment) Act, 2002 inserted Article 21-A in the Constitution of India to provide free and compulsory education to all children in the age group of six to fourteen years as a Fundamental Right in such a manner as the State may, by law, determine. The Right of Children to Free and Compulsory Education (RTE) Act, 2009, which represents the consequential legislation envisaged under Article 21-A, means that every child has a right to full time elementary education of satisfactory and equitable quality in a formal school, which satisfies certain essential norms and standards. The title of the RTE Act incorporates the words 'free and compulsory'. Free education is defined as 'removal of any financial barrier by the state that prevents a child from completing eight years of schooling'. 'Compulsory education' means the obligation of the appropriate government to provide free elementary education and ensure compulsory admission, attendance and completion of elementary education to every child in the six to fourteen age group.

The Act makes education a fundamental right of every child between the ages of six and fourteen and specifies minimum norms in elementary schools. It requires all private schools to reserve 25 per cent of seats to children from poor families (to be reimbursed by the state as part of the public-private partnership plan). It also prohibits all unrecognized schools from practice, and makes provisions for no donation or capitation fees and no interview of the child or parent for admission. The Act also provides that no child shall be held back, expelled, or required to pass a board examination until the completion of elementary education. There is also a provision for special training of school drop-outs to bring them at par with students of the same age.

Education and Financial Allocations

Since independence, education has been visualized in government policies as a precursor to national development as well as to better quality of life. Growth in public expenditure on education has not been impressive in terms of real prices and on per student basis. In the Education Policy of 1968, it was envisaged that public expenditure on education as a proportion of GDP will increase to six per cent over time. While GDP since increased 61 fold by 2002, expenditure on education has steadily risen from 0.64 per cent of GDP in 1951-52 to 2.31 per cent in 1970-71 and thereafter reached the peak of 4.26 per cent in 2000-01. However, it declined to 3.49 per cent in 2004-05. Currently, the budgetary allocations for education are pegged at 3.8 per cent of the GDP. Thus, raising public expenditure on education to a level of six per cent of GDP has remained a national commitment for nearly forty years now. The National Common Minimum Programme (NCMP) has also reiterated this commitment. To fulfil this commitment, in addition to augmenting budgetary support, the Government imposed an education cess on direct and indirect taxes in the Finance Act 2004-05 (No.2). The resource generating the capacity of the Government has got a boost after high growth rates in the Tenth FYP and the resulting exuberance should offer the right opportunity to meet this long pending commitment of expenditure on education, which would also help in converting the opportunity offered by demographic transition to a scenario of growth with social justice and its future sustainability.

In the Indian constitution, education comes under the purview of the states, and the Act has made state and local bodies accountable for the implementation. The states have been clamouring that they do not have the financial capacity to cover all the schools needed for universal education. Thus, it was clear that the central government (which collects most of the revenue) will be required to subsidize the states. A committee set up to study the funds requirement and funding initially estimated that ₹ 171,000 crore or 1.71 trillion (US$38.2 billion) would be required in the next five years to implement the Act, and in April 2010, the central government agreed to share the funding for implementing the law in the ratio of 65 to 35 between the centre and the states, and a ratio of 90 to 10 for the north-eastern states.

However, in mid 2010, this figure was upgraded to ₹ 231,000 crore and the centre agreed to raise its share to 68 per cent due to paucity of funds with the states. Of the total amount, ₹ 24,000 crore would come from the finance ministry and the remaining ₹ 207,000 crore from the Centre and the states. This, the government claimed, would prevent the states from being overly burdened. With the Supreme Court bringing all recognized schools under the Right to Education (RTE) Act, the government will have to boost spending on its flagship programme to meet the estimated ₹ 2.3 lakh crore needed to fund the initiative by 2014. The estimated: ₹ 2.3 lakh crore, to be shared between the Centre and states according to 68:32 ratio, is also expected to go up as it does not include subsidy that the government has to pay to private schools to implement a 25 per cent quota for economically disadvantaged students.

The education budget has also witnessed a rapid climb from ₹ 204 billion in 1997-2002 through ₹ 438 billion in 2002-2007, ₹ 52,060 crore in 2011, to a planned ₹ 61,407 crore in 2012, including ₹ 25,555 crore allocation to Right to Education (RTE) – Sarva Shiksha Abhiyan (SSA) showing an increase of 21.7 per cent. The Union government outlays for education have gone up marginally from 4.65 per cent as a proportion of the total Union Budget (in 2011-12 RE) to 4.97 per cent in 2012-13 (BE). Most of the money allotted for elementary education has been used to build school level inputs through a large education bureaucracy controlled and managed by the state and central governments.

To illustrate, PAISA analysed the elementary education budgets (SSA and State budgets) of seven states in the country for 2009-10 and 2010-11 to find that, on an average, 78 per cent of the education budget is invested in teachers and management costs. All critical teacher-related decision-making, for instance, hiring or salary payment, lies with the state administration. Following teachers, the next largest investment is on the creation of school infrastructure: 14 per cent of the budget. Funds for infrastructure development are often channelled to schools. However, key decisions related to sanctions and procurement are taken by the district. Importantly, while a school can demand infrastructure funds, it has no decision making power over the timing of receipt of these funds and de-facto funds have to be spent based on priorities set by the state and district administration.

As has been mentioned in the provisional data of Census, 2011, around 18.78 crore children are in school in our country today. But there are also hundreds of thousands of out-of-school kids involved in child labour or domestic work. In fact, of the children enrolled in school, 46 per cent drop out before they complete their primary education. Most of them are girls. At least 26 crore children in the country today are of school-going age. Going by the government statistics, 18 crore children are in school. What about the remaining eight crore? As per the key indicators provided by DISE, the total number of schools providing elementary education increased from 13,03,812 in 2009-10 to 13,62,324 in 2010-11 and primary schools from 8,09,974 in 2009-10 to 8,27,244 in 2010-11, but still lakhs of children are out of schools. According to current estimates, 80 per cent of all schools are government schools making the government the major provider of education. However, because of poor quality of public education, 27 per cent of Indian children are privately educated. It is strongly felt that RTE in India has certain obstacles to overcome. One major hindrance on the path of RTE, apart from several other factors, is insufficient allocation of financial resources.

Financial Challenges in the Implementation of the RTE Act

The main financial challenges in the implementation of the RTE Act are given below:

***Financing the Free Education*:** Under Section 3(2) of the RTE Act, it is stated that, "No child shall be liable to pay any kind of fee or charges or expenses, which may prevent him or her from pursuing and completing the elementary education..." The Act has been interpreted for the exemption of tuition fees for the children of 6-14 years in the form of free education, but it has not said clearly regarding other expenditures to be met by the children.

The allocations of resources for the provision of free textbooks, uniforms and addressing the problem of out of school children, account for just six per cent of the total investment in education, which is very less as compared to the requirements. Also, the Act is completely silent on the transportation cost to be borne by the children. The school expenses excluding tuition fees have risen from ₹ 35,000 in 2005 to ₹ 65,000 per annum in 2011, that too on a single child. Hence it is quite questionable as to how these expenses will be met for attaining the goal of cent per cent literacy in India.

***Dearth of Teachers due to Paucity of Funds*:** The norms of RTE provide to have a PTR of 30:1, which may extend maximum up to 40:1, which indicates that if 100 per cent GER has to be achieved, there will be a need of lakhs of teachers. According to the Union Human Resource Development Ministry, in 2010-11, 907,951 teacher posts have been lying vacant in primary schools across the country. Further, according to the ministry, in 45.76 per cent of primary schools, the teacher-student ratio is more than 1:30. Likewise, in 34.34 per cent of upper primary schools in the country, the teacher-student ratio has been over 30. What's more, almost 25 per cent of teachers in most states are para-teachers; in Jharkhand, for instance, almost half the teachers in schools are para-teachers. The question is how this gap of supply and demand of teachers will be met in order to follow the norms of RTE and even when we are concerned only with the education of children and ignoring the education of teachers.

***Teachers Pay and Training Costs*:** Section 23 of the Act, makes it compulsory that a teacher be trained and if it is strictly enforced, unrecognised schools will become unsustainable. Even though the RTE Act has provided a three year window (two of which are already almost over) for unrecognized schools to obtain recognition, in most cases, it is highly unlikely to happen. Among low-cost schools, on an average, teacher salary expenses equal 49 per cent of revenue. To replace the existing teachers of these schools with trained teachers and pay them salary at par with the salary earned by trained teachers in government schools, a low cost school will have to increase its average fees by 560 per cent. This is assuming that they maintain their existing PTR, which is much lower than what is mandated by the RTE. Even if they manage to increase their enrolment to the maximum level allowed by RTE (PTR of 40:1), they will have to increase their average fees by 294 per cent, to meet the increased salary expenses.

***Per-child Expenditure is Insufficient*:** Under Section 12 of the RTE Act, all private unaided schools are required to reserve 25 per cent of their seats in the entry-level class for children belonging to the economically weaker and disadvantaged groups in the neighbourhood. In exchange, the schools will be reimbursed an amount equal to the per-child expenditure of the state (or the actual amount charged to the child, whichever is less).

The per-child expenditure for the purpose of reimbursement with respect to the 25 per cent quota has been defined as the total annual recurring expenditure of the government on its own schools divided by the number of students enrolled in such schools. This amount may not be enough to cover the cost that the private schools actually incur. Apart from this, a higher reimbursement amount would probably engender less resistance to the 25 per cent quota from the private unaided schools. In the current scenario, schools may have to raise their fees to cover the increased expenses. This, in turn, would impose an inequitable burden on the parents of the non-quota students. The GoI will pay the school an annual sum of ₹ 1,190 per student admitted under the EWS scheme. For most private schools, that amount is too paltry in comparison to the fees they are charging from regular students. Moreover, it won't be possible to pay the proposed salaries to teachers if a large number of students are admitted at very low fees.

***Determination of Eligibility for Free Education in Aided Schools*:** The Act stipulates that all aided schools shall provide free education to such proportion of their students as the aid received by them from the government proportions to their total recurring expenditure. However, the Act is silent about what criteria aided schools shall use to determine the category of students that are eligible for free education under this provision.

***Corruption and Downward Filtration*:** While schools get money, data suggests that they don't always report receiving their entire entitlement. Unsurprisingly, the results of 2010-11 paint a depressing picture depicting 44 per cent primary schools receiving all the grants. Given that about half the schools reported receiving grants, this could mean that the general pattern is that grants arrive in bulk and schools either receive all their grants at one time or nothing. Upper primary grants tell a similar story—56 per cent upper primary schools reporting receipt of all the grants. The major problem in the financing of the RTE in India has been the devil of corruption in disbursement of funds, as it is following the downward filtration policy and only some percentage of the total funds actually reaches the schools.

***Closure of Unrecognized Schools*:** Sections 19(2) and 19(4) deal with the mandatory closure of schools that continue to remain unrecognised. Section 19(2) states: Where a school established before the commencement of this Act does not fulfil the norms and standards specified in the Schedule, it shall take steps to fulfil such norms and standards at its own expenses, within a period of three years from the date of such commencement. The proposed closure of all schools that remain unrecognized three years after the Act came into force. The provision to close down unrecognised schools, if implemented, will be counter-productive to the educational interests of the children. In fact, it will affect the schooling prospects of lakhs of children in the country besides adding financial burden to the state as well as the parents and also will eventually disturb the PTR of recognized schools again, reflecting the failure of providing education to the children.

Conclusion

Though the RTE Act is a milestone for the achievement of long awaited universalization of education, it is quite clear that there are many obstacles in the path of success. The funding of any project is the lifeblood of the project and in that sense, the RTE is suffering from acute anaemia. The funds are not only scarcely allocated, but whatever allocations are being done, they are not reaching to their right place. RTE has been plagued with fund shortfalls with the budgetary provision in the last two years being only half of what was estimated. The HRD ministry received ₹ 21,000 crore in 2011-12 instead of ₹ 43,903 crore. The allocation has gone up only marginally to ₹ 25,000 crore in the current 2012-13 budget. The Department of School Education and Literacy under the HRD Ministry, in fact, has only been given 60 per cent of its proposed demand for this financial year, a parliamentary standing committee on HRD ministry has observed. In other words, RTE scheme is facing a shortfall of ₹ 15,000 crore this year. Concerned over this "wide gap" between demand and actual Budget allocation, the standing committee, in a report tabled in the Parliament, expressed its apprehension on whether "insufficiency of funds would compel the department (of schools education and literacy) to cut down or withdraw from other schemes besides leading to hindrances in the implementation of the SSA-RTE programmes." In the light of above, it can be concluded that there is immediate requirement of resolving the differences among various authorities of education and coordination between the Finance and HRD Ministries should be established to overcome the financial challenges in the path of RTE.

References

1. Accountability Initiative Centre for Policy Research. (2011). PAISA, Do Schools get Their Money? http://www.accountabilityindia.in
2. Ambast, S. (2010). Funding The Right To Education, Working Paper No. 241. Centre for Civil Society, Delhi. http://ccsindia.org
3. Annual Status of Educational Report. (2011). Right to Education Report Card. http://pratham.org
4. Chopra, R. (2012, May 6). Kapil Sibal's RTE Act reeling under severe funds crunch. *India Today*.
5. Government of India (1968). National Policy on Education. http://www.ugc.ac.in/policy/policy.html
6. Government of India. (2010). Report of the 13th Finance Commission (2010-2015). http://fincomindia.nic.in

7. Government of India. (2010). Right to Education Act. http://vikramshila.org
8. Government of India. (2012). The Union Budget 2012-13. http://indiabudget.nic.in
9. Government of India. (May 2004). National Common Minimum Programme. http://pmindia.nic.in/cmp.pdf
10. Jandhyala, B.G.T. (n d). Financing Elementary Education in India. www.doccentre.net.
11. Marwaha, P. (n d) Challenges ahead to implement reservation for marginalized sections in Private schools; Long term solution lies in strengthening state run school education system: CRY. http://www.cry.org
12. Mittal, S. and Shah, P.J. (n d) Reservation In Private Schools Under The Right To Education Act: Model For Implementation. Viewpoint 10. Centre for Civil Society, Delhi. http://ccsindia.org
13. National University of Educational Planning and Administration. (2011). The Flash Statistics: Elementary Education in India, Progress towards UEE (2009-10). http://www.dise.in
14. National University of Educational Planning and Administration. (2012). The Flash Statistics: Elementary Education in India, Progress towards UEE (2010-11). http://www.dise.in
15. Rai, R. (2012). Challenges in implementing the RTE Act. http://infochangeindia.org
16. Reddy, A.N. (2008). Public Financing of Elementary Education in India. *Indian Journal of Social Development*, 8 (1), 19-36.
17. Singh, S. (2010). A Study of the Impact of Right to Education Act on Unrecognised Schools in Delhi, Working Paper No. 242, Centre for Civil Society, Delhi. http://ccsindia.org
18. Singh, S.K. and Pradhan, B.K. (n d). Policy Reforms and Financing of Elementary Education in India: A Study of the Quality of Service and Outcome. http://ideas.repec.org

Annexure-I

The Progress of RTE Act, 2009

The progress of Right of Children to Free and Compulsory Education Act, 2009 as on 1 April 2011 is summarized below:

1. Central RTE Rules notified in the Official Gazette on 8 April 2010; Model RTE Rules circulated to States.

2. Report of the Committee on Implementation of RTE Act and the Resultant Revamp of SSA finalized in April 2010.

3. SSA Framework of Implementation and Norms for Intervention revised to correspond with the provisions of the RTE Act.

4. Financial commitment of ₹ 2.31 lakh crore over five year period from 2010-11 to 2014-15; this includes the award of ₹ 24,068 crore of the 13th Finance Commission.

5. Fund sharing pattern for implementation of RTE-SSA programme revised from the earlier pattern in the sliding scale to 65:35 ratio between the Centre and States for a five year period from 2010-11 to 2014-15.

6. Central SSA outlays for 2010-11 enhanced from ₹ 15,000 crore to ₹ 19,838.23 crore: ₹ 4,000 crore provided in the 1st Supplementary Grant; ₹ 838.23 crore in the final Supplementary Grant.

7. Supplementary Annual Work Plans and Budgets approved for States in October-November 2010:

Sl. No.	*Item*	*Projected for meeting RTE provisions*	*Approved in 2010-11*
1	Additional Teachers (to be provided within 3 years)	5.08 lakh	4.55 lakh
2	Part time instructors for Art Education, Physical Education and Work Education (to be provided within 3 years)	3.10 lakh	1.13 lakh
3	Additional Classrooms (to be provided within 3 years)	14.25 lakh	2.74 lakh
4	Uniforms: estimated number of children annually	8.52 crore	7.21 crore
5	New KGBVs	1073	999
6	Residential Schools	655	111

8. NCTE notified as academic authority for Teacher Qualifications; new Teacher Qualifications notified in August 2010.

(a) NCTE has also notified Guidelines for conducting the Teacher Eligibility Test for teacher recruitment.
(b) NCTE has prepared Model syllabi for D.Ed. and B.Ed.

9. Initiatives taken by States:

Sl. No.	*Item*	*States*
1.	Notification of State RTE Rules	Andhra Pradesh, Arunachal Pradesh, Himachal Pradesh, Manipur, Orissa, Sikkim, Chhattisgarh, Madhya Pradesh, Rajasthan, Mizoram, have notified their State RTE Rules;
		A&N Islands, Chandigarh, Lakshadweep, Daman and Diu, Dadra & Nagar Haveli have adopted Central RTE Rules
		Assam, Bihar, Delhi, Gujarat, Jharkhand, Karnataka, Kerala, Maharashtra, Nagaland, Puducherry, Punjab, Tamil Nadu, Tripura, Uttar Pradesh, Uttarakhand, West Bengal have prepared the draft State RTE Rules
2.	Constitution of SCPCR/ REPA	Assam, Bihar, Chhattisgarh, Delhi, Haryana, J&K, Madhya Pradesh, Maharashtra, Mizoram, Rajasthan, Sikkim notified.
3.	Prohibition of detention, expulsion	A&N Islands, Andhra Pradesh, Arunachal Pradesh, Assam, Bihar, Chandigarh, Delhi, Gujarat, Haryana, Himachal Pradesh, J&K, Jharkhand, Kerala, Lakshadweep, Madhya Pradesh, Maharashtra, Orissa, Puducherry, Punjab, Rajasthan, Sikkim, Tamil Nadu, Tripura, Uttarakhand, West Bengal
4.	Prohibition of corporal punishment, mental harassment	A&N Islands, Andhra Pradesh, Arunachal Pradesh, Bihar, Chandigarh, Chhattisgarh, Delhi, Gujarat, Haryana, Himachal Pradesh, J&K, Jharkhand, Kerala, Lakshadweep, Madhya Pradesh, Maharashtra, Nagaland, Orissa, Puducherry, Punjab, Rajasthan, Sikkim, Tamil Nadu, Tripura, Uttar Pradesh, West Bengal
5.	No board examination till completion of elementary education	A&N Islands, Andhra Pradesh, Arunachal Pradesh, Bihar, Delhi, Gujarat, Haryana, Himachal Pradesh, J&K, Jharkhand, Kerala, Lakshadweep, Madhya Pradesh, Maharashtra, Manipur, Mizoram, Nagaland, Orissa, Puducherry, Punjab, Rajasthan, Sikkim, Tamil Nadu, Tripura, West Bengal

Contributors

Aarti Bhatnagar (Dr.), Research Scholar, Guru Gobind Singh Indraprastha University, Delhi, E-14/4 Krishna Nagar, Delhi-51, artibhatnagar3@gmail.com

Afaque Nadeem Khan (Dr.), Assistant Professor, College of Teacher Education, Bhopal-462001, Madhya Pradesh, afaquenadeem@yahoo.com

Akthar Parveen (Dr.), Assistant Professor, Maulana Azad National Urdu University, Hyderabad-500032, Andhra Pradesh, aktharparveen6@gmail.com

Charu Saini (Ms.), Assistant Professor, IIMT, Delhi, H-12A Street No. 7, Old Govind Pura Extn., Delhi-110051, charusaini1@gmail.com

D. Venkateshwarlu (Prof.), Professor of Education (Special Education), School of Education, IGNOU, New Delhi, dvenkatesh@ignou.ac.in

G.K. Tripathi (Mr.), District Programme Manager, District Aid Prevention & Control Unit, Allahabad, gktrpth@gmail.com

Indrajeet Dutta (Mr.), Assistant Professor, Maulana Azad National Urdu University, College of Teacher Education, Bhopal-462001, Madhya Pradesh, indraneet@gmail.com

Jeena K.G. (Dr.), Assistant Professor, Maulana Azad National Urdu University, College of Teacher Education, Bhopal-462001, Madhya Pradesh, kgjeena@gmail.com

Manju Negi (Ms.), Assistant Professor, Chet Ram Sharma College of Education, Noida, F-33, Sector-22, Noida-201301, U.P., manjunegi33@gmail.com

Naushad Husain (Mr.), Assistant Professor, Maulana Azad National Urdu University, College of Teacher Education, Bhopal-462001, Madhya Pradesh, nhctemanuu@rediffmail.com

Neeti Dutta (Dr.), Assistant Professor, Maulana Azad National Urdu University, College of Teacher Education, Bhopal-462001, Madhya Pradesh, tanudutta29@gmail.com

Noushad Husain (Dr.), Associate Professor, Maulana Azad National Urdu University, College of Teacher Education, Bhopal-462001, Madhya Pradesh, noushad_husain@rediffmail.com

Ravneet Gaur (Dr.), Assistant Professor, Manav Rachna College of Education, Faridabad, Flat No. 4, AIIMS Apartment, Sector–21D, Faridabad-121008, ravneetgaur@gmail.com

Sajid Jamal (Dr.), Incharge Principal, Maulana Azad National Urdu University, College of Teacher Education, Asansol, West Bengal, shadansj07@rediffmail.com

Shabana Ashraf (Dr.), Assistant Professor, Maulana Azad National Urdu University, College of Teacher Education, Bhopal-462001, Madhya Pradesh, sashrafshabana@gmail.com

Shobhit Wadhwa (Dr.), Assistant Professor, Ideal Institute of Management & Technology, 16-X, Karkardooma Institutional Area, Delhi-92, wadhwa.shobhit@gmail.com

Sonal Chabra (Dr.), Assistant Professor, Aravali College of Advanced Studies in Education, Faridabad., H.No. 809, Block-B, Sector-49, Faridabad-121001, Haryana, sonal.chabra77@gmail.com

Sucheta Arora Wadhwa (Dr.), Research Scholar, GBPU A&T, Pantnagar, Res.- F3, B-75, Ramprastha, Ghaziabad, U.P., arorasucheta3@gmail.com

Talmeez Fatma Naqvi (Dr.), Assistant Professor, Maulana Azad National Urdu University, College of Teacher Education, Bhopal-462001, Madhya Pradesh, talmeeznaqvi@rediffmail.com

Vanita Chopra (Dr.), Assistant Professor, Institute of Home Economics, Delhi University, C-247, Vikaspuri, New Delhi-110018, vinivpuri@yahoo.com, chopravanita1981@gmail.com

Wadudul Haque Siddiqui (Prof.), Professor & Principal, Maulana Azad National Urdu University, College of Teacher Education, Bhopal-462001, Madhya Pradesh, whsiddiqui@gmail.com

Syed Jamal [illegible], [illegible] Principal, Maulana Azad National Urdu University, College of Teacher Education, [illegible], West Bengal. [illegible]

[illegible] Ashraf [illegible], [illegible] Professor, Maulana Azad National Urdu University, College of Teacher Education, [illegible], Madhya Pradesh. [illegible]

[illegible], Assistant Professor, [illegible] Institute of Management [illegible], [illegible]. [illegible]

[illegible], [illegible] Professor, [illegible]

[illegible]

[illegible]

[illegible]

[illegible]